DAMAGED GOODS
American Evangelical Ethics

By
Maurice Martin

Dedication

For my grandchildren: Sam, Margaret, Milo, Rosemary, and Gus

"... clothe yourselves with compassion, kindness, humility, gentleness and patience ... and over all these virtues put on love, which binds them all together in perfect unity."
Colossians 3:12,14

Contents

Introduction   **5**

Preface   **8**

Part I: Ethics and Morality   **10**

Chapter 1   11
     A First Glance
     Ethics, Morals and Evangelicals
     Unintended Consequences
     Three Approaches to Knowing the Truth
        Correspondence Theory
        Pragmatic Theory
        Coherence Theory

Chapter 2   24
     Four Important Concepts
        Moralization
        Legitimation
        Alienation
        Determination

Chapter 3   48
     Ways of Looking at Ethics
        Descriptive Ethics
        Prescriptive Ethics
        Analytic Ethics
     Ethics and Morals
     Visible and Invisible, Me and Us
     Altitude Matters

Chapter 4   61
     Ethics in Context
        What is real?
        How do we think correctly?
        How do we know what is true?
        How should people govern and be governed?
        What is beautiful and why does it matter?

Chapter 5   86
     The "End" of Ethics
        outcome-based Ethics
        duty-based Ethics
           Tithing Mint and Rue
        character-based Ethics

Part II: Virtue and Vice   **111**

   Chapter 6   112

      Whose Virtue?

         Objectivism

      Retributive and Distributive Justice

   Chapter 7   126

      The Golden Mean

      The North Star

   Chapter 8   134

      Tension: Virtue, Responsibility and Rights

Part III: Sanctity of Life   **149**

   Chapter 9   150

      Just War

   Chapter 10   159

      Making America Great Again

      Other People's Sins

      Top Down Morality

   Chapter 11   173

      Poverty Matters

   Chapter 12   185

      "Thou Shalt Not Kill"

      The Eyes of the Beholder

   Chapter 13   203

      Slippery Slope

         Which Innocent Lives Matter?

         Abortion, Adoption, Accountability

         Rights, Religion and Roe

   Chapter 14   222

      Uncomfortable Truths

   Appendix 1: The Sermon on the Mount   226

   Appendix 2: The Sermon on the Plain   232

   Appendix 3: Letter to the Editor   235

   Appendix 4: "You will always have the poor among you ..."   240

   Appendix 5: Myths Regarding the Poor   243

Acknowledgments   **249**

Introduction

The following blog was written while I was serving as Chief Operating Officer and interim Chief Executive Officer of Food for the Hungry, a Christian organization which draws its name from Psalm 146: *"He upholds the cause of the oppressed and gives food to the hungry."*[1] The blog was posted just after the 2014 midterm elections and not long after my retirement from pastoral ministry in the Evangelical Presbyterian Church which I served for 25 years. All that follows reflects my thoughts and convictions and not those of either Food for the Hungry or the Evangelical Presbyterian Church.

American Christian or Christian American?

Is there a difference? At first glance, it might seem that there is not or that the distinction is a trivial one. The question needs a second glance.

Let me personalize this. I'm a graduate of the US Air Force Academy. My father graduated from West Point, two of my closest first cousins from the US Naval Academy. All four of us flew in Vietnam; my father in World War II and Korea as well. We are Americans to the core and we bleed red, white and blue ...

But that's not the whole story for me. During military flight training, I came to an intentional, intelligent (I like to think so anyway) faith in Christ and began a lifelong process of transformation. As that unfolded, I began to experience the tension between being an American Christian or a Christian American. There's a difference. Let me explain.

Midterm Elections

We've just come through [the 2014] midterm elections here in the States. Here we go again. Republicans had major gains, Democrats major losses in both the Senate and the House of Representatives. Republicans now

---

[1] Psalm 146:7. Unless noted otherwise, all Bible references are from the New International Version.

have their largest majority ever in the House. Democrats have had even larger majorities than this in the not too distant past. This year's story is familiar. Every second-term president from President Eisenhower to President Obama, regardless of party, has lost ground in the midterm election during his second term and has been faced with a divided government.

We Americans are capable of enormous opinion swings, but some things remain constant. Religion always plays a role in politics because the faith of many Americans informs how they vote. Those who have experienced great blessing as Americans, and are keen to conserve those blessings, often vote one way. Those who haven't experienced similar blessing often vote differently.

The American Dream

But there's a bigger "constant." In times of social turbulence and economic uncertainty, when the "American Dream" seems to be dimmed by present reality, Americans vote for change. Francis Schaeffer, noted Christian author, observed that most Americans, Christians included, have two controlling values that shouldn't be confused with the Gospel. They're what he called "personal peace" and "affluence" … core ingredients of the American Dream. His point was that we're generally content to follow whoever we believe will give us those.

In 1955, Will Herberg wrote a classic of American religious sociology: "Protestant – Catholic – Jew." Herberg, a Jew, noted that these had in common that they were Bible-based, Abrahamic faiths despite significant differences; however, what their adherents really valued, regardless of faith, were the "spiritual values" of "the American Way of Life" … the American Dream. He argued that many Americans made religion important for the wrong reasons. Schaeffer wouldn't disagree.

An American Christian, in my usage, modifies his Christianity by an often unconsciously equal or deeper commitment to the American Dream. A Christian American, on the other hand, modifies her commitment to the American Dream by her Christianity. She doesn't confuse the Gospel with

6

the American Dream, nor does she value them equally. The values of the Kingdom of God take priority over the values of American life.

Though many are possible, I'm only going to make one application. Jesus said, "Blessed are you who are poor for yours is the Kingdom of God." (Luke 6:20) In previous blogs, I've made the case that responding to the poverty of the poor is not peripheral to the Gospel, but central ... an essentially important Kingdom value. For many American Christians, Republicans, and Democrats, the poverty of the poor totally missed the cut among those issues of any significance in this past election. How incredibly sad. How about you?

Preface

"Why do you call me, 'Lord, Lord,' and do not do what I say?"
Jesus of Nazareth
Luke 6:46

The core of the ethic of Jesus is clearly laid out in the Sermon on the Mount and the distilled version is found in the Sermon on the Plain which is similar but much shorter. Each is reproduced in full in the first two appendices at the end of this book. My hope and my assumption is that you will have read both and that you will read what follows in the light of them. The ethical implications of the life and teaching of Jesus, the parables of Jesus and all of the spiritual practices, healing actions and sufferings of Jesus are brought into clear and sharp focus in these two powerful sermons. Though these are not the sum of all the ethical teachings of the Bible, they are central and their importance is underscored by Jesus, making his intent clear towards the end of the shorter sermon, *"Why do you call me, 'Lord, Lord,' and do not do what I say?"* In context, he was clearly referring to what he had just said and clearly expected His followers to embrace.

This ethic is not ethereal. That is, it is not something that can only be seen and understood by the followers of Christ or by a select few. The sermons are recorded in black and white, and the profound importance of the biblical record of His clear and pointed ethical teaching is that it is there for all the world to see. Christians and all who do not live up to the standard found in these can be forgiven, but when they ignore or reject that ethic it is an entirely different calculus. The idea that this ethic does not apply to politics, business, the military or nationalistic ideals is one that can be debated, but not for Christians who embrace the ethic of Jesus. G.K. Chesterton put it very succinctly: *"The Christian ideal has not been tried and found wanting. It has been found difficult; and left untried."*[2]

Given the current cultural divide in America, while many evangelicals feel as though they are being listened to for the first time in a long time, many others are wondering how Christians, evangelicals in particular, could be

---

[2] Chesterton, G.K. "What's Wrong With the World? Ch. 5: The Unfinished Temple." *The Literature Network: Online Classic Literature, Poems, and Quotes. Essays & Summaries.* www.online-literature.com/chesterton/wrong-with-the-world/5/. Accessed 6 March 2019.

supportive of so much that seems so antithetical to a traditional understanding of historic Christian belief and practice. Much of what follows can also be said of many who stand in opposition to the bulk of American evangelicals. The inexcusable occupies both sides of the American divide, but this book is going to focus primarily on the beliefs and actions of those who, by our own narrative, should know better.

Part I: Ethics and Morality

"If we did not bring to the examination of our instincts a knowledge of their comparative dignity we could never learn it from them. And that knowledge cannot itself be instinctive; the judge cannot be one of the parties judged; or, if he is, the decision is worthless and there is no ground for placing the preservation of the species above self-preservation or sexual appetite." [3]

C.S. Lewis

---

[3] Lewis, C.S. *The Abolition of Man: How Education Develops Man's Sense of Morality."* Macmillan Publishing Co., Inc, New York, Macmillan Paperback Edition, 1955, p.48.

Chapter 1

A First Glance

"The sermon on the mount is there for the purpose of being done." [4]
Dietrich Bonhoeffer

There must first **be something** before there can be a **damaged something**. For there to be damaged goods assumes the existence of goods that are undamaged. Though there's much more to it than this, a person's "ethics" or "ethic" is first a set of beliefs about what is morally good or bad, right or wrong. A damaged ethic assumes an already existing undamaged ethic. American evangelicals would be the first to tell you that American evangelical ethics are, first and foremost, Christian ethics. To the extent that evangelical ethics are understood by others to be Christian ethics, this book conveys the uncomfortable notion that Christian ethics have been damaged by American evangelicals ... of which I am one. This is not to say that all American evangelicals have contributed to this, nor that the damaging of Christian ethics was intended, but the damage is real and it is significant.

Christian ethics are close to the heart of the Christian faith, especially so for the evangelical understanding of the faith. There is no clearer or more comprehensive statement of the undamaged, personal ethic of Jesus than the Sermon on the Mount found in the New Testament (NT) Gospel of Matthew. Both the Lord's Prayer and the Golden Rule calling us to do to others what we would have them do to us are found in it. Any serious study of Christian ethics, evangelical or otherwise, must eventually address the Sermon on the Mount and the abbreviated similar account in the Gospel of Luke.

My aim in all that follows is not to convert, but to explain. Whether I am successful or not, there is much that needs explaining about the damage American evangelicals have done to Christian ethics. My intention, though, is not to end there. My intention is not only to describe the damage, but to suggest a path to repair. In the course of doing this, depending on the context, I will refer to evangelicals either using first person pronouns like

---

[4] Bonhoeffer, Dietrich. *Ethics.* Simon & Schuster, New York, 1995, p.46.

"we" or "our" or, when it is more appropriate, third-person pronouns like "they" or "their." For those reading this who are uncomfortable with references to the Bible, "God talk" or evangelical language, it is simply not possible to address this subject without using it.

My evangelical experience goes back nearly fifty years. It started while I was going through the Army helicopter training school following my graduation from the United States Air Force Academy. It was 1970 and there was a critical shortage of helicopter pilots due to the Vietnam war. Two weeks before graduation, our class was asked for volunteers and fourteen of us raised our hands to give up our already assigned Air Force pilot training slots to become the first Air Force pilots to go straight to the Army school and directly into helicopters. We reported to Ft. Wolters, Texas and entered the Army's well-oiled pipeline for producing pilots for Southeast Asia.

While learning to fly these challenging but incredibly useful machines, seven of us were also involved in a Bible study led by one of my AFA classmates. Over the next few months, I made a serious and life-changing decision to embrace Christ as Savior and Lord, as did my friends. Six of us were Air Force officers, one was an Army Warrant Officer. He died a few months after his arrival "in country" when his helicopter was shot down. I was the escort officer who accompanied his remains to his home in Massachusetts. Of the remaining six of us, five of us served in Vietnam and of that five, three of us eventually became Presbyterian ministers.[5] My ordination is in the Evangelical Presbyterian Church. One of my friends is ordained in the Presbyterian Church in America, the other in the Presbyterian Church USA.

Prior to helicopter training at Ft. Wolters, my ethics were largely those of my parents, my classmates, and our alma mater. My father was a 1943

---

[5] My initial assignment out of flight training was in the HH-3E "Jolly Green Giant" at Tyndall Air Force Base, Florida, supporting F-106 fighter weapons training. I served at Tan Son Nhut Air Base, Vietnam, with Detachment 14, 3rd Air Rescue and Recovery Group, during the summer of 1972. The detachment was deployed on short notice from April through September of 1972 and was staffed with volunteers from Air Rescue units from the US and overseas. Our mission was to evacuate Phnom Penh, Cambodia if necessary (actual evacuation not until 1975). We also had responsibility for air rescue operations in the Mei Kong Delta, VN. I was one of the volunteers who served in two month rotations. After Tan Son Nhut, I rotated back to my permanent base in the U.S. for upgrade training to Aircraft Commander and further assignment to Thule AFB, Greenland. During my time in VN, I flew 11 combat missions. My friends flew many more.

graduate of the United States Military Academy at West Point, and a career pilot, first with the Army Air Corps and then with the Air Force when it became a separate service. He and my devoutly Catholic mother instilled a deep sense of right and wrong in my sisters and me. The Academy's Honor Code also affected me deeply: "*We will not lie, steal, or cheat, nor tolerate among us anyone who does.*" Many of my fellow graduates will tell you that is the most valuable thing we brought with us out of the Academy. However, in the months and years that followed our graduation, I was introduced to an ethic that both re-awakened and surpassed the very best of what I had learned at home. It also went far beyond anything I learned at the Academy.

For two of my friends and me, our commitment to our newly forming Christian ethic was tested early on in a big way. Following our Army helicopter training, we were assigned to Hill Air Force Base (AFB), Utah for Air Force Combat Crew Training. Periodically the training wing scheduled an "Officer's Call," which was a large gathering of officers of all ranks to pass on needed information and address issues that pertained to our training. My two friends and I were late to the meeting and missed what was said right at first. We walked in and, trying to be as inconspicuous as possible, grabbed three remaining seats. The lights went out in the large room and a pornographic movie was projected onto the large screen at the front. This was meant to be "motivational training" for the then all male combat eligible officers. The three of us looked at each other, knowing that this didn't fit with our newly found faith, and without saying anything we got up and walked out.

You would think that a bomb had gone off. The doors to the room burst open, a sergeant ran out to bring us back in, the lights were now on, the film had stopped and hundreds of eyes were fixed on us. We were second lieutenants and there were many in the room who significantly outranked us. We really thought we were in trouble, but not a word was said to us. The Officer's Call ended after an hour or so, and for weeks after I was conscious of almost everyone in the training squadron keeping their distance or looking at us in an odd way. We hadn't planned it, we weren't even sure what exactly had happened or why, but something ethically meaningful had happened that we couldn't fully appreciate at the time.

Months later my two buddies were stationed in Thailand flying long range rescue missions into North Vietnam to pick up downed pilots. Both of their names are now etched in bronze at the Southeast Asia Memorial Pavilion at the Air Force Academy for their heroic duty. But there was another honor they received while still in Thailand. There was an Officer's Call for the rescue squadron they were assigned to, and one of the officers asked the commanding officer why he didn't show porn flicks to motivate the troops. He said he wasn't going to do that. With a nod to my friends, he said that when he had been going through Combat Crew Training at Hill AFB, some guys had gotten up and walked out when a porn flick had been shown, and he wished he had gotten up and left with them.

Ethics, Morals and Evangelicals

"If you are convinced that you are a guide for the blind, a light for those who are in the dark, an instructor of the foolish, a teacher of little children, because you have in the law the embodiment of knowledge and truth — you, then, who teach others, do you not teach yourself?"
Romans 2:19-21

Let me make a distinction between ethics and morals. The words are sometimes used interchangeably, but for our purposes, I am going to use "ethic" or "ethics" to refer to beliefs about what is right or wrong or the character shaped by those beliefs. I am going to use "morals" to refer to the behaviors that spring from those beliefs or from the character shaped by them. The word "ethic" comes from the Greek word "ethos" which is often translated "character."[6] The word "morals" comes from the Latin "moralis" which usually refers to "customs." The relationship between the two is like that between a tree and its fruit as in the biblical notion that good trees produce good fruit and bad trees produce bad fruit.[7]

Evangelicalism is more like a spectrum than a container. A container has definite boundaries while a spectrum has distinct colors that are shaded into by another color on one side and then shade into yet another color on the other side. There is a fundamentalist side of the spectrum and a traditionalist side of the spectrum along with other nuances. Pentecostal Christians differ from Charismatic Christians, including Charismatic

---

[6] Depending on the context it can also be translated "custom," "usage," or "practice prescribed by law."
[7] Matthew 7:17.

Catholics, who differ from Christians who are evangelical but would not identify themselves as Charismatic Christians.[8] There are also evangelicals who shade toward mainline Christian denominational churches of Baptist, Presbyterian, Methodist, Lutheran or other denominational persuasions, including, though some would disagree, Roman Catholic. Like a spectrum, there is a large middle portion that is identifiable as a particular "color" even though differing shades are still visible. When I talk about American evangelicals it is this large middle portion I'm talking about.

In addition to these religious distinctions, "middle of the spectrum" American evangelicals include those who generally are deeply patriotic and believe the United States to be primarily a Christian nation founded on Christian principles. They are pro-life in the sense that they believe that abortion is wrong in and of itself, and they deeply oppose the notion of a woman's right to choose to have an abortion on ethical grounds. They strongly believe that homosexuality is morally wrong. They want to draw their ethical beliefs from the Bible and generally believe it should be read as literally as possible.

Most would read the US Constitution in much the same way as they read their Bibles, and are deeply opposed to what they consider judicial abuse, which they believe takes place when judges look for deeper principles behind the words of the Constitution or the words of our nation's laws. Many, not all, are advocates of that current interpretation of the Second Amendment allowing liberal access to guns on the grounds of the right of self-defense. Though most are white, some are African American, Asian or Latino, and most white evangelicals take offense at any suggestion of their being considered racially prejudiced. In the 2016 US presidential election some of these people were deeply troubled by both major party candidates, but 80 percent of those who self-identified as white evangelicals voted for the Republican candidate.[9]

---

[8] Pentecostal Christians draw their identity from the NT biblical account of the first "Pentecost" when the Holy Spirit descended upon new believers soon after the resurrection and ascension of Jesus. This mainly Protestant form of Christianity emphasizes a Baptism of the Holy Spirit accompanied by speaking in tongues, prophecy, miraculous healing and the exorcism of evil spirits. Charismatic Christians also believe in a personal encounter with God through the Holy Spirit, the practice of spiritual gifts and miraculous healing, but are far less separatist than are Pentecostals and often belong to more mainstream evangelical or traditional churches.

[9] Bailey, Sarah Pulliam. "White Evangelicals voted overwhelmingly for Donald Trump, exit polls show." *The Washington Post,* 9 November 2016. Others take issue with this saying that the polls are not specific enough in identifying evangelicals and that they only identify voters who self-identified as evangelicals in

In the same way that evangelicals are not alike in all particulars, Christian ethics aren't either. Differences in approach and in some of the contents are evident. For example, many protestants disagree with the Roman Catholic belief that the use of artificial contraception is wrong. The Catholic church believes that all the issues related to the value or sanctity of life are interconnected in what has been called a "seamless garment." For the Catholic church, sanctity of life convictions apply not only to issues like abortion, but also to contraception, stem cell research, war, torture, refugees, capital punishment, human experimentation and surgical alteration, and end of life issues.

Protestants may and often do differ from Catholics on one or a number of these issues. Though this is true, Catholics and Protestants, evangelicals included, the Orthodox churches of Eastern Europe, the Middle East and Northern Africa, as well as Christian churches throughout the rest of the world, have a shared core set of teachings regarding how people should behave in relation to one another. These are drawn specifically from the teaching of Jesus in the Gospels, particularly the Sermon on the Mount. When I talk about Christian ethics it is this shared core to which I am referring.

As mentioned before, Christian ethics are close to the heart of the Christian faith. The teachings of the Bible and the spreading of the Gospel (literally, the "good news") are critical for evangelicals. Both of these underscore the belief that "sin" is a very big deal. In this view, humanity's greatest problem is not poverty, disease or ignorance; rather, it is a moral problem called sin.[10] Evangelicals believe that though we are made in God's image and thus are inherently valuable, it is both our inherited nature and our practice to do what is wrong in God's sight. This applies to people universally and results in separation from God. Most evangelicals believe that if this is not remedied before one's death, it lasts forever. This separation can only be overcome by God who came into the world in a new and wonderful way in Jesus Christ. It is by Christ's death on the cross which paid for our sins,

---

exit polls. Regardless, one obvious fact is that 20% of self-identified evangelicals, not an insignificant number, did not vote for Trump; however, he could not even have come close to being elected apart from the 80% who did.

[10] In the words of Question 14 of the Westminster Shorter Catechism, "Sin is any want of conformity unto or transgression of the law of God."

and Christ's coming into our lives through faith, that we are brought back to a right and eternal relationship with God. In this new relationship, we are both called to and helped to live lives pleasing to God.

So whatever else it is, sin is an ethical issue of great importance for Christians. In a nutshell, Christian ethics become both the pattern and the goal for how we are to live. Other Christians who would not identify themselves as evangelicals either do agree or agree in large part with what has just been said above, but it is an essential part of the core of what evangelicals believe everywhere. Some would emphasize parts of this more or less, some would add things here or there, but this is basic evangelicalism. Embracing these core beliefs is what makes an American an American evangelical. So how could American evangelicals damage something so core to Christianity?

The answer to this is not a simple one, but part of the answer is found in the fact that Christians in America are insulated in ways that Christians elsewhere are not. In late 2004, I was assigned to a two year term as Country Director for Food for the Hungry in the Democratic Republic of Congo. Food for the Hungry is an evangelical organization dedicated to eradicating physical and spiritual poverty worldwide. Two weeks after my arrival in Bukavu, eastern Congo, our office and residence were overrun by Congolese soldiers. We were held under armed guard until evacuated by UN Peacekeepers. This two year experience of life in a living hell of grinding poverty and unchecked violence changed the way I understood life itself and even the good news of new life that Jesus proclaimed to all. It took being taken out of the life in America that I had come to take for granted. The consequences of this journey were ones I never intentionally sought out, but among them was a profound realization that a Christianity experienced only in the security and prosperity of the most secure and prosperous nation in history is one that is unfortunately insulated from much of the reality which faces a much larger world created, sustained and loved by God. Sadly, this insulation diminishes us in significant ways.

Unintended Consequences

"I tell you," he replied, "if they keep quiet, the stones will cry out."
Luke 19:40

The Jewish people never intended to be hated, but the almost universal hatred they have experienced throughout history stems largely from their refusal to give the kind of allegiance to the countries among whom they were dispersed that American evangelicals are giving to America today. Their allegiance and submission to the God of Abraham, Isaac, and Jacob superseded any other allegiance. Many evangelical Christians in the United States today proclaim that sort of allegiance to Christ, but in practice have so conflated faith in God with allegiance to America, more specifically, allegiance to a vision of America expressed through conservative American politics and principles, that it is almost impossible to distinguish the two. Were American Christians to have embraced a politics of the left instead, it would have been an equally grave mistake. As one keen observer put it, when you mix religion and politics you get politics. It is not so much a case of wrong politics as it is a case of confused identity and allegiance.

Donald Trump's support among white evangelicals propelled him to victory in the 2016 election, and he has been and continues to be promoted and defended by many evangelical leaders. Christians, evangelical and otherwise, have long maintained that truthfulness in private and in public is essential to meaningful life together. Evangelicals proclaimed this loudly and in unison when former President Bill Clinton was impeached for lying to the Special Counsel and for the incredible abuse of power regarding his relationship with Monica Lewinsky.

When Clinton was untruthful, evangelicals were among the loudest voices condemning him. When Trump is untruthful, they are conspicuously silent or, in the case of numerous evangelical leaders and many devoted followers of the president, they are vocally supportive of him and justify his untruthfulness as truth clothed in hyperbole or truth based on alternative facts. It is a truth understood to be such in the sense that, because it apparently supports large parts of the narrative of an evangelical America, it is either considered true or truly excusable.

Apparently, this relationship with truth can only be clearly understood and appreciated by those with special evangelical insight. Evangelicals claim to believe that Jesus is the personification of the truth, yet in high numbers trust and insist that their fellow citizens can trust a leader who is regularly and demonstrably untruthful, whether touting the crowd size at his inauguration, payments to pornstars, or even his height. The voices crying foul are legion and, for the most part, evangelicals are conspicuously absent. Perhaps the stones are crying out.

Whatever else it may be, one's face is that which is seen by others and that by which one is recognized by others. The face of Jesus may be the face evangelicals ideally see when they view one another and would like others to see, but it is not. We are responsible for the face we present to the world. Until recently and for many decades, Billy Graham, the revered evangelist, was arguably the human face of American evangelicalism. With his recent death in early 2018, the unintended consequence of evangelical conflation of Christianity with conservative American politics and principles is that many of those outside the evangelical fold, when they hear the word "evangelical," now see the face of Donald Trump.

It is hard to overstate how damaging this is to almost everything Christians have held dear historically. To say that we never intended it is not enough. To say that we didn't hire him to be a pastor, but a protector, a bodyguard, as one evangelical leader put it, is to evade the issue and obscure the incredible damage such evangelicals are doing to the Gospel and the kingdom of God which it proclaims. The message of American evangelicals that is being heard by the rest of the world is "America First" not "Jesus First."

This did not happen overnight and it is possible to trace it to the demise of Christian ethics, not just in America as a whole, but specifically among evangelicals. It is far more involved than simply this, but evangelicals hold particularly to their stands on abortion and homosexuality to buttress a conviction that theirs is a truly Christian ethic setting them apart in a God-honoring way from much of America. This, however, is both simplistic and symbolic at best and covers up the wholesale adoption and practice of an ethic that bears little resemblance to historic Christian ethics. This will be addressed in more detail later, but for now, it is enough to point out that our ethics involve not only what we hold, as in "hold to be true," but how we hold what we hold.

There are several substantial beliefs, deeply held by evangelicals, that cast long shadows. Anything solid casts a shadow when it blocks the light of the sun. The sun which produces the light is good and the solid substance may well be good. The shadow that emanates from it is a necessary part of reality and, though it is not the substance, it is unavoidably attached to it. Because of the way they are understood and lived by evangelicals themselves, these shadows obscure the truths from which the shadows come. It may come as a surprise, but the shadows of such substantial doctrines as justification by faith in Christ (being made "right with God" through faith in Jesus) and the second coming of Christ are understood and lived out in ways that can do deep damage to the ethic so clearly taught by Jesus and exemplified by his character. How can this be?

Three Approaches to Knowing the Truth

"There are three things that are never satisfied ..."
Proverbs 30:15

Among the ways of understanding what is true, three major ones are particularly relevant. These approaches or theories can be roughly described as a correspondence approach, a pragmatic approach and a coherence approach.

Correspondence Theory

A correspondence theory argues that truth must correspond with facts. In the broadest sense, this is a scientific approach to truth. Facts are accumulated and, from those facts, a framework is developed that forms a narrative or a theory that helps us to find and to test additional facts. This is an inductive approach to understanding what is true and submits the truthfulness of a narrative to the facts that support it. If the facts make another case, the narrative must change to accommodate the facts. For example, when facts proved otherwise, the "flat earth" theory had to be abandoned. It has been well argued that this way of understanding truth has its roots in the Judeo-Christian heritage of modern Europe and America, but it is not the primary way that American evangelicals understand truth and, for reasons we will see, many are uncomfortable with it even when recognizing its merits and achievements.

Pragmatic Theory

Closely related to a correspondence theory of truth is a common sense or pragmatic theory which argues that if "it works in the real world" it is true. In the broadest sense, this is an experience based approach to truth that is less philosophical than either of the others. The truthfulness of the "law of supply and demand" or to maxims like "God helps those who help themselves" are examples of this. This theory is comfortable with much of the practical wisdom found in the Bible but relies heavily on practical knowledge found in everyday life as well.

This approach allows one set of beliefs to apply to the "real" world in which we live and another set of beliefs to apply to an ideal world we cannot see or the world to come. To the extent that these beliefs just don't work in the real world, this pragmatic approach has great problems with the ethics of Jesus conveyed in the Sermon on the Mount or the shorter, abridged version in the Sermon on the Plain. These are seen to be sacred ideals that will be realized only in a future chapter of history if at all, and though helpful in many ways, are not applicable in a binding way in the secular here and now.

For example, the admonition to *"Give to the one who asks you, and do not turn away from the one who wants to borrow from you"*[11] is a beautiful sentiment, but for many, it is not a command that is taken seriously in the real world of 2019. An easy way to check your attitude about this will be to observe your feelings and actions the next time you come to a stop sign with a homeless person asking for help. Similarly, the command to *"love your enemies and pray for those who persecute you,"*[12] whatever it means, doesn't practically apply to those who espouse radical Islam or even the opposite side of the political divide in our own country. For Christians, how many times did you pray for the presidential candidate you opposed during the last election cycle? It's a serious question. Other commands like *"Do not store up for yourselves treasures on earth"*[13] or admonitions such as

---

[11] Matthew 5:42.
[12] Matthew 5:44.

"*You cannot serve God and money*"[14] are thought to be beautiful ideals, but not realistic directions for life and not particularly compatible with the American Dream.

The pragmatic approach to truth splits the "sacred" from the "secular" in this way, and it has become one of the primary ways that Americans, evangelicals included, understand truth particularly as it relates to ethics. That said, even for evangelicals, this is not the primary way of knowing what is true. For that, we need to look at a final theory.

Coherence Theory

A coherence theory argues that something is true if it coheres with an already accepted narrative. Whereas a correspondence approach to truth is inductive, a coherence approach is primarily deductive. According to this approach, any "facts" are understood in a context or narrative that is already believed to be true. In a broad sense, Christians have historically believed that what is "truly true" is that which God has revealed. Though different Christian denominations or groups do this a bit differently, all embrace some sort of a biblical narrative that reflects their understanding of what God has revealed. If so-called facts don't fit into that biblical narrative, they can't truly be facts.

When Galileo defended a view of the world with the sun at the center and not the earth, most of the religious leaders of his day rejected his thinking because it didn't cohere with the biblical narrative as they understood it.[15] This is essentially a deductive view of truth and evaluates the truthfulness of facts through the narrative lens that views them. The Bible, distilled through creeds, faith statements, confessions of faith and catechisms of the various churches, provides the outline of a narrative framework by which the truthfulness of facts is evaluated. Christians are predisposed to this way of thinking, and it is impossible to understand how evangelicals are acting in America today without understanding this predisposition.

---

[13] Matthew 6:19.
[14] Matthew 6:24.
[15] Sobel, Dava. "*Galileo's Daughter. Chapter XXII.*" Walker & Company, New York, 1999. Years of actual correspondence between Galileo and his daughter and others show how significant the pressure from the religious leaders of that day was on Galileo.

Each of these ways of understanding truth overlaps with the others, and we almost reflexively draw from all of them from time to time. That said, Christians have long held first to a coherence view of truth that explains why, for some Christians, any so-called scientific facts that don't fit the biblical narrative as they understand it can't be true. Many hold that what they believe corresponds with the "facts" and claim allegiance to the first theory in that way, but live according to the latter two theories.

For example, the relative lack of concern about environmental issues among many evangelicals, despite an enormous array of facts that warrant deep concern, springs from a narrative that subordinates the created world to man. It sees man not only as the "crown of creation" but the benefactor of and primary reason for the creation of the earth. Also part of that narrative is the belief that the world is going to end in a massive confrontation between the forces of good and evil, not as a result of environmental pollution, so why get worked up about it?

This view hit the American evangelical scene very powerfully with the publication of *The Late, Great Planet Earth* by Hal Lindsey in 1970 and the sixteen book "Left Behind" series by Tim LaHaye and Jerry B. Jenkins published between 1995 and 2007. Total sales of this series exceeded eighty million copies. Many evangelicals read the series not merely as fiction, but as a credible if not exact map of the future. Apart from this, one cannot fully appreciate the evangelical fervor by which the current nation of Israel is given great license, even in wrongdoing, and why huge numbers of evangelicals continue to support the Trump administration and attribute that support to their strongly held religious convictions. Suffice it to say here that this view of the end times is a late arrival in theological terms, and most of Christianity for most of history has had a different view.

Chapter 2

Four Important Concepts

"Under three things the earth trembles, under four it cannot bear up ..."
Proverbs 30:21

Four related concepts that are very relevant to the discussion of Ethics are moralization, legitimation, alienation, and determination (not "strong resolve," but the kind resulting from determinism). Though these concepts often carry a negative connotation, especially the first three, each has positive applications and each can unfold in a way that produces either good or bad results or a better or worse understanding of what is good or bad and why.

Moralization is a key element in the process by which a person or society comes to understand something to be right or wrong. Legitimation is a key part of the process by which a person or society comes to believe that something is real or unreal, true or false. Alienation is the act or process by which a person or a group of persons becomes separated, either physically or socially, from the rest of the community whether the community is a relationship, a family or any larger grouping of people. Determination, or more accurately, determinism, goes to the very heart of ethics because if some biological, psychological, or sociological factor determines my behavior then my choices do not matter or matter only secondarily.

Moralization

"Rabbi, who sinned, this man or his parents, that he was born blind?"
John 9:2

When something is moralized it means that it is seen as having positive, negative or neutral moral value often expressed through the terms moral, immoral or amoral. The last generally refers to that which has no moral values and it too can be understood positively or negatively. A fish or a lion has no moral values and we simply take that for granted in a positive sense because it is consistent with their nature. On the other hand, a person who has no moral values is a problem. The focus here will be on the process by which positive and negative values are assigned and it should be obvious when amorality shades into immorality.

Two aspects of moralization that need to be considered are the moralization of the normal and the moralization of disgust. Moralization of the normal takes place when there is a general consensus that *"this is the way things are"* or *"this is the way we do things"* and to do otherwise is considered not merely different, but morally wrong. There are all kinds of examples of this, some that most or all of us would agree upon, like *"it is morally wrong to drink to excess and drive because of the danger it poses for others."*

There are also examples that now would be considered as simply incorrect or much less likely to be agreed upon, like the historical treatment of left-handedness. Ninety percent of humans are right-handed, thus it is normal for people to be right-handed. For centuries being left-handed was often viewed not only as being abnormal but as being immoral. As noted in the Journal "Science" by author Daniel Casasanto:

> *"Today, being a lefty is a point of pride in the Western world. Historically, however, the left hand has been associated with atavism or corruption and its use has been discouraged, if not savagely punished. Kushner [Harold I. Kushner, author of "On the Other Hand"] reports that in the early 1900s, for example, Zulu children who could not remember to eat with their right hand would have their left hand immersed in boiling water. Less extreme measures to "retrain" natural left-handers were common in the United States as recently as the 1940s and are still practiced in parts of India, Africa, and Asia."* [16]

We may think that it is laughable to even consider anything so seemingly preposterous, but there are still proponents of this in our own time and country as well as in India, Africa, and Asia and there was a time in our country when it was much more widely believed.

---

[16] Casasanto, Daniel. "A history of handedness shows how attitudes can influence scientific conclusions." *Science*. 20 September 2017. blogs.sciencemag.org/books/2017/09/20/on-the-other-hand/. Accessed 6 March 2019.

The point is simply this: Human beings have a propensity to negatively moralize that which is not normal, even when it occurs regularly, if not frequently, in nature and it cannot be shown that differing from the norm harms anyone. People are inclined to make the assumption that what is normal ought to be. This is true in some circumstances, but cannot possibly be true in others. This is known as the "is/ought fallacy." As a general principle, we cannot move simply from what "is" to what "ought to be." We can't say that because something is not normal it is not right in the moral sense ... but we do it all the time.

The moralization of disgust is similar to and related to the moralization of the normal except for the obvious fact that it revolves around disgust, not normalcy. The current spate of horror pictures features alien beings that aren't merely scary, they are disgusting. With gushing and gooey saliva emanating from hideous bodies, they evoke not only fear but disgust. It is the disgust that makes them not just fearsome, but evil. However, as with the moralization of normalcy, we can't simply say that because something is disgusting to us that it is also wrong.

Perhaps you've heard the old adage that *"cleanliness is next to Godliness."* The idea is that God is clean and pure, therefore in order to be like God, we must be clean and pure. In the Old Testament (OT) sacrificial system, sacrifices weren't offered just for the sake of sacrificing, they were necessary to "propitiate" God. This means that only by means of a sacrifice, usually but not always by the killing of an animal, could someone be made clean in God's sight and therefore able to participate without stigma in the believing community. The whole ethos of Old Testament sacrifice was making things right between God and the community God called into being.

Many men, perhaps most men historically, view menstruation with an element of disgust. If you doubt it, there is an enormous trove of literature on the subject. In OT times, during her period, a woman was confined for seven days, and no one else could touch her without becoming "ceremonially" unclean.[17] Lest we think there weren't significant moral aspects involved in ceremonial uncleanness, there were. From an OT

---

[17] Leviticus 15:19-33.

perspective, if her menstruating didn't cause displeasure for God, any violation of the rules around it certainly did and they were harshly punishable. At the end of her period and the confinement that accompanied it, a woman was required to bring two turtledoves or two pigeons to the priest who would sacrifice them, and then she could be a fully participating member of the community without stigma once again.

Casting this in the best possible light, the ultimate and completely warranted purpose of her confinement may have been to prevent disease in a greater community that was struggling to understand how cleanliness or the lack of it related to disease. It is noteworthy, though, that the disgust associated with menstruation in OT times cannot be separated from the moralization of the practices regarding it. A woman's period made her unclean. If she didn't follow the ceremonial rules by which she could once again be made clean, her disobedience made her morally repugnant to both God and her community. For example, in Ezekiel 36:17, God is speaking: *"Son of man, when the house of Israel dwelt in their own land, they defiled it by their ways and their doings; their conduct before me was like the uncleanness of a woman in her impurity."* The behavior of the House of Israel was regarded as impure and offensive to God as a woman's period was.

Human excrement[18] and nakedness[19] were thought to be "indecent" to God in the same way as menstruation. So were nocturnal emissions, any male whose testicles had been crushed or whose penis had been cut off, and other physical deformity which disqualified men from acting as priests.[20] Many theologians have pointed out that God can't possibly be offended by what is common to a humanity created by God. The disgust reflected in these instances is human disgust projected onto God by a people still working out what legitimately needed to be regulated in human society and how that related to moral right and wrong.

Much more controversial, particularly for evangelicals, are the issues of homosexuality or biological sexuality that is neither clearly male or female. According to a study published by the National Institute of Health in 2000[21]

---

[18] Deuteronomy 23:12-14.
[19] Exodus 28: 42,43.
[20] Leviticus 21, Deuteronomy 23.

1.7 percent (possibly as high as 2 percent) of live births in the US, that is between sixty-eight thousand and eighty thousand out of approximately four million births annually, are of children who are born with either ambiguous genitalia (not clearly male or female), or do not have the normal genetic makeup with forty-six chromosomes that include XY (male) or XX (female) chromosomes, or have other biological irregularities related to their sexuality.[22]

If one multiplies the incidence of those "abnormalities" by sixty years, a considerably shorter than normal lifespan, there are as many or more than four million Americans who don't meet the norm. Psalm 139 beautifully portrays God as knitting us together in our mothers' wombs. Unless one takes the position that God erred while doing so, an idea which should be repugnant to evangelicals, these humans were put on earth by God as they are. This begs the question of non-conforming sexual identity or orientation which involves a much larger number of people. Yet, if there is significant measurable biological variance, is it a surprise that there would be significant variances in how people see and experience their own sexuality?

It is beyond the scope of this book to address the much wider issues of variant sexuality so I'll focus on one aspect of it. The fact that male homosexuality has been part of the human experience for almost as far back in history as we can see should give us pause. Somewhere around five percent of men identify as homosexual, and when they have been publicly identified as such, willingly or not, for most of history they have been brutally rewarded.[23] Why would anyone subject himself to this? This begins to feel suspiciously like left-handedness. Left-handedness is not

---

[21] Blackless M, Charuvastra A, Derryck A, Fausto-Sterling A, Lauzanne K, Lee E. "How sexually dimorphic are we? Review and synthesis." PubMed.gov, US National Library of Medicine, National Institutes of Health, March 2000. www.ncbi.nlm.nih.gov/pubmed/11534012. Accessed 6 March 2019. This study was criticized for including Late-Onset Congenital Adrenal Hyperplasia (CAH) in the count. The conditions accompanying CAH involve excessive or deficient production of sex steroids and can alter development of primary or secondary sex characteristics. A common form results in ambiguous genitalia at birth, but the impact of other forms is seen later in life.

[22] Ibid. The frequency of individuals receiving "corrective" genital surgery probably runs between 1 and 2 per 1,000 live births (0.1–0.2%). In recent years there has been increasing caution before performing sex assignment surgeries and for good reasons. Instead of 46 chromosomes, including the normal XY (male) or XX (female) chromosome pairs, some children are born 45X, 45Y, 47XXY, 47XYY or 47XXX or other.

[23] Two recent films that have handled this frankly, but sensitively, are "The Imitation Game" and "Boy Erased." Both illustrate that the ethical issue of our response is perhaps more important than the behaviors that evoked that response.

"normal," but it is not disgusting. Homosexuality is not only not the norm statistically but is disgusting to many, especially other men, who cannot imagine feeling a powerful same sex attraction or who have experienced such attraction and are disgusted with it in themselves.

In the same way that normalcy is moralized, so is disgust. In both instances, we need to tread very carefully because neither normalcy nor disgust requires moralization. The question becomes: Is it disgusting because it is wrong or is it thought to be wrong because it is disgusting? The ethical problem is not simply the behavior that departs from the norm or is disgusting, but our response to those inclined to behave in those ways. Apart from clear universal moral principles that do require morally normative behavior, it is very easy to confuse moral cause and physical effect. In one notable instance, Jesus' disciples attributed a moral cause to a physical effect and Jesus corrected them: *"His disciples asked him, 'Rabbi, who sinned, this man or his parents, that he was born blind?' 'Neither this man nor his parents sinned,' said Jesus, 'but this happened so that the works of God might be displayed in him.'"*[24] Being born blind isn't normal, but it doesn't warrant the presumption that there is a moral cause behind it.

What would you say about a person whose dedicated work shortened a world war and resulted in the saving of millions of lives? Alan Turing, known as the father of modern computing, was a homosexual. His groundbreaking work resulted in the breaking of the Nazi "Enigma Code" in World War II, shortening the war by as much as two years and saving an estimated 14,000,000 lives.[25] Most Christian people, if they knew nothing about his private life, would view a "good" of that magnitude as a clear manifestation of the grace of God. Turing either took his own life, died accidentally from cyanide poisoning (he had cyanide in a spare room for chemical experiments) or was murdered by the British secret service. This after being forced to undergo chemical castration rather than going to prison following his conviction for a liaison with another man. The coroner concluded that he had committed suicide due to mental imbalance. However, homosexuals were thought to be a threat to national security and

---

[24] John 9:42,43.
[25] Copeland, Jack. "Turing: The codebreaker who saved 'millions of lives.'" BBC News, 19 June 2012. www.bbc.com/news/technology-18419691. Accessed 6 March 2019.

he was so knowledgeable of cryptanalysis that murder could not be ruled out. In 2009 British Prime Minister Gordon Brown made a public apology for the appalling way Turing had been treated and Queen Elizabeth issued a rare full pardon.[26] The unreflective moralizing of the normal and the unguarded moralizing of disgust were dangerous in the time of Jesus and they are dangerous now.

Legitimation

"These commandments that I give you today are to be on your hearts. Impress them on your children."
Deuteronomy 6: 6,7

One of the key ways we come to know anything is by the testimony of respected others like parents, teachers, pastors, and coaches. They play a critical role in providing a way of looking at reality, often referred to as a world view or what sociologist Peter Berger has described as a "plausibility structure."[27] Another way of saying this is that these influential people in our lives provide a framework for belief, a narrative which helps to explain life and especially the really hard things in life. It is not too much to say that one cannot live without such a structure or structures, and when one's main plausibility structure falls apart, if not replaced by another, one's life falls apart.

My conversion to Christ in a personal way came when I felt my life was falling apart and resulted in the adoption of a plausibility structure that has underpinned my living for nearly fifty years. This is the experience of millions of evangelicals, but the fact remains that many people have developed frameworks for living that do not involve the faith commitments which evangelicals hold so dear. It is also true that even though that plausibility structure remains firmly in place for me, it has matured over the years, and I must at this point in my life firmly disidentify with many of the traditional guardians of that structure, as will become increasingly evident.

One's life experiences and education, however one acquires them, often result in the developing and replacing of immature or incomplete plausibility

---

[26] Copeland, B.J. "Alan Turing: British Mathematician and Logician." *Encyclopedia Britannica*, updated 23 January 2019, www.britannica.com/biography/Alan-Turing. Accessed 6 March 2019.
[27] Berger, Peter. *The Sacred Canopy*. Anchor Books, A Division of Random House, Inc, New York, 1990, p.156.

structures with new ones when necessary. When a person matures many other things go into the refining or replacing of plausibility structures in order to continue to make sense out of a much more complex, difficult and real world than was evident in childhood.

Many American parents go through this with their children regarding Santa Claus. Either actively or by default, parents teach or allow their children to be taught about Santa and all the lore that surrounds him. Children gladly receive it all as literally true. For kids under a certain age, he is as "real" as can be. Among his capabilities are the ability to provide good gifts along with the supposed ability to see into a child's life: *"He knows when you are sleeping, he knows when you're awake, he knows when you've been bad or good so be good for goodness sake!"* Half eaten cookies and partially consumed drinks that were left for Santa, as well as gifts from St. Nick on Christmas morning, are more proof that Santa is real.

The same is true of the Easter Bunny and the Tooth Fairy. By the time the plausibility structure that supports these beliefs is outgrown, there is a more substantial one that replaces it. The point is, though, that parents actively or passively legitimate the plausibility structure that permits belief in these fictitious characters. If children had never heard of them, though they may have eventually invented others, it is unlikely that they would invent with any degree of precision either Santa, the Easter Bunny or the Tooth Fairy. Someone had to precede them in legitimating these particular characters.

Many Christians are uncomfortable with this because it seems similar to the process by which we come to and some lose their faith in God. But there is also a world of difference, and I would argue that belief in Santa followed by a skillful replacing of that concept by a more real one may actually be a benefit to developing a mature belief in God who transcends all times and all cultures. All of us must learn how to make the transition from one plausibility structure to another when a deeper understanding of what is real requires it. It is a great gift to a child when a parent facilitates that gently and skillfully, and encourages the child to be patient with other children who have not yet come to that understanding. Many parents do this well.

In a very simple way, children thrive on knowing that someone "out there" knows them and wants to give them good things. This reflects a deeply innate desire and I would argue not just for children and not just for people from particular times, cultures, races or nations. It is also the case that all humans, as we mature, must learn to leave simpler concepts behind and increasingly experience the reality of a more complex world. Just as our concept of trees and actual trees are not the same thing, learning to make these critical transitions allows us to see that our concepts, real as they are to us, and the greater realities to which they point, are not the same thing. Critical as it is, even one's concept of God and God are not the same thing. This is the truth behind the strong biblical admonitions against making idols, whether material or conceptual.

As Berger points out, religious legitimations are the most powerful of all.[28] For evangelicals, the Bible is the primary source of all religious legitimations, but the preaching of evangelical pastors, teachers, and leaders is perhaps the most influential way that the Bible comes alive in evangelical faith communities. In using the word "preaching" I am using it in a very broad sense as the overall proclamation including the speaking, writing, film making and guiding of those who are accepted as reliable guides by evangelicals, whether formally or informally.

Also profoundly important for evangelicals is the interior "witness" of the Spirit of God by which the truths of the Bible, written and proclaimed, are understood to come to life in the believer. This witness of the Spirit confers a legitimacy that allows Christians to take for granted that which cannot be proven otherwise. When something achieves the status of being taken for granted then it has achieved a kind of legitimation that can hardly be challenged. With this kind of legitimation, no further examination or justification is needed. It is simply assumed to be true. This even applies to biblically debatable issues like one's view of the "end times" and other issues yet to be discussed.

As noted before, among the preponderance of American evangelicals it is simply assumed that abortion and homosexuality are morally wrong, and any further discussion of either is seen as an effort to undermine truth and

---

[28] Berger, *The Sacred Canopy*, p. 32.

Christian faith. Because non-believers are believed not to have an experience of God's Spirit in the same way, there is an implicit if not spoken belief that they cannot possibly understand that which is truly true as do those who have received the Spirit through faith.

The current moment of history in the US is a perfect example of the power of religious legitimation. Numerous evangelical leaders, including those of various denominations, pastors of large denominational and non-denominational churches, presidents of evangelical universities, seminaries and non-denominational ministries with national prominence, evangelical publications, evangelical politicians and lay leaders alike have loudly and consistently legitimated the presidency and administration of Donald Trump at an unprecedented level.[29] Are there evangelical pastors, leaders, and teachers who refuse to do so? Yes, but their voices are largely drowned out by the larger American evangelical choir.

How is this legitimation accomplished and why? Some of these leaders maintain that Trump has had a conversion experience though there is scant evidence of that in terms of his personal public behavior. If he has recently had such an experience, though, a convenient byproduct of that is that all his past transgressions have been forgiven and, for many evangelicals, they are rendered totally irrelevant. Even though his present behavior is indicative of a character that is consistent with his past behavior, it makes no difference what he may or may not have done before he became president, and for anyone to harken back to his prior life transgressions is viewed as more of a problem than the fact that he committed them.

For some evangelicals, this supposed personal experience of the president is decisive. For some, it doesn't really matter because of his policies and accomplishments and what he represents. The fact is that both before Trump's election as president and at this juncture, two years into his administration, evangelical support and the legitimation of Trump, not only as president but as a man, are as strong and loud as ever. The recent release of the docudrama "The Trump Prophecy" by students and staff of evangelical Liberty University is merely one of the latest examples. A Fox

---

[29] Shellnutt, Kate and Zylstra, Sarah. "Who's Who of Trump's 'Tremendous' Faith Advisors." *Christianity Today,* 22 June 2016. www.christianitytoday.com/ct/2016/june-web-only/whos-who-of-trumps-tremendous-faith-advisors.html. Accessed 6 March 2019.

News poll in February 2019 indicated that 25 percent of those polled believed that God wanted Trump to become president. According to the same poll, the number of white evangelicals who believed this was 55 percent compared to 36 percent of Protestants and 20 percent of Catholics.[30]

By one widely proffered argument, Trump is likened to the Persian king Cyrus who was instrumental in the return of the dispersed Jewish people to their homeland starting in the mid 500's BC.[31] He approved and supported the rebuilding of the temple which had been broken down when the Babylonians defeated and forced most of the remaining Jewish population into exile and captivity years earlier.[32] The Babylonian Empire gave way to the Persian Empire and Cyrus, a pagan Persian king, supported the Jews in their endeavor to rebuild. The analogy excuses Trump's personal behavior because, by this account, regardless of whether he has had a personal conversion experience, he is seen as God's man for the times and God's instrument whereby Christian values are being brought back to America in a powerful way.

This is classic religious legitimation and, if one doubts the power of it, just observe the magnitude of the division it is creating in the US today. Many on the evangelical side of the divide are absolutely convinced of the truth of their narrative and that God is on their side. Pesky facts that would refute that belief are irrelevant because they don't fit the narrative. This legitimation is profoundly dangerous because for many American evangelicals this is an "anointing" that is unassailable. If Trump is truly believed to be God's appointed leader there is virtually nothing in his personal life that would disqualify him. Personal behavior that would not be tolerated in the life of any other leader is "off-limits" or irrelevant when it comes to him because, by this anointing, anyone challenging him is challenging God.

Even though he was required to make a $25 million settlement to compensate the victims of the false advertising and unethical sales tactics

[30] Anapol, Avery. "One quarter say they believe God wanted Trump to become president: poll." *The Hill,* 13 February 2019. thehill.com/homenews/administration/429942-one-quarter-say-they-believe-god-wanted-trump-to-become-president. Accessed 6 March 2019.

[31] Garrison, Greg. "Why Evangelical Christians Support Trump." *Alabama Living,* 30 August 2018. www.al.com/living/index.ssf/2018/08/why_evangelical_christians_sup.html. Accessed 6 March 2019.

[32] Ezra 1-3.

of the bogus university run by the Trump organization,[33] this doesn't matter. Even though the charitable foundation he founded was dissolved under court supervision because of significant evidence of self-dealing and diverting money given for charitable purposes into his businesses and his presidential campaign,[34] this doesn't matter. Though Donald Trump has repeatedly demeaned John McCain, a greatly respected hero, even after his death, this doesn't matter. Justice Department precedent and policy precludes indicting a serving president. Though not indicted by the Special Counsel investigating him in the aftermath of the 2016 election, a whole cadre of those closely surrounding and reporting to him were. This too does not matter. If Trump is ever credibly shown to have committed tax evasion, obstruction of justice, perjury, campaign finance violations, sexual assault or anything else it will make no difference whatsoever for those for whom his religious legitimation is all that really matters. The takeaway in all of this? Donald Trump is not the problem. He is a symptom of the problem. The fact that the Cyrus analogy is highly problematic is of little concern to those who desperately want to believe that it has merit.

One major problem with the analogy is that Cyrus was a tyrant not chosen by the Jews, and Trump was freely and happily chosen by many evangelicals. A much better analogy is the original establishment of the monarchy in Israel, roughly 3000 years ago. Saul was anointed as the nation's first king to satisfy the demands of a people clamoring to be protected by a king. Samuel the prophet warned them of the dire consequences of their having rejected God as King by demanding a human one *"But the people refused to listen to Samuel. 'No!' they said. 'We want a king over us. Then we will be like all the other nations, with a king to lead us and to go out before us and fight our battles.'"*[35] Saul was physically imposing and met with early success, but he was devoid of character, thin-skinned and jealous of any who got the affection of his people or met with more success than he as did David, his successor. This is a familiar profile.

---

[33] Winter, Tom and Dartunorro, Clark. "Federal Court approves $25 million Trump University Settlement." *NBC News*, 6 February 2018. Accessed 20 March 2019. https://www.reuters.com/article/us-usa-trump-trump-foundation/trump-charity-to-dissolve-under-deal-with-ny-attorney-general-idUSKBN1OH1TH. Accessed 20 March 2019.

[34] Pierson, Brendan. "Trump charity to dissolve under deal with N.Y. attorney general." *Reuters,* 18 December 2018. www.reuters.com/article/us-usa-trump-trump-foundation/trump-charity-to-dissolve-under-deal-with-ny-attorney-general-idUSKBN1OH1TH. Accessed 20 March 2019.

[35] 1 Samuel 8:19.

The consequences of the people's choosing to have a king would be felt in the first generation when Saul's kingship unraveled, but the real impact would be felt generations later when a long succession of kings without moral fiber or character would lead to the destruction of Israel as a nation. The first faultline in the demise of the nation became a major division when Israel divided into northern and southern kingdoms after the reign of Solomon who succeeded his father, David. This division resulting from leadership without character is illustrative of both the divide in America today and the next concept to be examined here, namely alienation.

Alienation

"Send away male and female alike; send them outside the camp so they will not defile their camp, where I dwell among them."
Numbers 5:3

In what follows, "alienation" is defined very broadly. For many, the word may often seem too strong as it is being used, but the concept is a vital one. The essence of alienation is separation of a part from the whole.[36] Someone is alienated, briefly or otherwise, when they are excluded, ostracized, incarcerated, quarantined, shunned, marginalized, stigmatized, enslaved, segregated, put in detention, put in "time out" or otherwise separated from the group. They are separated either by themselves or others from the group, whether it be a family, a community, society, etc. All metaphorical uses of the word refer back to an actual physical separation of a part from a whole. Sometimes it is necessary as in the incarceration of violent criminals or the quarantine of people with virulent communicable diseases. The point here is not that alienation is always bad as we shall see below, but when it is bad it can be very, very bad.

In 1967, Arthur Koestler coined the term "holon." He was looking for a word to capture the idea that reality is composed of wholes and parts that are simultaneously whole parts of greater wholes. A whole atom is part of a whole molecule that is part of a whole cell that is part of a whole organ that is part of a whole human body.[37] An individual human, the product of a mother and a father, is part of a whole family that is part of a whole

---

[36] There is an enormous amount of material that has been written about alienation from psychological and philosophical perspectives. Here the term is being used much more simply and as defined above.
[37] Wilber, Ken. *A Brief History of Everything.* Shambhala Press, Boulder, Colorado, 1966, p.20.

community, etc. There are physical holons and social holons. My kidney or any other organ is a physical holon that is part of a greater whole which is my body. A legislative body like the US Congress is a social holon. The House of Representatives is a whole body that along with the Senate, another whole body, comprise the whole Congress. Each greater whole includes but transcends or goes beyond its constituent parts. The whole of reality transcends all of the parts and the sum of them. This ultimate wholeness is the province and essence of God alone. That is to say that God is not a part of reality along with other parts.

Paul was getting at this when he wrote, quoting an ancient Greek philosopher and poet, "'For in him we live and move and have our being.' As some of your own poets have said, 'We are his offspring.'"[38] Paul affirmed the truthfulness and applicability of this quote to a group of pagan Athenian philosophers whom he sought to convert. The parts, each human being and all humanity, exist "in" the Whole which God is. At the same time, God is not merely a part of this as are they.

As Berger describes it, in the normal process of growing up, alienation first occurs when social roles are built into the lives of children by their parents or others in the regular course of life. For a child, the social world is first encountered as an already existing reality. Certain things are not acceptable in this social world and very early in life children experience the effects of being shaped and molded against the resistance that naturally occurs when directionality or limits are applied to anything that is originally unshaped or unformed, children included.

Children are taught to live in a world that has behavioral boundaries usually applied by their parents starting in infancy. This is normal and necessary. When an infant does not obey when told not to go near a hot stove, he or she can simply be picked up and moved as all of us were in similar situations in our infancy. When we are separated from a dangerous physical situation it is appropriate, necessary alienation.

Reality for children is first defined by those responsible for their upbringing and the social world they live in seems as substantial as the natural world.

---

[38] Acts 17:28.

There is a difference though. The natural, material world is not created by humankind in the way that the social world is. To a small child, the difference is invisible. A child bumps into a tree and it hurts because the tree doesn't move. A child "bumps" into a parent trying to stop him from biting his sister, and ideally the parent doesn't move, and it hurts because he either gets scolded, a time-out or worse. Both are experiences of one large, already existing reality in the mind of the child.

As Berger describes it, this sort of molding happens of necessity because of the unfinished nature of our lives when we are born into this world.[39] Animals are born into an instinctual world. Humans are born into a world where, in addition to genetics and upbringing, choice and habit play a role similar to that which instinct does for an animal. Children don't yet know that they participate, not just by their having been born into society, but by their choices and actions both in the ongoing creation and the sustaining of that social world.

This molding and shaping of children by their parents is a good and necessary thing; however, it comes with a price. When a child resists being molded and shaped she is made aware of the fact that she is in that moment "alien" to the social world of which she is being made a compliant part. In a word: she is alienated; not for the purpose of excluding her in the long run, but for the good and necessary purpose (from the perspective of her parents and teachers) of making her a compliant part of a social world that was there before she was born and will be there after she dies as Berger indicates. She bumps up against something that is really there. When she complies and is embraced for her compliance, she no longer experiences the alienation that is the very mechanism by which compliance is taught and internalized.

The roles that the social world defines do not define us apart from our acceptance of or submission to those roles. Those definitions are either submitted to or accepted or agreed upon intentionally or unintentionally, consciously or unconsciously. Whatever else role definitions are, they are also creations of the societies which embrace and enforce them. Those with the power to do so make the rules, however that power came to be,

---

[39] Berger, *The Sacred Canopy,* pp. 4,5.

whether by parenthood, conquest, democracy or divine appointment as king or prophet or priest. Whatever else they may be, right and wrong are also such as are defined by the societies in which we live.

The Bible makes this point when it states that the law as summarized in the Ten Commandments came through Moses. In the NT gospel of John, we read: *"For the law was given through Moses; grace and truth came through Jesus Christ."*[40] Whatever the ultimate origin of the law that Moses brought to the people of Israel (the Bible clearly attributes it to God), nonetheless it was brought through a man and was applied and passed on by the human society of which he was the leader and in which it was embedded.

The result of alienation is that we seem to be aliens in this world as long as we are non-compliant whether for ignorance, willfulness or biological, psychological or sociological reasons. Both immigrants or refugees from another culture and a willful child experience alienation albeit for different reasons. We also experience being aliens in our own skins when we begin to internalize the roles into which we are being shaped. We are soon introduced to the concept of being a good boy or girl, a good son or good daughter, a good man or good woman. The components or boundaries implied by this are reinforced by our parents and teachers, and as we internalize these "ideal" roles we become aware that there is a deeper self that is not identical to this socialized self. In fact, the two come into conflict when we do not live up to the ideal. When there is a conflict between the two, as there inevitably is, we experience guilt and shame depending upon how successful the socializing process has been. Guilt is assigned by the guardians of the ideal, including one's conscience when it has been "successfully" formed, and shame is the emotion we experience when we believe we are guilty. This happens early and universally, both in infant humans and infant social structures.

For infant humans, bodily or corporal discipline is necessary in ways that it is no longer in adulthood.[41] Only talking to a very young child simply doesn't work. Sometimes a parent needs to pick up and move a small child from

---

[40] John 1:17.

[41] This doesn't have to be corporal punishment in the sense of spanking, but, as noted earlier, can be as simple as placing a child bodily in "time out" or picking up a child and moving him away from a wall socket.

danger or conflict, thus involving a corporal dimension even for those who are most sensitive to the negative issues related to potential abuse. In infant social structures, non-compliance with the structure of rules is a huge issue and is penalized physically and harshly, even by death, in many instances that make us shudder today. The history of Israel after the Exodus is an excellent example. Enemies could be beheaded as was Goliath by David in what is probably the most famous example.[42] Within the Israelite community, all sorts of infractions were punishable by death, whether by stoning or burning for various types of illicit sexual behavior and for sacrilege. We read about such practices related to ISIS in the news and we find it revolting. We read about it in the Bible and many of us do not find it revolting because we believe the world has changed since the writing of the Bible and what may have seemed acceptable in the past is no longer so today.

Being alienated and being sinful are not the same thing. In one's personal history, alienation is original in ways that sin is not. Before a child knows right from wrong he experiences that form of alienation which is a primary mechanism for teaching right and wrong. Alienation in this sense is obviously not bad, it simply is one way the human world molds and shapes its young. However, just as infancy needs to give way to maturity in a person, if an infant society does not mature it will continue alienating and punishing those who are outside the norm for reasons many of which are ultimately not moral ones. What may have been regarded as necessary at one stage of human social development can become terribly destructive and bad at a higher level of development.

The fact of one's having been alienated psychologically, socially or physically may or may not have a moral component, while sin, by its very definition, is wholly immoral as it is understood in Judaism and Christianity. If we fail to distinguish between the two, we make a very serious mistake, especially when we seek to address the moral aspects of both. Both immature societies and immature people often equate the two, and where they see difference from the normal they see sin. They ascribe a negative moral aspect to that which in reality is a natural, though not usual, part of

---

[42] 1 Samuel 17:50,51.

human experience and not inherently immoral; whether left-handedness, menstruation or physical or mental disability.

In reality, a menstruating woman is a normal woman and neither threatens nor contaminates others by her menstruating. In reality, people born with non-conforming genitals or a genetic makeup different from the usual XX or XY genetic structure are normal people in the sense that these circumstances occur regularly, if not frequently, in nature. Similar examples include conditions like epilepsy being attributed to evil demonic forces. Here the immorality is not necessarily ascribed to the individual, but the condition itself is seen as being rooted in something demonic and hence deeply evil or immoral. Because it is happening within a particular human body, though, it is nearly impossible to resist attributing some sort of evil to the one who embodies it. Those in America who have family members suffering from mental illness, and have seen their loved ones brutally treated by law enforcement personnel who attribute the aberrant behavior to mere criminality, know exactly what this means.

In infant cultures, physical deformity, many physical illnesses and mental illness are almost always considered evil and often the work of evil demons. I saw this first hand in a very powerful way while serving with Food for the Hungry in the Democratic Republic of Congo. There and throughout sub-Saharan Africa, AIDS is a huge problem. It is also popularly and widely understood not to be the result of sexual transmission. Although heterosexual transmission of HIV is the primary way the disease is transmitted in Africa,[43] it is widely believed actually to be the work of "spirits." In Congo, unless taught otherwise, *"everybody knows that"* and it is why it is such a difficult problem to combat.

Both physical deformity and mental illness regularly occur in nature and have from time immemorial. When something that regularly occurs in nature is attributed to something outside of nature or is seen as the just consequence of sin, a dangerous line has been crossed. When the

---

[43] In Africa, the transmission of HIV is predominantly heterosexual. Very large portions of the population, male and female, regularly have their heads shaved. Little attempt is made by barbers to clean the razors between "customers" and nicks are common. In some communities, enemas are regularly done and the tubes that are used, like the barbers' razors, are seldom clean. To the extent that needles are used for drug injection, legal or not, cleanliness of the needles is often not taken into consideration before use.

disciples asked Jesus *"who sinned, this man or his parents, that he was born blind?"* it was a logical question in a culture that assumed that abnormalities have a moral cause, either the direct consequence of sin or the work of an evil being. Jesus begged to differ.

All of this points to an even deeper separation that is as much a part of our present-day thinking as breathing is to any of us. This deeper separation results in a dualism that is an inherent part of the way we think. It is powerful and pervasive. It divides the world into supernatural and natural, sacred and secular, we and they, black and white, good and bad. It sees the north pole as distinct from the south pole as a first frame of reference rather than seeing the entire planet that makes them part of the same whole. It sees the poles as separate entities rather than the polarity of the whole earth which incorporates them both into one.

In the aftermath of the contentious hearings surrounding the confirmation of Judge Brett Kavanaugh to the Supreme Court, Donald Trump dismissed the sexual assault claim of Dr. Christine Blasey-Ford against Kavanaugh not just as mistaken, but as a "hoax," and those who support her claims as "evil" and part of a howling democratic mob that is unfit to govern. It takes no special powers of observation to see that by linking the narratives, credible charges of significant sexual impropriety by the president himself are seen to be just more clamorings of the howling mob, a hoax, and just more fake news. The media is regularly characterized as the "enemy of the people" and the purveyors of "fake news" not just occasionally, but continually. Trump's political opponents, whether Republican or Democrat, are belittled with demeaning names and outrageous innuendo or outright fabrications like the claim made during the 2016 presidential campaign that Sen. Ted Cruz's father was connected in some way with Lee Harvey Oswald and the assassination of President John Kennedy.

This is a politics of alienation at a level seldom if ever seen, particularly by a president of the United States. It is clearly the case that similar charges could be leveled at individuals and groups on the other side of the political divide, and that dirty politics of the left are as dangerous and unacceptable as those on the right. I agree completely. For our purposes, though, one huge difference is that evangelicals, as a distinctly identifiable group, are firmly and happily planted on only one side of the divide. Because the subject of this book is evangelical ethics, the focus here is on how those ethics are in play in our country today. By our own evangelical narrative, we are supposed to be committed to a better way.

By "anointing" Trump as God's man for America, that significant evangelical block that is the center of gravity of his support have forced all evangelicals, especially those who are on the conservative side of the divide but are not Trump "true believers," into an implicit identification with them. Increasingly convinced as they are that being on God's side is identical with support for Trump's presidency will increasingly divide not only America but evangelical Christianity itself. The power of religious moralization, legitimation and alienation is immense. When it has taken place "successfully" it looks much like America today. God help us.

Determination

"One of Crete's own prophets has said it: 'Cretans are always liars, evil brutes, lazy gluttons.' This saying is true ..."
Titus 1:12,13

Determination, as discussed here, is not determination like that of a determined man or woman. Rather, it is that which determines how our lives unfold. How responsible are we for our actions? If our actions are determined for us by any number of possible factors then we are less free than we might otherwise think. If not, how do we understand our own seemingly involuntary actions and those of others? Hard determinism would say that every effect, including our behaviors, has a prior cause and therefore all of our actions are caused by something else. In other words, we are programmed in some sense to do what we do.

In order of historical appearance, the extreme versions of the religious determinism of John Calvin, the physical determinism of Sir Isaac Newton, the historical determinism of Georg Hegel, the biological determinism of Charles Darwin, the economic determinism of Karl Marx and the behavioral determinism of Sigmund Freud and B.F. Skinner would all fit into this category.[44] By these, we are products either of divine predestination, laws of nature, our time and place in history, our genes, our economic class, our

---

[44] Thiroux, J and Krasemann, K. *Ethics Theory and Practice. Updated Eleventh Edition.* Pearson, Hoboken, New Jersey, 2016, pp. 61-64.

environment or our conditioning. Each would say that something else determines the course of our lives, but all would say that something stronger than our choices is responsible for our individual and collective behaviors. It is fair to say that the stronger the determinism, including religious determinism, the less important ethics become.

A "soft" determinism would say that any or all of these factors may influence us, but we as humans are free enough to make choices, including moral choices, that are not determined in a hard and fast way by these other factors. For example, understanding our personality types in terms like those defined either by Myers-Briggs or the Enneagram can be very useful. These two approaches to understanding our personalities, along with others, have been helpful for many. I have been helped in understanding why I am so inwardly oriented and my wife so outwardly oriented. I'm an introvert, she is an extrovert by Myers-Briggs definitions. I want to analyze everything and she is content to get on with doing what the experts say without further analysis because I am a "five" and she is a "six" in Enneagram parlance. According to these, either early life experience or internal wiring, both outside our control, determine our personality types. However, understanding what our types are not only helps to explain why we are the way we are but also gives us tools for personal growth. In other words, we are capable of overcoming limitations associated with our individual personality types by making informed choices that help us grow.

Indeterminism largely attributes to freedom of choice or to chance what hard determinism attributes to prior causes. William James, American psychologist and philosopher, was a strong proponent of this view.[45] Spontaneity and creativity are the hallmarks of indeterminism and, by this idea, we are largely free to do anything in the sense that we are unconstrained by any outside forces. Indeterminism, along with hard determinism and soft determinism, are philosophical concepts and each has been strongly argued pro and con through the years. Each has major ethical implications, but to understand them it is helpful to look at them more personally.

---

[45] James, William. "The Dilemma of Determinism." Republished in *The Will to Believe,* Dover, 1956. www.uky.edu/~eushe2/Pajares/JamesDilemmaOfDeterminism.html. Accessed 6 March 2019.

Some will have heard of Muggsy Bogues, Spud Webb, and Earl Boykins. They were professional basketball players in the National Basketball Association (NBA). What made them unusual is that they competed at the highest level even though all three were five feet seven inches tall or less. Hard determinism would tell us that it couldn't have happened any other way. Fate, destiny or God made it happen. Some cause that is physical, biological or divine or some combination of prior causes resulted in their success. Soft determinism would say that the three men played a vital role in their own success, one that can't be explained solely in terms of other causes. Their self-generated determination, hard work, and competitive spirit, along with their inborn talent, overcame their height limitations and resulted in their success. Indeterminism would tell us that if we are as determined as they are, work as hard, compete with the same ferocity and get the same breaks, then we too could get to the NBA.

The simple fact is that the success of these three men was highly unusual. Their outsize talent was indisputable. There is no rule that prevents short people from playing in the NBA; nonetheless, the rules are written in such a way that they favor those who, in addition to their talent, are tall, fast and strong. It isn't that it is impossible for short players to succeed, but that it hardly ever happens. The rules of the game make a huge difference. The rules, including the dimensions of the court and the height of the baskets, favor certain people.

No one has to play basketball. We are free to play and we are free not to play. That's the way games are. There are some things though that we are not free to do without substantial consequences. We are participants in a society where not only are we subject to the rules, but sometimes we are given the awesome responsibility of participating in writing the rules. Our ethics come fully back into play when it is not just impersonal forces or divine power that determine the course of our lives or the lives of others, but we ourselves are indispensably involved.

In the most recent midterm elections, one party in one state got 45 percent of the votes and 64 percent of the seats in the state legislature. Divine providence? Probably not. Survival of the fittest? Maybe, but if true that would be a concern for most evangelicals who reject this primary mechanism of evolution. Did the rules play a huge role in the outcome?

Yes, and the ethics or lack thereof of those who have written the rules to favor themselves and their interests over others.

Christianity has historically had a fraught relationship with determinism. Since the 1500s, the hard predestination attributed to Calvin has battled theologically with the free will doctrines championed during the Reformation by Jacob Arminius. These are the bookends, with hard determinism being one bookend and a more indeterminist theology the other. Catholicism and many varieties of Protestantism have generally held that free will or free choice demands more of a soft determinist or indeterminist view of our relationship with God and reality. Most evangelicals, certainly not all, tend more to a soft determinism with respect to "salvation." That means that choice plays a major role in one's coming to an experience of salvation. That said, with regard to the future, a very substantial number of evangelicals are hard determinists to the core. That is, they fervently believe that human choice has little or no control over the ultimate outcome of history.

By one popular understanding among evangelicals, things will just get worse and worse as history unfolds, and the end is probably coming soon. It will involve a war of the most epic proportions between the forces of good sided with the nation of Israel against the forces of evil. At some point in all of this, Christians will be taken out of the world as we know it in a "rapture" that will bring Christians immediately into the presence of God. According to one stream of this thought, all the rest of the world, except for a small remnant of faithful ones, will be left on an earth destined to experience increasing darkness and despair until a wrathful divine consummation of history when Christ comes in judgment. Seeking a lasting world-wide peace is a fool's errand for those who believe this. The current Secretary of State, Mike Pompeo, is a firm believer in the rapture[46] and this certainly has implications for an American foreign policy that is being presently shaped by his convictions.

Though some variation of this view of end times is held by many evangelicals, most of Christianity for most of history has not believed this.

---

[46] "Mike Pompeo Holy War and Rapture." *YouTube*. Published 26 April 2018. www.youtube.com/watch?v=3N2bOVd9_n8. Accessed 6 March 2019. Pompeo made these remarks at Summit Church in Kansas on July 8, 2015.

The post-millennial theology of mainstream Protestantism in the US and the amillennial theology of Catholics and many Reformed Protestants places far more emphasis on collective responsibility for making the world as good a place as possible. Both of these theologies are optimistic in that sense and reject the deterministic, pessimistic theology embraced by many evangelicals and fundamentalists. Both of these other views reflect the teaching of Jesus in many parables, such as the parable of the "talents" (a talent was a weight of precious metal that could be used as a form of currency). In this and other parables, a master entrusts his servants with his wealth or property, goes away for a long period of time, and comes back, in the end, rewarding those who used what had been given them wisely and holding those who didn't accountable for their irresponsibility.[47]

Relative lack of concern about environmental issues, issues of social justice and efforts to seriously reduce poverty world-wide fit easily in the "end is coming soon" line of thought. Evangelical animus towards Islam and unconditional support for Israel are powerfully consistent with this evangelical narrative. Sin is the real problem and abortion and non-traditional sexuality are primary exemplars of that which God really hates. The environment, social injustice, and poverty all pale in comparison. Actually, they are beside the point. What really matters is being on the right side when all hell breaks loose. Being on the right side involves a simple transaction with God in which the sinner gives God his sins and receives God's forgiveness and eternal life through Christ. This assures that one will be "taken up" and not experience the dire consequences or be held accountable for that which humanity, including evangelical humans, has brought upon itself. We don't know exactly when the end or the beginning of the end will happen, but many evangelicals feel that it probably won't be long. Sadly, with this often comes the view that the best we can do is circle the wagons and protect what we've got while we wait for God to straighten everyone else out once and for all.

---

[47] Matthew 25:14-30.

Chapter 3

Ways of Looking at Ethics

"Then you will understand what is right and just and fair - every good path."
Proverbs 2:9

The same sort of distinction we made between ethics and morality can be made between culture and society.[48] Though the words are sometimes used interchangeably, for our purposes here, one is the root and the other is the fruit. Human societies are rooted in human cultures. Christians believe their ethics are rooted in the moral law of God. So do the followers of the other major monotheistic faiths, Judaism and Islam. Despite their significant differences, these three faiths all trace their spiritual lineage back to Abraham. But why would others who don't share a belief in the God of Abraham be concerned with ethics? People all over the world, in every culture, have thought about and been concerned with what is right and good in the context of their culture. Even Christian ethics assume an already existing ethic from which the uniquely Christian aspects of ethics can be distinguished. Christianity is rooted in Judaism and Christian ethics are certainly rooted in the ethics of Judaism, but there is also a difference. In trying to understand this and other differences, there are three key ways of looking at and understanding ethics: descriptively, prescriptively and analytically.

Descriptive Ethics

"At the descriptive level, certainly, you would expect different cultures to develop different sorts of ethics and obviously they have; that doesn't mean that you can't think of overarching ethical principles you would want people to follow in all kinds of places."[49]
Peter Singer

For Christians, the ethics of the Bible come to full fruition in the New Testament. It is possible to distinguish Christian ethics, not only from those of Judaism, but also from the ethics of Confucius, Buddha and the classical Greek philosophers, all of whom preceded Christianity historically. Thus, Christian ethics can be distinguished from and compared with these. When

[48] Wilber. *A Brief History of Everything*, p. 77.
[49] "Peter Singer Quotes." BrainyQuote.com. BrainyMedia Inc, 2019.
www.brainyquote.com/quotes/peter_singer_649393. Accessed 6 March 2019.

we study Christian ethics in this way, as a subject, apart from the behavior that Christian ethics is meant to guide, we are engaging in "descriptive ethics." Looking at or studying ethics this way is valid and good, but it is not enough.

Prescriptive Ethics

"This is my commandment, that you love one another as I have loved you. ..."
John 15:12

There is another major way of looking at ethics. We can rightly look at them descriptively as I just mentioned, but that is not what my friends and I were doing when we got up and walked out of Officer's Call. In that moment we were looking at them "prescriptively." Think of your doctor writing a prescription. When we break down the word, "pre" means before and "script" means writing. So the doctor is writing an order ahead of time. When we walked out, we felt it was in obedience to a moral order that had been written ahead of time and we were supposed to follow it.

Analytic Ethics

"You know how to interpret the appearance of the earth and sky. How is it that you don't know how to interpret this present time?"
Luke 12:56

There is also a third, analytic, way of looking at ethics. This perspective examines what lies behind our ethical beliefs and moral practices. It shows how ethical beliefs develop in cultures, how those cultures influence us individually and corporately and how we act out those beliefs in human behavior. When ethical beliefs are written down in codes or creeds or laws like the Ten Commandments or the Sermon on the Mount or the Academy's Honor Code, they become objectively real and visible in human society. When those codes, creeds or laws are taught and followed by an individual or a society, they become part of individual and collective morality.

This way of looking at ethics also allows us to look behind or beyond ethics. Meta-ethics, a key aspect of analytic ethics, looks behind particular ethical values or the laws or customs that result from them. People the world over long for things like security, health, peace, purpose in life, prosperity, happiness, and freedom. Many of these are beautifully expressed in the unmatched King James Version[50] of Psalm 23. Though it is of special importance for Jews and Christians, and reflective of what draws them to the God of the Bible, what we find here reflects many of the things people everywhere long for:

> "The Lord is my shepherd; I shall not want.
>
> He maketh me to lie down in green pastures: he leadeth me beside the still waters.
>
> He restoreth my soul: he leadeth me in the paths of righteousness for his name's sake.
>
> Yea, though I walk through the valley of the shadow of death, I will fear no evil: for thou art with me; thy rod and thy staff they comfort me.
>
> Thou preparest a table before me in the presence of mine enemies: thou anointest my head with oil; my cup runneth over.
>
> Surely goodness and mercy shall follow me all the days of my life: and I will dwell in the house of the Lord forever."

The sense of abundance, serenity, security, freedom and rich relationship conveyed by green pastures, still waters, fearing no evil, a table prepared in the presence of one's enemies, an overflowing cup and the promise of goodness and mercy being shown towards us now and forever … these are things for which we all long. We can't make laws like "Thou shalt be secure" or "Thou shalt be prosperous" or "Thou shalt be free" because these are things that depend on much more than what any individual longs for or can do or attain alone.

Security, health, peace, purposefulness, prosperity, happiness, and freedom are so collectively valued by humanity, so longed for by people everywhere, that they become that around which life itself is ordered. In ordering our lives, ethics plays an enormous role. These values, these longings stand behind or beyond ethics as goals that ethics help us attain. We don't do ethics simply for ethics' sake, we do it for the sake of these things. From a strictly human perspective, these longings are what make

---

[50] The abbreviation for King James Version is KJV.

ethics necessary. From a Christian perspective, these longings begin to be fulfilled here and now in Christ, and are ultimately fulfilled by God in eternity. But the longings for which Christians seek fulfillment both now and in eternity are very similar to those that all humans seek whether they embrace the Christian message or not.

Ethics and Morals

"Likewise, every good tree bears good fruit, but a bad tree bears bad fruit."
Matthew 7:17

In the Air Force and the other branches of the military, you must be able to count on others and others must be able to count on you. Lives depend upon it. In US military culture, honesty, dependability, and trustworthiness are critical. These values are the roots of codes like the Academy's Honor Code. Values like these are internal. They can't be seen except when someone actually acts truthfully or behaves in a dependable or trustworthy way. When an autopsy is done, you won't find values like truthfulness or dependability; however, when these values are externalized in a code they become visible. They become a standard, something that can be taught and followed.

At the Academy, we received hours and hours of training about how to apply the honor code in everyday life. We were put under intense pressure and learned that the only acceptable answer when we didn't live up to one of the many stringent rules was *"No excuse, sir!"* With upperclassmen shouting in our faces while we stood at stiff attention, for most of us there was a great temptation to lie or quibble about why we were late to formation or didn't get around to polishing our shoes to a nearly impossible standard. But we were not allowed to get away with it. Months and months of intense training yielded a new way of thinking and acting. For a young man like I was then, it was a gift of great value. These values of the military community became my own values. Not only could they be seen in a code which had become my code, but they came to be seen in actual practice.

The late 1960s and early 70s were difficult years to be in the military. Opposition to the war in Vietnam was loud and growing. Our short hair and military bearing were not popular among people our age, but as young men in our late teens and early 20's, there was a strong desire to be like and to be liked by those our age. Drug use was rampant. During the summer following my graduation from the Academy, before reporting for helicopter training, I was at a party and smoked marijuana. Unlike one of our past presidents who was slammed by political opponents for smoking pot in his youth, but insisted that he hadn't inhaled, I did inhale. Though I enjoyed the experience, it was not something I did regularly nor did I do it at all during my flying career.

After completing helicopter training, first with the Army and then in Air Force Combat Crew Training, my first assignment was to Tyndall AFB, Florida, recently destroyed by Hurricane Michael. It was 1971 and the Air Force was cracking down on drug use. All pilots had to sign a form indicating whether they had ever used illegal drugs. By then I believed that the commandment "*Thou shalt not bear false witness*" prevented me from lying on the form. It was a real dilemma for me because I believed that my flying career hung in the balance. I went to my commanding officer, Lt. Col. Williams, and explained my dilemma. He sat in his chair, feet up on the desk, smoking a cigar, and asked me a few questions. He then told me to sign the form and give it to him. He never told me what he intended to do because I believe he knew that I would object if he told me he intended to falsify it. I never heard another word about it and feel that I owe my thirty year flying career in large part to him. I also learned an outstanding lesson in leadership.

The point of the last few paragraphs is not just to tell a story, but to show that ethics and morals are in a dance together. Though we can make a distinction between ethics and morals, it is damaging to both when we make a division between them. Christians, evangelicals especially, make a distinction between faith and works. However, a real difficulty arises when faith is not just distinguished from works but is separated from works. The New Testament makes it clear that one cannot say that he or she has faith if there is no evidence for it. As the NT book of James puts it:

> "What good is it my brothers, if a man claims to have faith but has no deeds? Can such a faith save him? Suppose a brother or sister is without clothes and daily food. If one of you says to him, 'Go I wish you well, keep warm and well fed,' but does nothing about his

physical needs, what good is it? In the same way, faith by itself, if it is not accompanied by action, is dead."[51]

Berger describes three movements that occur universally in human life.[52] As noted before, he observes that humans are born curiously unfinished. At birth, we are incapable of living apart from the care we receive from others. We are necessarily a part of a society that can be understood in either very simple family terms or in much more complex national terms. As mentioned previously, animals are born with the instincts they need to survive and thrive. They mature rapidly in comparison with humans and what they do largely by instinct, humans have to learn to do in the process of maturation, including becoming a functioning part of society.

Humans collectively "externalize" themselves. This is the first movement. For example, one key way we externalize ourselves is in conflict. Conflict is as old as humanity itself. In the biblical narrative, Cain, the son of Adam and Eve, killed his brother, Abel, out of jealousy at the dawn of humanity.[53] The narrative soon chronicles deadly conflicts between groups of people, with revenge for past wrongs a central part of the story.

Through trial and error and the desire to survive, certain values prove to be necessary in order to assure victory that leads not only to survival but to the enhancement of life for the victors. These values are "objectivated" in warrior codes and the like and ultimately in codes like the Air Force Academy Honor Code. Objectivation is the second movement. This objectivated reality then acts back upon the group and the individuals in the group through "internalization." This is the third movement. The Honor Code, now a reality itself, is the fruit of the seed of such values as the need for honesty and dependability. It becomes an objectivated standard that can be taught and, as it is learned and internalized, it acts back upon both the group and the individual to refine and perpetuate the very things that it states.

---

[51] James 2:17.
[52] Berger, *The Sacred Canopy*, p. 4.
[53] Genesis 4:8.

Visible and Invisible, Me and Us

"By faith we understand that the universe was formed at God's command, so that what is seen was not made out of what was visible."
Hebrews 11:3

The following diagram, based on the insight of author Ken Wilber, provides an excellent analytic framework for understanding how ethics and morals play out in our lives.[54]

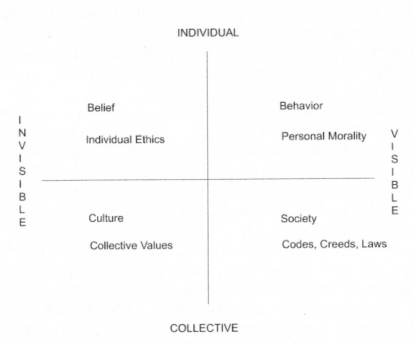

The diagram allows distinctions to be made among four integrally related quadrants, each representing a major aspect of human living. Notice that everything left of the vertical line is invisible. Everything right of the vertical line is visible. Everything above the horizontal line is individual. Everything below it is collective. By visible we're not talking only about things that can be seen with our eyes but anything that can be perceived by our senses. So anything tangible or measurable, anything we can see, touch or hear is visible in this sense and is right of the vertical line. My friends and I believed that it was wrong to stay in the room and watch the porn flick. Our belief was something inside us, so in that sense it was invisible. We got up and walked out. That was visible.

---

[54] Wilber, Ken. *A Brief History of Everything.* p.71.

Everything above the horizontal pertains to one person, everything below it pertains to groups of people. Another way of saying this is that everything above the horizontal line is singular, everything below it is plural. Christian corporate culture believes that degrading women is wrong. This invisible belief is held corporately, but each of my friends and I had come to embrace that corporate value individually. What was true corporately below the line became true individually above the line. So it wasn't just a group that believed that what was happening was degrading, each of us believed it. It wasn't just a group that walked out of the room, each of us walked out of the room. But it didn't start with each of us. It started as a corporately held belief that we later embraced individually.

Note that, like a dance, there is movement in multiple directions. The values of the Kingdom of God are *externalized*, to use the term coined by Berger, in the life and teaching of Jesus. The values and teachings of Jesus are objectivated in the doctrines and teachings of the church. The values and teachings of the church, when internalized, first shape the values and then the behavior of individual Christians. If this works out the way it is supposed to, there is also significant movement in the other direction. The values and behavior of Christians, corporately and individually, are supposed to affect those around them.

When we walked out of Officer's Call it stopped what was going on at that moment, but months later it also affected the decisions of a commander who refused to show a porn flick at another Officer's Call. Individual values can change corporate values and the change in corporate values can change corporate behavior which results in a change in the behavior of individuals who are part of that corporate group. If we lose sight of this fluid, dynamic process, we lose sight of a critical piece of the "big picture."

The damage being done to Christian ethics by American evangelicals is not being done by all evangelicals. It is often done in ignorance and fear. It involves embracing and prioritizing values that may not be bad in and of themselves, but when elevated as they are by many evangelicals, they displace the most significant Christian values. It also involves the damaging application of popularly held theological beliefs in the evangelical community.[55] When these elements are embedded in politics the damage is multiplied. When influential evangelical leaders legitimize all of this, the damage to Christian ethics is profound.

Altitude Matters

"And, while with silent lifting mind I've trod
The high untrespassed sanctity of space,
Put out my hand, and touched the face of God."
"High Flight"
John Gillespie Magee

There are some things that just can't be seen without altitude. This is true both literally and figuratively. In the biblical account, Moses encountered God on Mt. Sinai and saw things in a way that he had never before seen them. His receiving and delivering the Ten Commandments on tablets of stone dramatically shaped Jewish culture. This then greatly influenced Christian culture. Together, Jewish and Christian cultures have powerfully impacted world history. Moses later saw something at the top of Mt. Pisgah[56] right before he died that he had never before seen. It was a panoramic view of the "Promised Land" that enabled him to encourage Joshua with a vision of where he was to lead the people of Israel.[57] Both Moses and Elijah lived many hundreds of years before Christ. During what is called the Transfiguration, however, Jesus saw both Moses and Elijah on Mt.Tabor preparing him for what lay before him in his suffering and death. Peter, James, and John, who had accompanied him to the mountain, saw Jesus in a way they had never before seen him.[58] What we often describe as "mountain top experiences" are aptly named.

If I stand at my ground floor front door I can see part of one house near mine, some grass and the line of trees in front of my house. What I see is real and it is truly there, but we all know that there is more. If I stand on my second-floor balcony, I now can see a nearby mountain, several hills and many houses in my neighborhood. If I stand on the hill above my house I can see several mountains, neighborhoods beyond my neighborhood and

---

[55] These include end-time beliefs popularized years ago by Hal Lindsey in his book "The Late, Great Planet Earth" and more recently in the "Left Behind" series of books. These and other popularly held beliefs are discussed elsewhere.

[56] Deuteronomy 34:1-4. Sometimes translated Mt. Nebo.

[57] Deuteronomy 34:1-9.

[58] Matthew 17:1–8, Mark 9:2–8, Luke 9:28–36.

the city center. At lower altitudes, there are some things that I just can't see, literally and figuratively.

The famous Swiss child psychologist, Jean Piaget, did an experiment in which young children were given a ball that was red on one side and green on the other. The ball was then placed between the children and an interviewer. When asked the question, "what color do you see?" The young children answered that it was green. When asked by the interviewer, "what color do I see?" The children answered "green." They were unable to see the ball from the interviewer's point of view, not because they were unintelligent, but because they were at a stage of cognitive development where it just wasn't possible for them. Older children were regularly able to say "I see green" and "you see red."[59]

Building on Piaget's work, Harvard professor, Lawrence Kohlberg described three major levels (altitudes if you will) of human moral development. He called them pre-conventional, conventional and post-conventional. He identified additional stages within the levels, but these are three very general categories of human moral development. Another way these same levels can be described is egocentric, ethnocentric and omnicentric.[60]

At the pre-conventional, egocentric level or altitude I see what is good for me and those right around me, but am relatively unaware of or unconcerned with what is good for others outside that tight circle. At the conventional, ethnocentric level I see what is good for me and what is good for "us" but am less aware of and less concerned with what is good for "them" or for all. At the post-conventional, omnicentric level my concern is not just what is good for me and good for us, but what is good for all.

Yet another way of describing these is in terms of concentric circles of concern and responsibility that expand when we move from one level to another. Think of movement from one of these levels to another more like going up steps to reach the next levels rather than in an elevator moving from one distinct floor to the next. In either case, it is necessary to go through one level to get to the next or higher ones. It is also possible to get

---

[59] Wilber. *A Brief History of Everything.* P. 174.
[60] Ibid. pp. 180-183. Wilber uses "world-centric" but I prefer omnicentric as more descriptive.

off at a particular floor and stay at that level. Similarly, people often plateau before reaching the highest levels of moral development.

Based on the work of Piaget and Kohlberg, a Christian author, James Fowler, took Kohlberg's levels and stages and applied them to understanding how people are able to understand and grow in their faith. Fowler connected levels and stages of human cognitive and moral development with levels and stages of growth in one's faith.[61] One of the noteworthy implications of Fowler's work is that the levels and stages of human cognitive and moral development hold for Christians in the same way as they do for all people. The apostle Paul was getting at this when he wrote, *"When I was a child, I talked like a child, I thought like a child, I reasoned like a child. When I became a man, I put the ways of childhood behind me."*[62] Here it isn't a matter of being Christian or non-Christian, "spiritual" or "unspiritual," but being a child or being an adult developmentally.

One's spirituality and one's level of human cognitive, moral, or faith development, though not the same thing, are closely related. At the pre-conventional, egocentric level we may understand the consequences of our actions, but not the morality of them. At the conventional, ethnocentric level we understand the morality of our actions, but not the universality of our responsibility and what lies behind our morality. At the post-conventional level we understand not only the morality of our actions, but what that morality is aiming at, why it is there and why our responsibility is not just to ourselves, our family or our people, but to all people.

Small children are pre-conventional and egocentric. Their world is the world right around them and they don't yet understand "conventions" or rules. They primarily respond to their parents' or another adult's authority. As they develop, most young people mature into the conventional, ethnocentric stages and level. Whether they follow them or not, they understand why there are rules. Within their peer groups they establish "rules" that apply there even if they reject the rules of their parents. Many adults plateau at this level, including many Christians, though they are uncomfortable with the thought of this because they see little or no relationship between what

---

[61] Fowler,James W. *Faith Development and Pastoral Care.* Fortress Press, Philadelphia, 1989, p. 53ff.
[62] 1 Corinthians 13:11.

they consider spiritual maturity and levels of human development. They see the relevant world as including, but larger than, their immediate families. It now can encompass more relevant people in their lives including those in their schools, their places of worship, their community, their party, their race, their nation, their faith, but at this stage what is really important in life is what is important for "us" or "our people." At this level people respond to expectations and rules or conventions thus the term "conventional." They are strong advocates of law and order and value firm boundaries. Fewer people develop further to the post-conventional, omnicentric level where they realize that moral obligations extend not just to our immediate families, not just to "our people," but to all people. Many Christians do develop to this level, but many do not.

Keep in mind that we are not talking about intelligence here. I have a granddaughter who is developmentally pre-conventional and egocentric. She doesn't understand that it is wrong to hit or bite her brother, but she does understand that every time she does she ends up in "time out" or worse. She is highly intelligent, it's just that her intelligence and her stage of human development are not the same thing. Nor are spirituality and level of human development the same thing; however, both intelligence and spirituality show themselves in ways that are consistent with a person's level of cognitive, moral or faith development.

The Nazis were highly intelligent, but their level of human development was essentially conventional and ethnocentric. They had all sorts of laws and rules that they took very seriously. They believed that things like following orders were of huge importance, but they also firmly believed in the supremacy of their Aryan race and heritage and could not or would not see beyond that to the full humanity and value of the Jewish people they slaughtered. One's level of human moral development, in addition to other notable factors yet to be discussed, is a question of altitude, not intelligence.

When Jesus said, "*Do unto others as you would have them do unto you*" and "*love your neighbor as yourself*"[63] he was speaking from a post-conventional, omnicentric level. "Others" were not simply those around him,

---

[63] Matthew 22:39 KJV.

or those who were his people, but all of us. This was brought home forcefully in the parable of the "Good Samaritan" where Jesus answered the question "Who is my neighbor?" In the parable, the true "neighbor" turns out to be a stranger encountering and caring for a person in need who is of a different ethnicity and religion.[64] The upshot? Included among my neighbors are those whom I have never met who are in need and are of different ethnicities and religions. Commending the Good Samaritan, Jesus said, "*Go and do likewise.*" This is post-conventional, Christian morality.

During the civil rights movement of the 1960's, when many African Americans and a handful of others engaged in nonviolent civil disobedience, they broke laws regarding who could eat in which restaurant or use which bathroom or occupy which seats on a bus. They did so because our laws are supposed to protect all people and these laws didn't do that. They weren't avoiding the law. On the contrary, they thought the law was necessary, but that these laws were unjust. Because they understood the importance of the law, they were willing to suffer the consequences of the law and go to jail in order to demonstrate how unjust the laws were. The Christian theology behind this is beautifully expressed in Dr. Martin Luther King Jr.'s "Letter from the Birmingham Jail" which is an exceptionally powerful piece of post-conventional Christian moral writing. One of the great "misses" for American evangelicals is that they were, for all practical purposes, "no shows" for the American civil rights movement which was arguably the most significant social-spiritual movement of the 20th century in America.

In the Great Commission, which is so central for evangelicals, Jesus sent his followers out to "*make disciples of all nations.*"[65] The Greek word for nations is "ethne" from which we get the English "ethnicities." His message was not for some, but for all. When Jesus talked about "*having eyes to see and ears to hear*"[66] he was talking about an ability or inability to perceive things, not just "spiritually," but from a higher level or altitude, and in every case it was an implicit or explicit call to rise to the higher level.

---

[64] Luke 10:25-37.
[65] Matthew 28:19.
[66] Matthew 13:16, Mark 8:18 as well as many similar usages in both Old and New Testaments.

Chapter 4

Ethics in Context

"Rarely perhaps has any generation shown so little interest as ours does in any kind of theoretical or systematic ethics."[67]
Dietrich Bonhoeffer

Ethics, Christian or otherwise, damaged or not, cannot be studied or practiced alone. Ethics, as a set of beliefs or as a subject, does not exist alone and cannot be understood in isolation from other related and complementary disciplines. For centuries before the time of Christ and for centuries afterwards, up to and including the present, those who take ethics seriously have seen it as part of a larger quest for wisdom.

The literal meaning of "philosophy" is the love of wisdom. It has been pursued both within the Judeo-Christian worlds and in many others. Confucius, Buddha and the Greek philosophers, notably Socrates, Plato and Aristotle, all sought to understand what it meant to live wisely hundreds of years before Christ. The wisdom books of the Old Testament also were written hundreds of years before Christ. Proverbs, Ecclesiastes and Job are examples of the importance to and love for wisdom among the Jewish people. Within Christianity, the early church fathers, followed by people like Augustine, Aquinas, Teresa of Avila, Luther, Calvin and Wesley were part of this quest in centuries past. In the last century, people like GK Chesterton, Simone Weil, Dietrich Bonhoeffer, Dorothy Sayers, C.S. Lewis, Francis Schaeffer and, more recently, thinkers like N.T. Wright, Timothy Keller and pastors and teachers in many seminaries, churches and study groups have been indispensable for our Christian understanding of truth and wisdom.

The Apostle Paul cautioned Christians against being caught up in what the King James version of the Bible describes as *"philosophy and vain deceit"* and a more recent translation describes as *"hollow and deceptive philosophy."*[68] Recall our earlier conversation about damaged goods requiring the prior existence of undamaged goods. It is appropriate to note

---

[67] Bonhoeffer, *Ethics*, p.66.
[68] Colossians 2:8 NIV.

that Paul was not, as many evangelicals believe, warning us off from philosophy, the love of wisdom, but from hollow or deceptive philosophy. There is a huge difference. Even in his strong criticism of worldly philosophy, what he called *"the wisdom of the wise,"*[69] Paul was not disparaging real wisdom which he believed and taught to be fulfilled in Christ.

Though it is possible to speak of Christian philosophy generally, it is also possible to discern subtle and sometimes very clear differences in philosophy even among New Testament authors. The apostles Peter, James, and John had different philosophical approaches to the same great truths from that of Paul. Peter noted that *"our dear brother Paul also wrote you with the wisdom God gave him ... he writes the same way in all his letters, speaking in them of these matters."*[70]

God gave Paul a unique wisdom and Peter encouraged his readers to embrace that wisdom and not to distort it. The New Testament tells us that *"Jesus grew in wisdom and stature and favor with God and men."*[71] The point being simply that the love of wisdom, philosophy, is vitally necessary and has been for Christians since the beginning. Ethics is a vital part of philosophy because it is the quest for wisdom in moral matters, in matters of good and bad, right and wrong, for Christians and non-Christians alike.

For centuries both classical philosophy and Christian philosophy have sought to answer many of the same questions. Even in his strongest criticism of worldly wisdom, Paul did not criticize the questions that worldly philosophers have raised since antiquity; rather, he criticized their answers to those questions because they did not take into account God's wisdom as revealed in Christ. His criticism is not with the endeavor of philosophy, but with the insufficiency of its answers apart from Christ.

In a debate with Athenian philosophers, Paul quoted Greek philosophers and affirmed the truthfulness of their observations. When he quoted Epimenides, saying *"For in him [God] we live and move and have our being"* and Aratus saying *"For we are his [God's] offspring,"* Paul applied

---

[69] 1 Corinthians 1:18-31.
[70] 2 Peter 3:15,16.
[71] Luke 2:52.

those truths uncensored to Christians and non-Christians alike. He then went on to build on those truths and show how they were fulfilled by and in Christ.[72]

The main questions classical philosophy seeks to answer are questions like these: What is real? How do we think correctly? What is true and how do we know it? What is morally right? How should human societies be organized and how should one govern or be governed? What has beauty or value in what we produce (art for sure, but more generally in all that humans produce)? The discussion of what is morally right and wrong is central to every part of this book so, in the next few paragraphs, we will look briefly at these other classic philosophical questions and how they relate to our understanding of ethics. There are one-word terms like "ethics" for the study of each of these questions. Before getting to those terms though, consider this:

The Nazis had answers to all of these questions. They had a vision of what was ultimately real. They believed their thought processes were right and that they were clear in their thinking. Thus, they were confident that they knew what was true. In light of their beliefs about what was real and true, they had a particular view of what was right and wrong. Because they felt their beliefs in all these areas were right and true, they had a particular vision of how to govern and how people should respond to that governance. Their beliefs in these other areas gave them an appreciation for beauty and art and they valued both very highly. In short, they had a view of the world, reality, truth, and beauty that affected virtually every aspect of life. This powerfully affected how they actually lived and behaved. They were also frighteningly immoral.

The following list is not meant to be all-inclusive; rather it is meant to illustrate a salient point. Communists under Lenin and Stalin also had answers to these questions, as did the Egyptian, Persian, Babylonian, Greek and Roman Empires, the Chinese dynasties, the British monarchy, African tribal kingdoms, Islam in its several manifestations and, though we often don't like seeing ourselves in lists like this, Christians in general and

---

[72] Acts 17: 28.

American evangelicals in particular. Philosophy, the love of true wisdom, is important. Denying its necessity or power is foolish and dangerous.

What follows is not the usual fare for either Bible studies or book clubs, but if understanding the necessity for and the power and the importance of ethics in our lives is appealing to you, it can't be done apart from grappling with the answers to these next five questions. When we get the answers to one or more of these questions wrong or fail to see their relationship to the others, we soon find ourselves in dangerous ethical territory.

What is real?

"Why, sometimes I've believed as many as six impossible things before breakfast."
Alice in Wonderland
Lewis Carroll

The one-word term for the study of what is real is metaphysics.[73] It refers to what is beyond the physical or material. "Meta" means after, along with or beyond. "Physics" refers to the material, the physical. Metaphysics involves those beliefs that come after or go along with or beyond what we can perceive with our senses. Most of our religious beliefs are metaphysical, but there is much more to it. Remember the diagram introduced earlier? Most everything to the left of the vertical line, things like "values" or "beliefs" are metaphysical in nature. They are invisible in the sense intended in that diagram. If you believe something to be real, but it isn't material in nature, it is metaphysical. If you do surgery or an autopsy you won't find it, but that doesn't mean that it isn't real. On the contrary.

If you do an autopsy on a man or woman you will not find a character, a conscience, a nature, a soul. Nor will you find wisdom or justice or compassion or goodness or evil. You will find a brain that is a physical correlate of a mind (it goes "along with" a mind), but you won't find a mind. A neurosurgeon can tell me almost everything about my brain, including what kinds of thoughts or emotions originate in and activate different parts of my brain. Unless I tell her, though, she can't tell me the content of a single one of my thoughts.[74] The brain and the mind go hand in hand, but they are not the same. Likewise, you will find a physical heart, but not the

---

[73] Ontology, a branch of metaphysics, focuses on major aspects of this.
[74] Wilber, Ken. *A Brief History of Everything*, p. 86.

kind of "heart" that a person with compassion has. These are metaphysical realities. We can see evidence of them in a person's life, but we can't "see" any of them. They are invisible. But I believe, as do many or most, that they are real in a very essential sense. Metaphysics is the study of what is real in just this sense.

A brief aside here: as Wilber points out, the Nazis had strongly held metaphysical beliefs about the origin and supremacy of the Aryan race and the destiny of the Third Reich. Because of firmly held beliefs about this destiny they believed they were on the right side of history. These beliefs were firmly held to be true and they informed virtually everything the Nazis did. What's the point? If you get the metaphysics wrong, if you have the wrong assumptions about what is real, along with and beyond the physical, you will get much of the rest of it wrong too.

Some say that we just use words like character or conscience or nature or soul or mind or heart simply to describe the products of biological or sociological processes. They don't have a reality of their own. By this thinking, words like justice, wisdom, compassion, and goodness are just shorthand for culturally conditioned activity and behaviors that we name with those names. But to believe this is as much a metaphysical belief as believing that they are real. People do math, but behind the math that we do are these real relationships between numbers that exist "out there," whether we believe in or do the math correctly or not. As a pilot, if I thought the numbers weren't real or got the math wrong about my fuel quantity and consumption rate, I could actually run out of fuel and crash.

When Christians talk of each of us having a sinful nature, we are referring not just to a propensity to do bad things or think bad thoughts, but a flawed reality within from which sinful behaviors come. When Christians speak of each of us having a soul, we are speaking of a non-material reality that transcends our physical bodies. When Christians speak of conscience or character, we understand them to be realities that must be shaped or formed, not just generally, but in a specifically Christian way, if we are to be faithful to our calling.

One last point before moving on: the real and the true are closely related, but they are not the same thing. A lie may be real, but it is not true. A mistaken belief like "at this rate of fuel burn I have enough fuel to make it to my destination" may be my real belief, but it is not true if I have not calculated correctly and I may well crash.

How we think is as consequential as what we think because it largely determines what we think. Those of us who believe that characters, consciences, natures, souls, minds, and hearts are real, believe that they are real in much the same sense that numbers and the relationships between numbers are real. To understand their reality, though, we have to go beyond the physical. That being said, it is not enough simply to go beyond the physical to get to the real, and that leads us to a next pressing question.

How do we think correctly?

"If you don't know where you are going any road can take you there."
Alice in Wonderland
Lewis Carroll

The one-word term for the study of how we think correctly is logic. Our English term comes from the Greek word "logos" which, depending on the context, can mean logic, word or reason. For Christians this is of special interest if for no other reason than in the Gospel of John, Jesus is referred to as the "logos" or, in most English translations of the Bible, the "Word." When John writes *"In the beginning was the Word (logos) and the Word was with God and the Word was God,"* he is writing about Jesus.[75] By the time John wrote his gospel, the Greek word logos had been in use for hundreds of years in connection with the formal study of logic as well as otherwise so we could almost as easily say, "In the beginning was the One in Whom all things fit together logically." In this sense, Jesus is the embodiment or personification of logic and, though never a formal student of logic, he was a master practitioner.

Logic is a complex subject and it would be easy to get bogged down in a deep discussion that doesn't help us much when it comes to examining our ethics. So at the risk of oversimplifying it, logic serves knowledge and truth by helping us to think and reason correctly about that which is real, whether it is visible or invisible. Logic is a means to an end and not an end in itself.

---

[75] John 1:1.

The simple point is that if our ethical beliefs are illogical then, at best, it is questionable whether they are right and true and, what is equally or more disturbing, we have no way of knowing one way or the other.

We are all familiar with simple addition and subtraction. When we add, we take something known and add it to something else that is known and we get something new that is greater than either of the things with which we started. In the study of logic, a similar kind of process is known as induction. Induction takes us from particular facts to a larger general truth. Sherlock Holmes did this all the time. He would start with a particular clue, add to it other clues and then would sum it all up in a way that solved the mystery.

Subtraction, on the other hand, starts with a known and larger whole and takes away a part of it leaving another part which we can often know with precision. In logic, a similar process is known as deduction. Deduction starts with a general truth and moves to a particular truth. Sherlock Holmes did this all the time too. For example, he would follow a process something like this: *"We know from indisputable testimony that everyone in this gang was involved in this crime. We know that this particular man was part of the gang when the crime took place, therefore we know that he was involved in the crime."* This is called a syllogism. If the major premise is true and the minor premise is true then the conclusion is true.

Without getting into mathematical concepts like negative numbers, addition has no upper limit as one can always add more to a sum. Subtraction, however, starts with an upper limit, a known number from which one starts, but in addition to this upper limit, it also has zero as a lower limit. One can always add to an inductive argument. One cannot always subtract from a deductive one. There is a limit and it is this limit that allows a precision in a deductive process that an inductive process can never produce. Though both addition and subtraction can produce clear and indisputable mathematical results, in logic a deductive process is capable of producing more certainty than is an inductive process provided that you start from something known to be true.

Evangelicals believe that something that the Bible clearly teaches is the kind of general truth from which other truths can be deduced.[76] For example, we believe that the Bible teaches that God only does good.[77] From this general truth, we can reason as follows: God only does good. God did this; therefore it is good. Similarly, evangelicals generally believe anything Jesus taught is true; therefore, if anything contradicts the teaching of Jesus it cannot be true.

On the other hand, Aristotle believed that you could only arrive at general truths which he called "first principles" or "universals" by induction.[78] Aristotle is right ... unless you start with an authoritative assumption, as evangelicals do by faith when they declare the Bible to be true, God to be good and Jesus to be the Son of God. These beliefs are all based on the internal teaching of the Bible made personal for evangelicals by the internal witness or illumination of God's Spirit. Evangelicals believe they are justified and right to assume those truths, but not for the same kind of reason with which Aristotle would have been comfortable.

If one can come to the same Christian conclusions inductively by providing evidence outside the Bible, well and good, but for evangelicals that is not necessary in the way Aristotle thought it was. For example, Christians believe that Jesus was crucified and rose from the dead whether any concrete evidence outside the Bible supports this or not. Whether the Shroud of Turin could be proved to be the burial cloth that covered a crucified Jesus or not, Christians believe Christ was crucified and rose again based on the testimony of the first disciples recorded in the Bible. Anything outside of the Bible that might lead one to believe otherwise is overruled by the Biblical narrative. For evangelicals, the Bible is evidence and, for many, that is evidence enough in the areas to which it speaks. Aristotle's general truths were based on induction; for the evangelical Christian, general truths of the faith are based first on the authority of the Bible and secondarily on inductive evidence outside the Bible.

---

[76] Westminster Confession of Faith, Chapter II, paragraph VI "The whole counsel of God concerning all things necessary for His own glory, man's salvation, faith and life, is either expressly set down in Scripture, or by good and necessary consequence may be **deduced** from Scripture: unto which nothing at any time is to be added, whether by new revelations of the Spirit, or traditions of men."

[77] Psalm 119:68 "You are good and do only good; teach me your decrees" (New Living Translation)

[78] Aristotle, The *Nicomachean Ethics.* Penguin Books, London. Translation by J.A.K. Thomson, Revised edition 1976, Further revised edition 2004. p.148 "all teaching starts from what is already known ... because it proceeds either by induction or by deduction. Induction introduces us to first principles and universals, while deduction starts from universals. Therefore, there are principles from which deduction starts which are not deducible; therefore they are reached by induction." Christians would say that first principles are also revealed by God.

Our legal system depends on induction as when in court we take particular pieces of evidence, "add" them together and come up with a general conclusion of guilt or innocence. This kind of process cannot lead to absolute certainty, but it does establish guilt or innocence based on whether the facts show a person to be guilty *"beyond a reasonable doubt"* or not. The challenge with induction is that if there are other pieces of evidence "out there" that were not originally added in, then it is possible that if they are introduced they will change the conclusion. For example, since the development of the capability to analyze DNA evidence, the convictions of many "criminals" have been overturned. The "new" facts changed the verdict.

Jesus used induction very powerfully in his life and teaching. In the well known account of a woman caught in the act of adultery,[79] Jesus used an inductive process to shape the outcome of the incident. The "facts" appeared to be clear. She was caught in the act and Old Testament law required that those caught in the act of adultery were to be stoned to death. For the accusers, this was a pretty cut and dried deductive argument for her stoning. However, there were other facts that hadn't been factored into the equation. The Old Testament law required that both parties be stoned. If there was no other party involved then she couldn't have been caught in an act that requires two parties. Suspiciously, there was no mention of the man who was also caught in the act by the men who were ready to stone her. When Jesus said *"let him who is without sin cast the first stone"* he made this a confrontation about the men and their injustice, not about the woman. There was the real law prohibiting and calling for the punishment of adultery, the real circumstances of those having been caught in adultery, the real leaving out of pertinent facts like her partner's complicity, the real fact of her accusers' immoral selective application of the law, all building to a proof of their injustice and the total inappropriateness of their self-appointment as judges, jury and executioners.

The genius in this is that he did not condone adultery generally or excuse her adultery in particular; rather, he powerfully exposed their profound injustice. They understood it clearly: *"At this, those who heard began to go*

---

[79] John 7:53 - 8:11.

away one at a time, the older ones first, until only Jesus was left, with the woman still standing there.[80] His process was one of sophisticated induction, but it was much more than that. In this instance, when those who were in an overwhelming position of power, the power of life or death, were arrayed against one, who though not innocent herself, had no power, Jesus intervened on behalf of the powerless woman.

Jesus also used deductive logic often and powerfully. For example, when confronted by religious opponents who did not believe his teaching about the resurrection of the dead, he appealed to the Scripture that they did believe which said, "*I **am** the God of Abraham, the God of Isaac and the God of Jacob.*"[81] Abraham predated Jesus and all who were present that day by perhaps as much as 2000 years. The Scripture, speaking of God's relationship with Abraham in the present tense, was believed to have been written by or under the direction of Moses hundreds of years after Abraham's death. So Jesus went on to say "*He is the God not of the dead, but of the living.*" Then the Scripture continues, *"When the crowds heard this, they were astonished at his teaching."*[82] Jesus' logic? He asserts that God is the God of the living, and then deduces that because God **is** the God of Abraham therefore Abraham still lives despite having died 2000 years ago, so the resurrection of the dead is real and true. Whether we think this is a valid deductive argument and whether we believe it or not is a separate matter. One remarkable thing, though, is that the largely uneducated crowd who heard Jesus say this got both his logic and his point.

Back to the Nazis. They were murderously logical. They started with faulty premises like the belief that Jews were inferior to Aryans and dangerous. Then, when they identified people like the family of Anne Frank and millions more as inferior and dangerous, they logically but immorally concluded that because they were inferior and dangerous, it justified something like the Holocaust. Ugh.

Surely, though, this couldn't happen among Christians, could it? When many white Americans, including many Christians, believed that Native

---

[80] John 8:9.
[81] Exodus 3:6.
[82] Matthew 22:32, 33.

Americans and Africans were inferior, they justified confiscating Native American land, confining Native Americans on reservations and enslaving Africans. Excluding the Jewish population, Nazi Germany was approximately half Catholic and half Lutheran so it could happen among at least nominally Christian people. But it certainly couldn't happen among evangelicals, could it? An evangelical dictator in Guatemala named Rios Montt, embraced enthusiastically by American evangelical leaders like Jerry Falwell, Pat Robertson and Luis Palau, was responsible in 1982-1983 for the murders and rapes of huge numbers of his countrymen and women, particularly indigenous Guatemalans. The genocide in Rwanda in 1994 involved thousands and thousands of conservative Christians, perpetrators and victims. It can happen.

Logic is important, but as a means to an end and not as an end in itself. As a necessary means to the end of knowing what is real and true, logical induction and deduction are essential to ethics and to Christian ethics in particular. Where evangelicals have failed to realize that even strongly held opinions formed by faulty induction or deduction are suspect at best, they can cause real damage. We will examine this in more detail in Chapters 8-13, but at this point, it can be pointed out that the theology that gives us a "rapture" is an inductive one that patches together verses from here and there to construct an inductively rickety view of the future. It provides an "off ramp" for Christians, literally taking them out of the world, "saving" them from having to seriously address the most serious ethical concerns specifically addressed by Jesus. It is an exercise in profoundly faulty induction. On the other hand, the kind of theology that unreflectively equates abnormality or disgust with evil and deduces from that the conclusion that those who are not normal or evoke disgust are necessarily evil is likewise faulty.

How do we know what is true?

"Well, I never heard it before, but it sounds uncommon nonsense."
Alice in Wonderland
Lewis Carroll

The one word term for the study of what is true and how we know it is epistemology. The Greek root words are "episteme" meaning knowledge, science or understanding and "logos." Anytime you see the suffix "ology" it usually means "the study of." So epistemology is the study of knowledge. Knowledge and truth are closely related, but they are not the same thing. I can truly know the contents of Hitler's book "Mein Kampf" but it doesn't mean that what I know is true. Epistemology tries to bring knowledge and truth together and it is imperative that we know something about it.

One of the major ways that we know things is through our senses. Other ways we know things include the kind of introspection through which we have awareness of our own consciousness and knowledge of our own thoughts and feelings. Reason, memory and the testimony of trusted others like parents, teachers, coaches and, for Christians, Jesus and the Bible are other key ways that we know. Together they account for our experience which is secondary to them as far as what we know because it requires one or more of them. That doesn't mean that experience is less important.

Some of the most basic things I know, like the love of my mother, are based on experience, certainly not study. My experiences, though, come largely through my senses and consist also in my memories of them, my reflections upon them, my reasoning about them and the testimony of others about the importance or unimportance of them. These ways of knowing what is true are as necessary for evangelicals as they are for anyone else.

When Christian leaders decline to push back on what is demonstrably untrue in our public discourse the damage done to Christian ethics is palpable. It is one thing to say that we have difficult problems regarding immigration, but when a ragtag bunch of desperate people moving towards our border with Mexico are portrayed as an invasion force and the fears of the American people that rapists and murderers are swarming over our border are stoked to a fever pitch, it calls to mind the clear teaching of Jesus that *"whoever is dishonest with very little will also be dishonest with much"*[83] and *"I tell you that every careless word that people speak, they shall give an accounting for it in the day of judgment."*[84]

It is self-evident that perception of the real world through the senses is essential to our knowing. Evangelicals, along with many others, believe

---

[83] Luke 16:10.
[84] Matthew 12:36 New American Standard Bible.

there is a limit to what we can know through the senses, but that our senses are indispensable nonetheless. In addition to everything else we know through our senses, one key way Christians believe they know things to be true is if they are taught in the Bible. Still, we have to see them in a printed Bible or hear what is in the Bible when it is preached. Paul made the key point that *"faith comes by hearing and hearing by the Word of God."*[85] We don't just get this through osmosis; rather, the senses are vital to what we know and knowing what is true. However, just because we physically sense something doesn't guarantee that we can know it is true. People who have lost a limb often still feel pain in their missing limb. The pain is real, the perception that it is in a missing limb is not. We obviously need more than just our senses.

Memory, the recollection of mental, emotional, or physical experience, also plays a vital role in what we know. The people of Israel were told again and again to remember what God had done for them in bringing them out of slavery and into the promised land. What God had done in the past was their basis for confidence in God's provision in the present and in the future. The New Testament is full of encouragement to remember or not forget what has been done for us in being brought into right relationship with God.[86] But memories too can be faulty. I vividly remember watching the original "Star Wars" right after it opened and while my wife was pregnant with our first son. When describing this to one of my son's friends, a Star Wars fanatic, he did the arithmetic and pointed out that my son was born more than a year after Star Wars opened so either I didn't see it right after it opened or my wife wasn't pregnant with my son when I saw it. I was totally convinced that I had remembered it correctly. Memory has to be corroborated by reason or testimony.

Consciousness and introspection are mutually dependent and cannot be separated; rather, they often operate simultaneously. Consciousness involves not only being aware of what is happening outside ourselves through our senses, but also of looking within ourselves at what we actually feel, understand, believe, etc. Consciousness takes what we perceive through our senses and connects it with what and who we are internally. When my friends and I walked out of Officer's Call we were intensely aware

---

[85] Romans 10:17.
[86] Galatians 1:6ff, 2 Timothy 2:8, James 1:25.

of what was going on in the room around us and, at the same time, what was going on inside ourselves. Among other things, through introspection, consciousness connects ethics and morals. It connects what we believe with what we should do. Remember the analytic diagram? Consciousness and introspection connect the left side of the vertical line with the right side. In that moment we knew not only what was right, but also that we had to do something about it.

Paul admonished Christians to *"examine yourselves to see whether you are in the faith."*[87] The entire NT book of James is a prolonged call to look into our lives and see whether they give evidence of the things we say we believe. Introspection, in this sense, is vital. But it too needs more. There is a morbid kind of introspection that can be extremely unhealthy and dangerous particularly when it devolves into guilt, shame, and self-condemnation.

Richard Rohr, Franciscan priest and noted speaker and author, made the incisive observation that *"we don't see people as they are, we see them as we are."*[88] His point was that we often project our own guilt and shame onto others. Long before this observation or ones like it were made, Jesus asked, *"Why do you see the speck in your neighbor's eye, but do not notice the log in your own eye?"*[89] The effective use of penetrating questions was calculated to lead his hearers to look inside themselves, to use conscious introspection along with their reason to understand even deeper truths.

Reason and reasoning are obviously critical to what we know. Some Christians minimize the importance of reason and find reason to conflict with faith. Big mistake. Dietrich Bonhoeffer was a German pastor, theologian and a founder of the "Confessing Church" which stood strongly against the atrocities of the Nazi regime. He was hanged by the Nazis for his role in a plot to assassinate Hitler. Bonhoeffer put it plainly and clearly: *"Contempt for the age of rationalism is a suspicious sign of failure to feel the need for truthfulness."*[90] Reason and faith go hand in hand from the biblical account of creation onward. God's first creative acts begin to bring

---

[87] 2 Corinthians 13:5.
[88] This was not original to him. Stephen Covey has also used it in his teaching. French novelist Anais Nin perhaps first spoke this, but she too may have read or heard it elsewhere.
[89] Matthew 7:3.
[90] Bonhoeffer. *Ethics*. P. 98.

order out of chaos making the world understandable. God's call to the prophet Isaiah is, *"Come now, let us reason together."*[91] Paul's carefully reasoned arguments in his letter to the church in Rome have been a mainstay of Christian understanding of God's plan and purpose for all of humankind. One of the major points of the Gospel (the "good news") is to convince us through reason of God's love, our need for forgiveness and the benefits of responding by faith. As critical in this as anything else for Christians is the teaching of Jesus. Jesus used parables and stories to lead people from what they could relate to or knew to help them understand even deeper truths. His teaching both required and led to the ability to reason well.

This leads us to testimony as a source of knowledge. Testimony is that which we hear from sources we trust that gives us knowledge that we don't already have and might never have apart from what they tell us and teach us. Each of us first learns enormous amounts of what we need to know from our parents or original caregivers, even when they do a bad job of it. Most of us, regardless of any faith commitments we do or don't have, have learned many of the most necessary things in life from teachers, coaches or mentors who have helped us learn and grow.

For evangelicals, the testimony of the Bible, the testimony of God's Spirit in one's life and the testimony of other Christians, what they say and what they have written, are key factors in knowing especially the spiritual truths of the Bible, but also in putting all of life together in a meaningful whole. In a trial, witnesses take an oath to *"tell the truth, the whole truth and nothing but the truth."* Honest testimony under oath is intended to enable the judge and jury to know what actually happened and then to decide wisely and fairly. When false witnesses, including national leaders and Christian leaders, more concerned with ideology than with the truth, betray the trust of unsuspecting people, it is a basic violation of something essential for life together.

All of these factors: perception through our senses, memory, consciousness and introspection, reason and testimony are primary ways of human knowing. Though this is a simple treatment of these issues related to our "knowing," it is enough to help us understand that what we

---

[91] Isaiah 1:18.

know and how we know what we know are serious questions that deserve our attention. But these questions are part of the picture, not the whole of it. Nazi political leaders, military leaders, doctors and scientists had a great deal of valid knowledge and they nearly brought the world to its knees. Knowledge, even valid knowledge, mixed with bad metaphysics and bad ethics is as bad as it gets. Closer to home, the disregard for truth in our current public discourse finds evangelicals to be not just victims of the problem, but contributors to it.

What does this look like? When asked if it wasn't hypocritical for evangelical leaders to support a president who regularly lies, is a proven adulterer and has advocated violence, Jerry Falwell Jr. replied, *"When Jesus said we're all sinners, he really meant all of us, everybody. I don't think you can choose a president based on their personal behavior ... you choose a president based on what their policies are. That's why I don't think it's hypocritical."*[92] This "testimony" is simply preposterous. The officership of the US military is taught from the first day that the character and moral behavior of the officer is essential for leadership in the military. The idea that it is not a necessary qualification for the Commander in Chief and the most powerful leader in the world is unthinkable. This legitimation of inexcusable behavior, not just past behavior, by a Christian leader appealing to the teaching of Jesus is powerfully harmful.

The one thing Falwell gets right here is that evangelicals have selected the President for his policies and, in so doing, own those policies. These are policies that go counter to aspects of our public life that have been most influenced by our Christian heritage, but are being torn down by a man who has no respect for that aspect of our heritage. Those policies that marginalize and work against the poor, allow our President to demean our allies and the alliances that have kept the larger world at peace for decades, weaken the institutions that made America greater than it is today, and allow a sitting President to lie about hush payments, protect his own family and business interests when they run afoul of the law, demean his opponents, including men like John McCain and the generals who have left his administration in disgust; these policies, his policies, are in effect in large part thanks to an evangelical America that is simultaneously

[92] Gstalter, Morgan."Jerry Falwell Jr.: You don't choose a president based on how good they are." *The Hill,* 01 Jan 2019. apple.news/ASjzqLzk_TPOnbuRfZMmjRw. Accessed 19 March 2019.

feathering and fouling its own nest. Leaders like Falwell who are so desperate for legitimacy and influence are willing to religiously legitimate that which is directly contrary to the deepest ethical principles of the Saviour they claim to serve.

How should people govern and be governed?

"This is also why you pay taxes, for the authorities are God's servants, who give their full time to governing."
Romans 13:6

The one word classical term for addressing how people should rule and be ruled is politics. It comes from the Greek word "polis" meaning city. For the Greek philosophers politics represented their thinking and beliefs related to citizenship and governance in their Greek city-states like Athens, Thebes and Sparta. Today we would recognize it most readily as the study of political science and the practice of governance. Aristotle believed politics to be the science that studies what is the supreme good for humankind.[93] To say that ethics does or should affect our politics is a huge understatement, but it is also true that politics affect ethics and can enhance or contaminate ethics in a powerful way.

One of the great values in studying abnormal psychology is that it really helps in our understanding of normal psychology. By the same principle, studying failed states and political systems can help us understand what a just and thriving state should look like. Understanding one particular failed state, one resulting from failed politics, has implications for Americans and American evangelicals on a number of different levels.

The night of September 10, 2001 is one I will never forget. By then I was living a long held dream of being a pastor. After a military and civilian flying career of more than 25 years, I was serving the congregation of Cherry Creek Presbyterian Church in Denver as the Executive Pastor of this large, solidly evangelical church. What made that particular night so memorable was not just the awful events of the next day, the inerasable images of planes flying into the World Trade Center on September 11th, but because I experienced something in the media that I had never experienced in such a life changing way. I was surfing through the channels and came to rest on

---

[93] Aristotle. *The Nicomachean Ethics*. p.4

"Nightline" hosted by Ted Koppel. He started the show by apologizing both for himself and for his colleagues in the media. He said that there was something going on that he and his colleagues in media had known about for quite some time without reporting, but things had gotten so bad that he could no longer keep silent.

Koppel's program was entitled "Still the Heart of Darkness: The Killing in the Congo." The title picked up on the title of Joseph Conrad's novel *The Heart of Darkness* written more than a hundred years before this broadcast. The novel was about the travesty of the colonization of Congo by the Belgian monarch, King Leopold. The "heart of darkness" was not the Congo itself or that of the Congolese people, but that of their brutal colonizers and, more broadly, the darkness of the human heart. Koppel was going to do a five part series between September 10th and 14th. When the horrible events of the next day occurred, he discontinued the series and picked it up months later when a volcano erupted in eastern Congo. Once again the plight of the Congolese people was brought to the world's attention. But this first night, as Koppel made the link between the awful atrocity of the genocide in Rwanda and its aftermath in Congo, I began to feel sicker and sicker.

Here is the transcript of Koppel's opening to the series:

> "At the heart of the continent, genocide in a tiny country [Rwanda], a genocide that horrified the world, brought chaos to a country almost 100 times its size [Democratic Republic of Congo], and you probably haven't heard a word. Young boys serving time in prisoner of war camps with mass murderers. You think that's bad? It's the best thing that's happened to them in years. What these children have endured is almost unimaginable. She resisted when soldiers were kidnapping children from her village [imagine here a gut wrenching photo/video of a young woman who has been savagely brutalized]. Animals that have always been protected [elephants, gorillas] have been slaughtered by people who simply need the meat. It has claimed more lives than all the other current wars around the world combined. But outside of Africa, no one seems to have noticed. Three years, two and a half million dead. We thought someone should tell you. Tonight, the first in a weeklong series: Still the Heart of Darkness." [94]

Multiply the death toll on September 11th by nearly a thousand and you begin to feel Koppel's angst the same way I did. Three years later, on loan from the church and because of past operational and logistical management experience both in the military and in civilian life, I was appointed to a two year term as Country Director for Food for the Hungry (FH) in the Democratic Republic of Congo (DRC). By the end of my contract term, the death toll in Congo had close to doubled from the time of Koppel's report.

FH is a Christian organization. Its essential work is tangibly demonstrating the love of Christ through international development with a special focus on the well being of children. Though there is substantial funding from private donors, over the years much of its funding has also come from government agencies like the British Department for International Development (DFID), the Canadian International Development Agency (CIDA) and the United States Agency for International Development (USAID). Because of the size and scope of the programs, FH and similar organizations are often the targets of corrupt soldiers and government officials. As mentioned before, two weeks after my arrival in the city of Bukavu in eastern Congo, the FH office and residence were overrun by Congolese soldiers and we were evacuated by UN Peacekeepers. It was a sobering introduction to the reality of the next two years of my life. Congo is the definition of a failed state and nothing is quite as frightening.

The point is, failed politics, when married to contaminated ethics, is one of the deadliest unions on earth. Nazi Germany, Stalinist Russia, Communist Cambodia under Pol Pot, Rwanda at the time of the genocide, the Democratic Republic of Congo for most of the past sixty years, the bloodbath in Syria, Yemen and other middle eastern countries today, all are tragic evidence of this. But this doesn't happen overnight. It is often that the full extent of the problem isn't seen until the momentum is almost unstoppable.

In the Congo, the rot started at the top. One analyst clearly identified the problem: "*During the 32-year-long rule of the kleptocratic Mobutu Sese*

---

[94] Koppel, Ted. ABC News. "Heart of Darkness." *Nightline,* ABC News, 10 September 2001. abcnews.go.com/Nightline/story?id=128597. Accessed 20 March 2019.

Seko, the Congolese used to cite an unwritten clause in the constitution known in bitter jest as Article 15: "Débrouillez-vous pour vivre."[95] This means roughly "sort yourselves out to stay alive" or "fend for yourselves." Mobutu certainly did, looting between four and fifteen billion dollars during his reign and encouraging those under him, both in government and the military, to do the same, resulting in growing poverty and chaos for the Congolese people. To his military he said, *"You have guns, you don't need a salary."*[96] Things have improved very little since then.

Why should this matter to Americans and American evangelicals? One reason is that Mobutu came into power with American support, and continued to be tolerated for decades because it was perceived to be in the best interests of America. Part of the reason for this is that Congo has some of the richest uranium deposits in the world. The uranium used in the bombs dropped on Nagasaki and Hiroshima came from Congo, as have the nuclear materials for much of our nuclear arsenal, and there was a strong desire to prevent additional nuclear materials going anywhere else in the world. We, along with many other nations, including Rwanda after the genocide, have benefitted mightily from Congolese minerals, but have done relatively little to mitigate the poverty of some of the most impoverished people in the world.

Though Mobutu has been gone from power for more than 20 years, his legacy remains in a tragic way and continues to influence how politics are done in one of the saddest nations on earth. Apart from the fact that most Americans are preoccupied with our own well-being and know little about this, to the extent that American evangelicals embrace a philosophy that seriously thinks that it is right and good to take the interests of America, whatever they may be, to be of foremost importance regardless of potentially deadly consequences for others, it represents a major point of departure from Christian ethics.

The fact that a policy may be expedient, strategic or beneficial is different from whether it is right or good. Mobutu's philosophy and the deadly ethics

---

[95] The Economist,"Lullabies of the Abandoned." 1 October 2009. www.economist.com/middle-east-and-africa/2009/10/01/lullabies-of-the-abandoned. Accessed 19 March 2019.
[96] Mobutu's quote is attributed to Michael G. Schatzberg, "The dialectics of oppression in Zaire," Bloomington: Indiana University Press, 1988; found in Jason K. Stearns, "Dancing in the Glory of Monsters," (New York: Public Affairs, 2012), p. 116.

that both informed it and flowed from it, though an example from a deeply flawed state, are reflective of one of the major ways that ethics are understood universally. Magnifying the problem through such an extreme example helps us to see flaws that might otherwise remain invisible.

When self-interest becomes the measure for what is right, there has been a radical departure from Christian ethics. On the international scale, when national interest is the primary measure of what constitutes right, the problem is simply multiplied. This is a way of seeing ethics that American evangelicals are increasingly comfortable with, even though many would not hesitate to condemn Mobutu's extreme use of it.

Much closer to today, Pat Robertson, longtime evangelical minister and television celebrity, in support of President Trump's publicly stated desires, voiced support for the US maintaining strong relations with Saudi Arabia for economic reasons related to a highly exaggerated one hundred billion dollars worth of projected US arms sales and the American jobs that would protect and promote.[97] This in the aftermath of the Saudi leadership's murder and dismembering of a journalist, a US resident named Jamal Khashoggi, who was working for the Washington Post. Khashoggi had focused his writing on Saudi abuses of human rights. Following his October 2, 2018 murder, the president subsequently said that we will never know whether the Crown Prince of Saudi Arabia actually ordered the killing, but it doesn't matter because we need Saudi Arabian cooperation to keep oil prices low and arms sales high. Do we think Jesus would support the Saudi regime and we should too because it is good for American jobs and low prices at American gas pumps? Good grief. If you think that Pat Robertson is not an influential evangelical leader, think again. He may not be particularly esteemed by some faith groups, but he has been very influential in shaping the thinking of many conservative Christians.

---

[97] Burton, Tara. "Pat Robertson, prominent evangelical leader, on Khashoggi crisis: let's not risk '$100 billion worth of arms sales.'" *Vox,* 17 October 2018. www.vox.com/2018/10/17/17990268/pat-robertson-khashoggi-saudi-arabia-trump-crisis. Accessed 19 March 2019.

What is beautiful and why does It matter?

"He has made everything beautiful in its time."
Ecclesiastes 3:10

Of all the major questions philosophy has posed over the centuries, in some ways this question is most like the fundamental ethical question, "what is morally right and good?" On the surface, though, that is not obvious. Ethics deals with moral values while aesthetics deals with what has value in how men and women perceive things and in what they produce. The word "aesthetics" comes from the Greek word that refers to what we perceive with our senses. Many years later it came to be understood more narrowly as that which we perceive to be beautiful, but even that understanding was based on thoughts about beauty and art that Plato and Aristotle expressed long before the birth of Christ.

Plato believed that a beautiful work of art was something we could see or hear that participated in something else. That is, it was a visible or audible expression of an invisible beauty that was greater than the work itself. Though it is difficult to pinpoint when and where he might have said it, the great sculptor, Michelangelo, thought of it this way, *"I saw the angel in the marble and carved until I set him free."*[98] The point being that there is an interior, invisible reality that is behind, before and greater than what we experience through our senses. In this way of thinking, the true, the real and the beautiful are closely related. What we understand to be true participates in a greater truth. What we understand to be real participates in a greater reality. What we understand to be beautiful participates in a greater beauty.

This idea of participation is a meaningful one, especially so for Christians. In the same way that a good work of art participates in an invisible beauty of which it is a reflection, Christian character is a participation in and

---

[98] Attributed in numerous sources to Michelangelo, but the attribution is open to question.

reflection of the character of Christ. When Jesus taught the importance of trusting rather than worrying in the Sermon on the Mount, he compared the beauty of the lilies of the field with the magnificent clothing of one of Israel's greatest kings. He said *"Yet I tell you that not even Solomon in all his splendor was dressed like one of these."*[99] The beauty of the lilies was something that came from their nature, from their character. It involved not only their external beauty, but their capacity not to worry. Peter made the same point when encouraging Christian women in the first century. Just as Jesus had said about Solomon, Peter said, *"Your beauty should not come from outward adornment, such as elaborate hairstyles and the wearing of gold jewelry or fine clothes. Rather, it should be that of your inner self, the unfading beauty of a gentle and quiet spirit, which is of great worth in God's sight."*[100]

It is not that good hair, jewelry and clothes are wrong either for women or for men, it is that they can't provide what is at the very heart of beauty. For the Christian, that beauty comes from participation in the character of Christ. When we dig down deep to discover the essence of beauty, it is like Michelangelo carving the marble to free something inside it. The angel is already there, it just needs to be found. It involves a cutting away of the superficial or non-essential.

In the same way, our participation in the character of Christ is active, not passive. It's there, but one must cut away that which is not compatible with it. Building on the same idea, but flipping the image, Paul wrote to all Christians, men and women, *"Therefore, as God's chosen people, holy and dearly loved, clothe yourselves with compassion, kindness, humility, gentleness and patience ... And over all these virtues put on love, which binds them all together in perfect unity."*[101] There is, in each of us, an inner beauty and reality that, on the one hand, must be loosed by carving away what needs carving away, but must also be adorned with that which has lasting value. This deepest inner reality is what Christians refer to when echoing the Bible's teaching that we are made in the image of God.

---

[99] Matthew 6:29.
[100] 1 Peter 3:3,4.
[101] Colossians 3:12,14.

Aristotle said, *"Every art is concerned with bringing something into being, and the practice of art is the study of how to bring into being something that is capable either of being or not being, and the cause of which is in the producer and not in the product."*[102] Art has to do with what humanity creates, not with what God has created. I may perceive that a sunset is beautiful and though that may be real and true, it is not art. When I produce a photograph of it or a painting or express my feeling about it in poetry or music, then what is real and true also becomes art. Aristotle goes on to say, *"Art … is a productive state that is truly reasoned, while its contrary non-art is a productive state that is falsely reasoned."*[103]

Art does not exist in the same way that nature exists. Art is produced by humans which means it must be caused. It is something that is done. This brings into focus the very important idea of causation and this brings art or aesthetics and ethics together even more closely. If I cause something I am responsible for it. If I cause something good, I am responsible for something good. If I cause something bad, I am responsible for something bad. In the same way that Aristotle says there can be bad art if it flows out of false reason, there can be bad ethics if those ethics flow out of false reason. False reason produces bad art and it produces bad ethics. Ethics and morality, just like art, cannot exist apart from the idea of actual cause and responsibility. If I say that God made me do it, like many on opposing sides of holy wars have done, then I am denying responsibility. If I say that the devil made me do it, like the comedian Flip Wilson used to say, then I am saying that I am not responsible.

Aristotle thought differently. Though the words I'm going to use aren't identical in every case to those he used, the thinking is rooted in his. Imagine that there is a glass on the table and I knock it off. It falls and breaks. What caused the glass to break? I am the *effective cause* of the glass breaking. If I didn't knock it off the table it wouldn't have broken. But gravity made the glass fall. Gravity is a *contingent cause*. The floor is the *immediate cause* of the glass breaking. Before its impact with the floor, I had already knocked the glass off the table and gravity had already caused it to fall. If it had landed on a cushion it wouldn't have broken so just my knocking it off the table and gravity can't explain its breaking.

---

[102] Aristotle. *The Nicomachean Ethics,* p. 149.
[103] Ibid.

But none of this could have happened apart from the existence of a world in which I exist and can act; one in which tables, floors and glasses can be produced and gravity exists. Non-theists would attribute this to a more ultimate reality that is caused by non-personal forces, Christians would attribute it to God. In either case there is an *ultimate cause* that goes beyond the particular events related to the glass breaking. Without me, gravity, the floor and God or some other ultimate reality, the glass would not break.

Now imagine that the glass was an inherited crystal glass that my wife values deeply and I knocked the glass off the table because I was mad at her. I am morally responsible for the act while gravity, the floor and God are not. A bad thing happened. It couldn't have happened apart from God keeping the real world going as it really does, but I am at fault for that which I cause. Any meaningful discussion of ethics, Christian or not, depends on responsibility and responsibility is inseparably linked with the ability to actually cause something good or bad … whether in art or ethics.

Chapter 5

The "End" of Ethics

"Man's chief end is to glorify God and to enjoy Him forever."
Westminster Shorter Catechism

Ethics has a purpose. Thus ethics has an end; it aims at something. In general ethics aims at that which is ultimately good and, on the way to that, what is morally right and good here and now. Aristotle put it this way: *"So if there is only one final end, this will be the good of which we are in search; and if there are more than one, it will be the most final of these."*[104] For Christians it looks something like Bonhoeffer"s assertion that: *"It is evident that the only appropriate conduct of men before God is the doing of His will."*[105] The end, or purpose, is that God's will be done as Christians everywhere pray regularly in the Lord's Prayer: *"Thy kingdom come, Thy will be done on earth as it is in heaven."* However, knowing God's will and knowing how to do it aren't the same.

Aristotle believed that *"every action and every pursuit is considered to aim at some good. Hence the good has been rightly defined as 'that at which all things aim.'"*[106] When one looks at all the attempts in history to put together a cohesive ethical framework, ancient and modern, modern and postmodern, secular and religious, Christian and otherwise, they can be divided into three basic camps, all of which aim at some "good." Each has a different "good" at which it aims. Some aim at good outcomes or consequences. Some aim at good actions or following rules that ensure our doing what we should, doing our duty. Some aim at good character or virtue.

outcome-based ethics, duty-based ethics and character-based ethics are not unrelated. Each is concerned with and uses words like consequences, virtue and character, but they understand these in different ways. They define them differently and they prioritize them differently. This may not

---

[104] Aristotle, *The Nicomachean Ethics,* p.14.
[105] Bonhoeffer. *Ethics,* p.16.
[106] Aristotle. *The Nicomachean Ethics,* p.1.

seem like it is particularly significant, but it is. In fact, it makes an enormous difference. Some examples are needed.

Outcome-based Ethics

"My happiness is not the means to any end. It is the end. It is its own goal. It is its own purpose."
Ayn Rand, Anthem

The view that ethics should be based on outcomes or consequences goes by the name of "consequentialism." The term was coined by Elizabeth Anscombe in her 1958 essay "Modern Moral Philosophy,"[107] but it can be properly applied in many instances looking back in history as well. In fact, it is as old as humanity. In this view, the consequences of our actions are what really count. If one's actions produce a good outcome from the point of view of an individual or a grouping of individuals, then what has been done is good. It is less important how you get to the outcome, what matters most is that the outcome produces benefit to the individual or group. By the terms of this ethic, the end justifies the means.

According to a consequentialist morality, the decision by President Truman to drop atom bombs on Hiroshima and Nagasaki was a morally good decision because it resulted in what was believed to be a higher moral good. Justice was served by the ending of World War II, the ending of Japanese aggression, the saving of the lives of many American soldiers and a widespread peace won through the defeat of a mortal enemy.

What if things had worked out differently? Had the Japanese emperor dropped atom bombs on the US to end the war thus saving the lives of many Japanese soldiers and resulting in peace from worldwide conflict won through the defeat of a mortal enemy, would that have been a moral action? Would justice have been served? The Japanese would have said yes. This begs the question, was America right and just in fighting World War II? Most of us would answer with an unqualified "yes." But to answer this question we have to look past the good outcome to a good motive, to a higher good than the outcome alone allows us to see. In both world and personal affairs, consequentialism works for the winners in the sense that if

---

[107] Anscombe, G.E.M. "Modern Moral Philosophy". *Philosophy,* vol.33, no. 124, Cambridge University Press, Cambridge, January 1958. Published online 25 February 2009. doi.org/10.1017/S0031819100037943.

the outcome is good for their interests then the route to the outcome is justified. It leaves unanswered, apart from our interests and what is to our benefit, what is actually good and good for whom.

Answers of a certain sort are provided to these questions by the two major categories of consequentialism: ethical egoism and utilitarianism.[108] Ethical egoism should not be confused with egotism which is psychological in nature while ethical egoism is a serious, if not adequate, theory of what is right generally.[109] Ethical egoism defines good in terms of individual interest. Ayn Rand, the author of *Atlas Shrugged* and *The Fountainhead* has heavily influenced many contemporary American politicians and Americans in general. She is a well-known proponent of universal ethical egoism which is the theory that everyone should do what is in his or her best interest and that this will produce the best overall outcome for all.

Her personal philosophy which has been called "Objectivism" is much more complex than this, but the ethic that flows out of Objectivism is universal ethical egoism. Universal ethical egoism is to Objectivism what any ethic is to the philosophy from which it comes. According to Objectivism, *"Each individual must choose his values and actions by the standards of man's life - in order to achieve the purpose of maintaining and enjoying his own life."* Thus, according to one of the foremost voices of this philosophy, *"Objectivism advocates egoism - the pursuit of self-interest - the policy of selfishness."*[110]

The Art of the Deal by Donald Trump is a textbook for personal ethical egoism which is similar to universal ethical egoism but it is even more individualized. *"My style of deal-making is quite simple and straightforward. I aim very high, and then I just keep pushing and pushing and pushing to get what I'm after. Sometimes I settle for less than I sought, but in most cases I still end up with what I want."*[111] The primary concern here is not whether a particular deal is morally right or whether there is any means of

---

[108] Thiroux and Krasemann. *Ethics Theory and Practice. Updated Eleventh Edition,* pp. 22-26.
[109] Ibid.
[110] Peikoff, Leonard. *Objectivism: The Philosophy of Ayn Rand.* Meridian, a member of the Penguin Group (USA), New York, 1993, p.230.
[111] Trump, Donald. *"The Art of the Deal,"* Ballantine Books Trade Paperback Edition, New York, 2015, p.45.

making a deal that is ruled out by moral considerations. What really has value is getting what one wants and that is the measure of a "good" deal.

In his chapter entitled "The Cincinnati Kid: Prudence Pays" Trump proudly describes a deal in which he knowingly sold at a huge profit a property that he knew was going to go down in value substantially from the value the purchasers thought they were getting in the deal.[112] Legal? It was probably defensible in court especially with tough enough lawyers. Moral? This is morally problematic when your morality is based on a principle other than individual interest, such as *"do unto others as you would have them do unto you."* The principle of "caveat emptor" or "buyer beware" certainly has standing in our law, but law and morality are not the same thing. What is or is not allowed by law and what ought to be are not the same thing, especially for Christians.

For a picture of the dark underside of this approach to ethics, we can look back to the previously cited history of Mobutu Sese Seko in Congo. *"Débrouillez-vous pour vivre"* or *"fend for yourself"* was not just a saying, it was an actual political and personal strategy for life. What mattered most to Mobutu were his interests and the interests of those closest to him. Whatever it took to realize those interests was fair game. This is consequentialism in its rawest form.

Unlike personal ethical egoism that is based on individual interests, utilitarianism strives for the most good for the greatest number of people. Good here is measured in terms of benefit or usefulness (or utility, hence "utilitarianism"), but instead of it being considered simply for an individual, it is usefulness or benefit for the greatest number of people affected by whatever it is one does.

This was illustrated in a famous thought problem called the "Trolley Problem" first put forward by ethicist Philippa Foot.[113] There have been various modifications of the problem over time, but it is often presented this way: with no other knowledge of any of the people in the problem and no options other than what is given in the problem, imagine a train track with a

---

[112] Ibid. pp. 90-92.

[113] Foot, Philippa. "The Problem of Abortion and the Doctrine of the Double Effect." *Oxford Review, Number 5,* 1968. philpapers.org/archive/FOOTPO-2.pdf. Accessed 19 March 2019.

rail car or trolley on the track moving towards a group of five workmen who don't see it and will be killed if it hits them. You are a switchman and you see that if you throw the switch it will divert the trolley to a side track where there is one man working who also doesn't see it. Instead of killing five others it will only kill him. What will you do? If you do nothing several people will die. If you throw the switch one person will die.

Most of the students in the Ethics classes I have taught would throw the switch, but a persistent minority would not because they feel that doing so makes them personally responsible for the death of an innocent person in a way that not flipping the switch does not. It is possible to view this dilemma from other perspectives, but a utilitarian, with no other knowledge of any of the people who are in danger and no options other than those given in the problem, will throw the switch in order to provide the most good for the most number of people affected by his or her action. Many of us would agree.

This may seem like too artificial a problem, but consider the men and women in our military who are faced with either writing the directives that determine when to fire drone-mounted weapons or the drone pilots who actually fire those weapons while controlling drones which have targeted terrorist suspects. Though the procedures are designed to minimize this, the suspects may be accompanied by innocent non-combatants who are killed along with the targeted person. The justification for doing this at all is that the greater security needs of the US warrant the killing of these suspects even when there may be "collateral damage" in the form of killing innocent bystanders like children who are immediate family members.

It's the same problem faced by President Harry Truman when he ordered the dropping of the atomic bombs, but on a much smaller scale. These are hard choices, but they are based on something other than individual interest. What is thought to be right and good in this case is what is right and good for the ultimate security of the American people. The goodness of the choices are not ultimately based on a conception of what is right or good in and of itself, but what has the most benefit or utility for our national circle of concern, for American interests.

Consequentialism is not simply based on good outcomes, but on outcomes that are defined as good when they meet my interests, our interests or provide the most usefulness for the greatest number of people, usually "our people," affected by the acts which produce those outcomes. Actions are not good or bad in and of themselves, but are deemed to be good or bad based on what they produce. This is a very pragmatic approach, but one with which historic Christianity has been very uncomfortable.

Both personal and universal ethical egoism are based on self interest. Personal ethical egoism is the belief that I should always act in my self interest and personal morality is based on doing that which is best for me. Universal ethical egoism is the belief that everyone should act in his or her self interest and that, it is believed, will produce what is good for all. Whether personal egoism or universal egoism, the measure of what is good is self interest. "Trickle down economics," the idea that increased benefit to the wealthy will trickle down to those lower on the economic totem pole, is an example of universal ethical egoism.

For utilitarianism, the measure of what is good is not based on the inherent qualities of the action taken or on merely personal self interest, but on what produces the greatest good for the greatest number. The belief that what is good is not intrinsic in the actions that we take, but in the outcomes they produce, is what separates outcome-based ethics, consequentialism, from both duty-based and character-based ethics.

Duty-based Ethics

"Do not let this Book of the Law depart from your mouth; meditate on it day and night, so that you may be careful to do everything written in it."
Joshua 1:8

Much different from the outcome-based ethics of consequentialism are the duty-based ethics of non-consequentialism or what is often called deontological ethics. This comes from the Greek word "deon" usually translated as "duty." Duty and responsibility go hand in hand. If I am responsible for something or someone then I have an obligation to it or to them. Whereas consequentialism is primarily concerned with outcomes or ends, this approach to ethics is more concerned with the means or how we get to the ends.

Consequentialism holds that the ends justify the means. A duty ethic holds that if you do the right thing, do what you are responsible for and obligated to do, you will get the right outcome … whatever it is. In other words, there may be any number of things that you can't do just because they are wrong in themselves. Likewise, there are things that you must do. This holds even if you think that doing them, if they are right, or not doing them, if they are wrong, hurts your self-interest.

A classic example of this is the story of Eric Liddell portrayed very powerfully in the Academy Award winning film "Chariots of Fire." Liddell, a devout Scottish Presbyterian, ran in the 1924 Olympics in Paris. Considered the fastest man in the United Kingdom, he was favored to win the 100 meter dash which was his best event. Months before the Olympics, the preliminaries for the race were scheduled to take place on a Sunday. He believed that this was in violation of the commandment to *"Remember the Sabbath Day by keeping it holy."*[114] Accordingly, he refused to run in the preliminaries which the Olympic Committee would not reschedule. This disqualified him from participating in the finals. In addition to his own hopes, the hopes of his countrymen had been riding on him. His non-participation in the 100 meter race was a great disappointment, but more important to him than winning the medal for himself and his country was fulfilling what he believed to be his moral duty.

As it turned out, one of his countrymen, whom he had previously beaten in the 100 meters, went on to win it. Liddell ran in the 400 meters and, in a stunning performance in a race not well suited to his style, he won the gold medal. It's hard to find a better story to convey the principle of doing the right thing and letting the outcome fall where it may, but there's more to the story. During World War II, while serving as a missionary in an impoverished community in China, Liddell was placed in a Japanese internment camp. He had sent his pregnant wife and family home due to the growing dangers from the Japanese occupation. Those in the camp with him held him in the highest regard for his selflessness and devotion to the community of those who had been imprisoned with him. He died there

---

[114] Exodus 20:8.

without ever seeing his youngest daughter. Sometimes the fulfilling of one's duty can prove to be very detrimental to one's individual interest.

This ethic is not immune to or unconcerned with the consequences or outcome of what is done, but it clearly prioritizes doing the right thing over doing whatever it takes to get the "right" outcome. There are approaches to duty ethics not specifically based on religion or distinctly religious values, like the ethics of Immanuel Kant (1724-1804) and Sir William David Ross (1877-1940), but in the Judeo-Christian tradition, "Divine Command" duty ethics have been of central importance.[115] This is the ethic of moral absolutes such as the Ten Commandments. As some have wryly observed, these are not ten suggestions. Rather, in historic Judaism and Christianity, the Ten Commandments have been understood to be a summary of the moral laws of God, incumbent upon all humans for all times.

John Murray, a Scottish-born theologian, first taught at Princeton Seminary. He left Princeton for Westminster Theological Seminary in protest of the theological liberalism increasingly embraced by Princeton. Murray's book *Principles of Conduct* was based on the Payton Lectures he did in 1955 at Fuller Theological Seminary,[116] one of America's foremost evangelical seminaries. In it he wrote:

> "It is symptomatic of a pattern of thought current in many evangelical circles that the idea of keeping the commandments of God is not consonant with the liberty and spontaneity of the Christian man, that keeping the law has its affinities with legalism and with the principle of works rather than the principle of grace. It is strange indeed that this kind of antipathy to the notion of keeping commandments should be entertained by any believer who is a serious student of the New Testament. Did not our Lord say, 'If ye keep my commandments, ye shall abide in my love, even as I have kept my Father's commandments and abide in his love' (John 15:10)? It was John who recorded these sayings of our Lord and it was he, of all the disciples, who was mindful of the Lord's teaching and example regarding love, and reproduces that teaching so conspicuously in his first Epistle … 'For this is the love of God, that we keep his commandments' (1 John

---

[115] Thiroux and Krasemann, *Ethics: Theory and Practice.* pp.49-55.
[116] Ibid., p.7.

5:3). If we are surprised to find this virtual identification of love to God and the keeping of his commandments, it is because we have overlooked the words of our Lord himself ... 'He that hath my commandments and keepeth them, he it is that loveth me' (John 14:21)." [117]

This is a classic exposition of "Divine Command"[118] duty ethics. This was the ethic demonstrated by Eric Liddell and it has as its goal or aim doing the will of God. In short, there is a right and wrong that depends on the commands of God, not the outcome, good or bad, from the perspective of my or our interests. For Christian ethics, duty is not just any duty, but duty defined by the commandments of God. This duty supersedes all other duties.

In his chapter entitled "The Sanctity of Truth," Murray cites the biblical story of Rahab from the Old Testament book of Joshua. The people of Israel had just crossed into the promised land and, under Joshua's leadership, were about to capture the city of Jericho. Rahab, a prostitute living in Jericho, hid two Jewish spies whom Joshua had sent to spy out the city. She lied to protect them enabling them to escape and bring their report back to Joshua. Ultimately her vital role resulted in an overwhelming victory for the Israelites.[119]

Though this outcome was a key beginning to Israel's conquest of the land they believed God had promised to them, Murray asserts that *"neither Scripture itself nor the theological inferences derived from Scripture provide us with any warrant for the vindication of Rahab's untruth and this instance, consequently, does not support the position that under certain circumstances we may justifiably utter an untruth."*[120] In a footnote supporting this statement, he refers to John Calvin's statement:

> *"For those who hold what is called a dutiful lie (mendacium officiosum) to be altogether excusable, do not sufficiently consider how precious truth is in the sight of God. Therefore, although our*

---

[117] Murray, John. *Principles of Conduct*. Wm. B. Eerdmans Publishing Co., Grand Rapids, Michigan, 1957, Eighth printing 1981, pp. 182, 183.
[118] Thiroux and Krasemann, *Ethics: Theory and Practice*. p.33.
[119] Joshua 2:1-24.
[120] Murray. *Principles of Conduct,* p.139.

purpose be to assist our brethren, to consult for their safety and relieve them, it never can be lawful to lie, because that cannot be right which is contrary to the nature of God. And God is truth. And still the act of Rahab is not devoid of the praise of virtue, although it was not spotlessly pure."[121]

duty-based ethics are believed to rest upon moral absolutes and Murray's convictions support that traditional understanding of Christian ethics. But, how can these moral absolutes apply to those who have never heard the Ten Commandments or the teaching of Jesus? C.S. Lewis was a strong proponent of "Natural Law" which, in the Christian tradition, is the idea that the moral law of God is built into humanity. The apostle Paul alluded to this when he wrote,

"Indeed, when Gentiles, who do not have the law, do by nature things required by the law, they are a law for themselves, even though they do not have the law, since they show that the requirements of the law are written on their hearts, their consciences also bearing witness, and their thoughts now accusing them, now even defending them."[122]

C.S. Lewis put it this way:

"The laws of nature, as applied to stones or trees, may only mean 'what Nature, in fact, does.' But if you turn to the Law of Human Nature [Natural Law], the Law of Decent Behavior, it is a different matter. That law certainly does not mean 'what human beings, in fact, do'; for as I said before, many of them do not obey this law at all, and none of them obey it completely. The law of gravity tells you what stones do if you drop them; but the Law of Human Nature tells you what human beings ought to do and do not." [123]

Whether the moral law is written on stone tablets or on human hearts, the point is that the requirements of that law are central to traditional Christian ethics. From this perspective, the fact that we all fall short does not give us

---

[121] Ibid.

[122] Romans 2:14,15.

[123] Lewis,C.S. *"Mere Christianity."* Macmillan Publishing Company, New York, First paperback edition 1960. pp. 27,28.

warrant to do away with it or water it down or explain it away or excuse ourselves when we fall short. But there is more to discuss.

Tithing Mint and Rue

"Woe to you, teachers of the law and Pharisees, you hypocrites! You give a tenth of your spices—mint, dill and cumin. But you have neglected the more important matters of the law—justice, mercy and faithfulness. You should have practiced the latter, without neglecting the former."
Matthew 23:23

There is a difference between absolutism and absolutes. John Murray and John Calvin believed that we have an absolute duty to tell the truth regardless of the consequences. Eric Liddell believed he had an absolute duty to keep the Lord's Day holy by not running in the Olympic Trials for the 100 meter race on a Sunday regardless of the consequences. There were moral absolutes that drove not just their conversation or their writing, but their actions as well.

In the NT gospel accounts, the Pharisees believed they had an absolute duty to tithe, that is to give God one tenth of what they earned or produced. Jesus, however, called them to task because of their neglect of the virtues that lay behind the law and for which the law existed. They tithed things like garden herbs (mint and rue) that can be measured, but they neglected much more substantial things like justice and the love of God which cannot be easily measured. This is the difference between absolutes and absolutism.

Absolutism leaves no room for deviation, but misses the main point. It treats whatever it already believes as absolute whether, in fact, that which it believes is absolute or not. Absolutism applies one standard to the things important to the absolutist and another to those things not important or distasteful to the absolutist. American evangelicals, in great numbers, have embraced absolutism regardless of whether the objects of their beliefs are absolute or not. In fairness, this is also true of many who are not evangelicals and many who are on the opposite sides of the issues being discussed, but that is not an excuse for evangelicals who, according to the Scriptures, ought to know better. Absolutism is not a virtue. It was not a virtue for the Pharisees and it is not a virtue for evangelicals. An example is necessary.

Many American evangelicals, as a large part of their commitment to conservative political principles, believe that access to guns is essential for freedom. Legal and largely unrestricted access to guns is believed to be necessary because the right to bear arms for self-defense (whether against individuals or the government when deemed necessary) is of paramount importance. The argument is that guns do not cause killings; rather, people do. Guns, in this estimation, are inanimate objects and, as such, are neither good or bad. Weapons, including assault weapons, are thought to be necessary for self-defense or recreation. They are weapons designed not for hunting or simply for target practice, but ultimately for the wounding or killing of human beings. It is argued that they actually deter killings in addition to providing recreational value.

When the discussion turns to condoms or birth control pills, also inanimate objects, we find that these are apparently more powerful than guns. They are particularly heinous because, whereas guns are not religiously objectionable, birth control somehow is. Guns don't cause killings, but condoms and birth control pills apparently have the power to cause potentially illicit couplings. Legislation currently being proposed by a deeply conservative U.S Congress, strongly supported by most evangelicals, eliminates the current legal requirement that US employers pay for birth control in employee healthcare plans, regardless of the marital status of the employees, because it offends the religious sensibilities of some employers. It is a powerful absolutism that demands that we must have protected access to guns, but we cannot have protected access to birth control.

Once again, absolutism applies one standard to the things important to the absolutist and another to those things not important or distasteful to the absolutist. In either case, absolutism is not a virtue. Absolutism is much more about how one holds what one holds than it is about what one holds. In this regard, absolutism has only a passing relationship to any real moral absolute. Jesus abhorred an absolutism that tithed garden herbs, an absolutism that totally missed the point regarding justice and love of God.

In the conflation of conservative American politics with Christianity, many evangelicals are doing just this.

Character-based Ethics

"Therefore every teacher of the law who has become a disciple in the kingdom of heaven is like the owner of a house who brings out of his storeroom new treasures as well as old."
Matthew 13:52

character-based ethics or virtue ethics are not a newcomer to the general discussion of ethics. Confucius, Buddha and Greek philosophers, Socrates, Plato and Aristotle notably, were discussing, defining and teaching variations of this hundreds of years before Jesus was born. There are many differences in what they believed to be virtuous and why, but all agreed that central to any understanding of ethics was the question of character or virtue and virtuous behavior. All believed that it didn't just happen, but had to be taught, learned and practiced.

The Sermon on the Mount is strongly in this vein. Christian discipleship has great affinity with many of the principles found in these other efforts to understand and set forth what is right and good and how we should live. Jesus' Great Commission to *"Go and make disciples of all nations ... teaching them to observe all that I have commanded you"* reflected the understanding that our faith, particularly the ethical and moral aspects of our faith, has to be taught, learned and practiced.

Any discussion of character-based ethics has to start with a basic understanding of character itself. Some have tried to reduce character to the behaviors that we have traditionally associated with character. Behavior is certainly weighty evidence of character, but the two can't be equated. It is like equating intelligence with intelligent answers or choices. They are related but they aren't the same. Intelligence involves a capacity that goes far beyond specific intelligent answers or choices. The same is true of character. It is both a capacity and a quality that goes beyond particular acts that flow from it. Positively speaking, character's capacity is a capacity for virtue and its quality is the quality of the virtues it contains. When the Apostle Paul wrote, *"the fruit of the Spirit is love, joy, peace, patience, kindness, goodness, faithfulness, gentleness and self-control"*[124] he listed qualities or virtues that constitute Christian character. The list is representative, not exhaustive. Each of these qualities is a virtue that we are to nurture and together they give us a picture of the kind of character to which a Christian should aspire.

Fruit trees produce fruit. The tree and the fruit have the same genetic makeup or character, but we can distinguish between the two. Though genetically identical, the tree and the fruit are different. The capacity of the tree is greater than that of any individual piece of fruit because it can produce many pieces of fruit. The character or quality of the tree, whether it is an orange tree or an apple tree, determines the character or quality of each and all of the pieces of fruit. There is a process of growth and ripening through which each piece of fruit must develop. When Jesus said, *"A good tree cannot bear bad fruit, and a bad tree cannot bear good fruit,"*[125] he was simply illustrating the essence of character for us. When Jesus said, *"You will know them by their fruits"*[126] he was providing very practical guidance both for knowing ourselves and challenging ourselves to grow, but also for knowing who to trust and who to follow in a world that is often hostile and dangerous.[127]

Virtue and character go hand in glove. If the hand and all its fingers are virtues then character is the glove that contains them all. Both testaments of the Bible address character and its virtues extensively. For example, Proverbs 31, written centuries before Christ, is a famous passage of Scripture describing the noble character of a virtuous woman. It describes virtue after virtue while building a picture of a truly noble woman whose nobility has nothing to do with her social status, but has everything to do with her character. Christians have been thinking and writing about virtue from the very beginning of the church. Catholics have distilled much of that thinking and writing in the "Catechism of the Catholic Church" which contains a clear, concise description both of virtue in general and four "cardinal virtues" that encompass all the rest: prudence, justice, fortitude, and temperance. We will discuss each of these a bit later and why they are

---

[124] Galatians 5:22.
[125] Matthew 7:18.
[126] Matthew 7:20.
[127] Matthew 7:15-20; John 16:33.

considered cardinal virtues when we look at different perspectives on virtue, including these essential ones.

The Catechism describes virtue this way: *"A virtue is an habitual and firm disposition to do the good. It allows the person not only to perform good acts, but to give the best of himself. The virtuous person tends toward the good with all his sensory and spiritual powers; he pursues the good and chooses it in concrete actions."*[128] St. Gregory of Nyssa (c. 335-395 AD), revered by Catholics, Orthodox and Protestants (Lutherans and Anglicans especially) for his contributions to our understanding of the Trinity, wrote: *"The goal of the Christian life is to become like God."* [129]

Virtues, from the Christian perspective, are the virtues of God, those which comprise the character of God. This really matters in helping us to distinguish one understanding of ethics from another. outcome-based ethics, duty-based ethics and character or virtue-based ethics all hold and defend particular virtues and all think that virtues are of central importance in ethics. But the virtues they see as most important are radically different. Only the "Divine Command" duty ethics of our Judeo-Christian heritage and Christian virtue ethics assign those virtues to the character of God. This is not so much a defense of these views, but a clear statement of what they are and how they have been understood historically by Jews and Christians. Outcome-based ethics or consequentialism has a very different set of core virtues and they are found not in God or God's commands, but in that which is good in terms of my individual interest or our collective interest.

Why does this matter? It makes a huge difference whether we base our ethics on what we believe to be the commands or character of God or if we base them on individual or collective interests. If we fail to see the difference between these we fail to see something that is central to Christianity. To put this in terms that are meaningful to evangelicals, it is equivalent in magnitude to saying that there is no difference between basing one's salvation on faith or basing it on good works. Relying on the teaching in the New Testament Epistle to the Ephesians *"For it is by grace*

---

[128] *Catechism of the Catholic Church, Article 7, Section 1803.* Liguori Publications, Liguori, Missouri. English translation Copyright 1994, United States Catholic Conference, Inc. - Libreria Editrice Vaticana.
[129] Ibid.

*you have been saved, through faith—and this is not from yourselves, it is
the gift of God— not by works, so that no one can boast"*[130] evangelicals
would say that basing one's salvation on good works violates the core of
Christianity. Basing our ethics, individual or collective, on something other
than God's character or commands likewise violates the core of Christianity
and, with increasingly thoughtless ease, evangelicals are doing just that.

Christianity has a great "North Star." It is the guide star for all Christian
ethics. As noted before, when Jesus was asked what was the greatest of
all the commandments, not just the broadest but that which was the
foundation of all the others, he answered: *"Love the Lord your God with all
your heart and with all your soul and with all your mind. This is the first and
greatest commandment. And the second is like it: Love your neighbor as
yourself."*[131] The greatest commandment is two inseparable
commandments: love God and love your neighbor. They aren't just first and
second, they are heads and tails. Together they orient us to that which is
most important in life, that to which we are called and accountable. As
Richard Rohr pointed out in one of his many seminars, the value of the
North Star is not in our actually reaching it, but in the fact that it keeps us
oriented.

How do character-based ethics, virtue ethics, differ from duty-based ethics?
In many ways the two are compatible and both have strong roots in
Christian ethics. I have no doubt, for example, that Eric Liddell was a man
of great character and that his strong commitment to moral duty was a
reflection of his character. But for Christianity, the two ethical approaches
are subtly and sometimes significantly different. How so? One is essentially
a rule based ethic, whether the rules are written or unwritten, divine or
human, while the other is not. A character-based ethic both values and
uses rules when needed, but does not see rules as ends in themselves. It
understands that the rules are not there for their own sake, but for the sake
of something else. Those who are committed to a hard notion of moral
absolutes are uncomfortable with any behavior that compromises what they
believe to be absolute rules that cannot be broken. A duty-based ethic
says that the rules, certain ones of them anyway, always apply. A

---

[130] Ephesians 2: 8,9.
[131] Matthew 22:37-39.

character-based or virtue ethic, says that is not necessarily so, but for far different reasons than an outcome-based, consequentialist ethic would.

Many readers of this will be familiar with the story of Corrie ten Boom and her family from the book, *The Hiding Place*, that later was made into a film. Her family was Dutch and all were deeply committed Christians. They were watchmakers who lived in the city of Haarlem until their imprisonment during World War II. Corrie's father had strong sympathy for his Jewish neighbors believing that the status of the Jews as the originally chosen people of God required it. Corrie and her sister Betsie shared that conviction. The family built a secret room in their house and hid Jewish families and resistance workers from the Nazis. They never tried to convert those who stayed with them to Christianity. Later, during their own imprisonment, they were revered for their care for those imprisoned with them. Betsie died before being released from Ravensbruck women's labor camp. Before the war's end, Corrie was released from the same camp as a result of a clerical error that saved her life. After her release, she went on to hide and care for mentally ill people who were being targeted for destruction by the Nazis.

Corrie was willing to lie to protect the people whom they were helping, Betsie was not. The two sisters loved each other and both were deeply committed to their faith, but they took different principled positions with regard to this incredibly difficult dilemma. Their different stands powerfully illustrate both the close connection and the essential difference between Christian duty-based ethics and Christian character-based ethics. To be sure, both women were women of strong character, but one felt the freedom, even the necessity, to lie on behalf of those in their care while the other did not. Betsie maintained her conviction that lying, even under the most trying circumstances, was wrong.

Does this mean Corrie was acting from a non-Christian, outcome-based ethic in the sense that she justified her lying only because of the probable terrible consequence of not lying to protect those in need? That her lying protected those whom she was concealing from the Nazis certainly was the case, but there is much more behind her actions. There is a huge difference between someone who believes that lying is wrong, but permits or requires herself to do it when the very purpose of life itself and all that is good is threatened, and someone who believes that lying can be right or wrong depending on whether it provides the best outcome-based on either personal interest or the most benefit for the most people. Corrie was deeply committed to truthfulness and the truth. *The Hiding Place* paints a beautiful picture of her being brought up from childhood with a strong conviction that it was necessary to honor God by living according to the moral precepts of the Bible. Christian duty-based ethics and Christian character-based ethics start from the same point. Both are rooted in the need for truthfulness and the truth and both believe that these are needed because they reflect the character of God.

How then, under any circumstances, even extreme ones, could she lie? Is this one of those dreaded slippery slopes where one justification of a wrong leads to a whole host of others? Envisioning circumstances just like those facing Corrie ten Boom, Dietrich Bonhoeffer explained the morality of actions like hers in terms of what he called "living truth." He knew there was need for extreme caution against going too far but in his words,

> *"There is a truth which is of Satan. Its essence is that under the semblance of truth, it denies everything that is real … The dangers which are involved in the concept of living truth must never impel one to abandon this concept in favor of the formal and cynical concept of truth. We must try to make this clear. Every utterance or word lives and has its home in a particular environment."*[132]

For Bonhoeffer, when the environment was one in which all that was right and good in God's creation was threatened, any blame for a lie intended to counter such a threat fell back entirely on the one or ones who created the threatening situation.[133] Corrie's protection of her neighbors was a positive fulfilling of the great commandment. In Bonhoeffer's language she spoke the "right word" not a "formal and cynical" word which could have destroyed those in her care even though it was technically true. Bonhoeffer struggled mightily with his duty as a Christian citizen of Germany and his growing conviction that Hitler needed to be assassinated. Doing so would surely be construed as murder by many of his religious countrymen. It was not something he could justify on the surface, but he became increasingly

---

[132] Bonhoeffer, *Ethics.* p.361.
[133] Ibid., p.362.

convinced that the Nazi regime was an affront to all that was right and good in the sight of God. This struggle took place in one who, like Corrie ten Boom, had been raised from infancy with a moral compass based on obedience to God's commands.

Only someone who has been raised and schooled in the truth and its importance knows how to speak "the right word." Bonhoeffer wrote, *"'Telling the truth,' therefore, is not solely a matter of moral character; it is also a matter of correct appreciation of real situations and of serious reflection upon them ... Telling the truth is, therefore, something which must be learnt."*[134] Ideally, this learning to tell the truth is central to Christian discipleship. The upbringing of these two giants of the faith is a beautiful example of how that can be done in the context of our families.

There is a significant scriptural principle behind the actions of these two. There is a gospel account of Jesus' disciples picking grain in a field on the Sabbath because they were hungry. They were confronted by the Pharisees, a Jewish religious group who prided themselves on their knowledge of and commitment to the Hebrew Scriptures. Intentional Sabbath breaking was a grave offense in the law of Moses and they were, at the very least, deeply offended by the disciples' apparent disrespect for the Law.

> *"One Sabbath Jesus was going through the grainfields, and as his disciples walked along, they began to pick some heads of grain. The Pharisees said to him, 'Look, why are they doing what is unlawful on the Sabbath?' He answered, 'Have you never read what David did when he and his companions were hungry and in need? In the days of Abiathar the high priest, he entered the house of God and ate the consecrated bread, which is lawful only for priests to eat. And he also gave some to his companions.' Then he said to them, 'The Sabbath was made for man, not man for the Sabbath. So the Son of Man is Lord even of the Sabbath.'"* [135]

The principle that the Sabbath was made for man, not man for the Sabbath is critical for understanding Christian character-based ethics. For the

---

134 Ibid., p.359.
135 Mark 2:23-28.

Jewish people, the Sabbath and the keeping of the Sabbath were right at the heart of their Law and of their relationship with God. Jesus was deeply committed to the principle of the Sabbath and was not in any way lessening the importance of it. The statement that *"the Son of Man [Jesus] is Lord of the Sabbath"* has meaning only if the Sabbath actually has meaning and relevance; otherwise, he is Lord of something meaningless and irrelevant. He was surely not saying or conveying that.

Though it means more than this, the point of the Sabbath day is not that God needs man's worship and acknowledgment, but that man needs God's rest and provision; not just generally, but in a structured rest that is built into life. Resting from work on the Sabbath meant that God's people had to trust God to provide their needs even when they rested from their labors. The point of the Sabbath was not to prohibit doing what was needed to meet basic daily needs as the disciples were doing and to which the Pharisees objected. The law doesn't exist for the sake of the law. It ultimately exists so that humanity's deepest needs and longings can be met. Apart from what it is meant to protect and produce in us, the rightness of the law is not intrinsic to the law, even the moral Law of God.

What then is the relationship between law and character? For one thing, law is foundational to character, but is not the same thing. The relatedness and the difference can be illustrated by a short story. On July 26, 1971 my helicopter crew was assigned responsibility for clearing the launch window for the Apollo 15 space mission. We were dispatched to Cape Kennedy, Florida and were tasked with moving a flotilla of various sized boats wanting to get as close to the launch site as possible. Many were just curious onlookers, but there was always the possibility that among them were some with less innocent intentions. There was also the possibility that an explosion of the Apollo on takeoff could result in the deaths of the onlookers.

Our helicopter, an HH-3E "Jolly Green Giant," created a very powerful rotor wash and that was needed to move the boats back from the launch site. They would move only as far as someone made them move. We used our loudhailer to tell them what to do then enforced it by hovering up to the boats till their antennas whipped in the downwash to the point that the crews feared they would be ripped off the boats. Then they moved. We were like a sheepdog moving back and forth along this huge line of boats, moving the whole bunch of them back. This allowed something important and good to happen and ensured the safety of all.

Just before liftoff, we landed at a small airstrip close to the launch site. When the Saturn 5 rocket ignited we could feel it before we could hear it or see it. The ground literally shook and then we heard the deafening roar and, as the dense smoke from the ignition of the rocket billowed upwards, we eventually saw the thirty-six story high Apollo vehicle emerge out of the smoke. It was awesome.

Unknown NASA employee, scanned by Kipp Teague -
http://www.hq.nasa.gov/alsj/a17/images17.html *(Image number KSC-72PC-589)* Direct link:
http://www.hq.nasa.gov/alsj/a17/ap17-KSC-72PC-589.jpg

At the launch pad, there was a huge superstructure which attached to the Apollo spacecraft. It remained attached after ignition to provide vertical stability and one other vital function. Included in the structure were four "hold down arms" that prevented it from lifting off prematurely as the thrust following ignition built to the level needed for flight. When it reached near full thrust the hold-down arms detached. As it lifted off, having done its job, the rest of the superstructure fell away from the Apollo. Once liftoff had been achieved the spacecraft had to rely entirely on its internal guidance system. Had the superstructure remained attached, internal guidance system or no, the craft would never have been able to fly. It would have never left the atmosphere and never gotten into space.

Without carrying the analogy too far, character-based ethics are like an internal guidance system that could never function as designed apart from the external stability and restraint provided by the superstructure at the very beginning. But when the superstructure had served its purpose, it needed to give way to internal guidance. Christian virtue ethics, character-based ethics, share the same superstructure as Christian "Divine Command" duty-based ethics. Neither is possible apart from the substance of God's moral law. But the idea that the superstructure must necessarily fall away belongs in a special way to character-based ethics, virtue ethics.

There is another point to be made here about the relationship between law and character. In this context, I mean the principle of law, not only the moral law of God or formal laws that are in place in society but the need for rules generally, rules that need to be followed in the home or elsewhere in society as a matter of necessity for living together at all. For children at the pre-conventional, egocentric level of human cognitive and moral development, law is absolutely necessary. It is foundational to the development of character which is almost impossible apart from it. When a child grows up in a home where rules for living, including respect for parents and siblings and behavior that is necessary for living socially with others, are not taught and enforced, it is a tragic formula for failure in life. There is no grace or freedom in this kind of lawlessness. On the other hand, when this is done right it is pure grace even though it consists in laying down the law. On a societal level, the same thing is true.

When the law of Moses, including the Ten Commandments, was given to the people of Israel they had just come out of 400 years of slavery. Centuries before the Exodus, after a famine in their historic homeland, Abraham's grandson, Jacob, and all his sons and their families migrated to Egypt. Those familiar with the biblical account know that Jacob's sons, jealous of their brother, Joseph, had long before sold him to slave traders who sold him to an Egyptian official. Despite several misadventures, he eventually rose to a position of great prominence. When famine threatened the entire Middle East, Joseph's brothers went to Egypt in search of food. There he met his brothers again, forgave them and brought all of them, their families and their father, Jacob, to Egypt where they were provided for by the Egyptian Pharaoh who had appointed Joseph to a position second only to himself over the entire nation.

Years later, after Joseph's death and another Pharaoh had come to power, the Egyptians became increasingly jealous and suspicious of the immigrant Israelites. The Israelites were reduced to a slavery that lasted four hundred years. Depending on whose assumptions one uses, Moses was born and lived sometime around 1300-1500 BC. Shortly after his birth, through God's providence, he was brought into the family of the Egyptian Pharaoh's daughter who raised him. He fell into disgrace after having killed an Egyptian who was abusing a fellow Israelite. He fled into exile and eventually was called by God to lead his people out of Egypt and back to the land that had been promised to their ancestor, Abraham. Moses led the Israelites out of their slavery in Egypt in what is known as the Exodus and ultimately led them to the boundary of their historic homeland just before his death. Enroute to the promised land, the law that would be the defining aspect of their culture was given to them through Moses.

The Israelites being led out of slavery by Moses were an entire society that was essentially pre-conventional in Kohlberg's terms. After four centuries of enslavement, their whole sense of identity was that of being the property of someone else. They were essentially children whose morality was largely dictated by those above them. After escaping from Egypt, when they encountered extreme hunger and thirst while in the wilderness of what we now call the Sinai peninsula, their first instinct was to return to the place of their enslavement where at least they had food and water. It was all they knew. In the biblical account, despite the inclinations of the people to return to Egypt, Moses urged them forward and God miraculously provided both food and water.

When God gave them the law through Moses, summarized in the Ten Commandments, it was a gift of pure grace. It provided them an entirely new identity. Now they were the people of God, not the property of others. They were given a basic structure of expected behavior and justice, a basic system of public health, a form of government that was appropriate both to their level of development and their circumstances. They were given an ethnic unity formed by allegiance to a transcendent God who not only ordered their collective and individual behavior through a firm moral law but also protected and provided for them and gave them hope for a stable, prosperous life in a promised land. They could not thrive apart from any of these things and could not have been given a more gracious gift. Their national character and their character as individuals now had a center around which both could form. It was the character of God, the God of Abraham, Isaac, and Jacob, that was to shape their character, individually and nationally. In the process, they moved from a pre-conventional altitude to an ethnocentric, conventional one.

More than 1000 years later, the Apostle Paul would write, astonishingly, *"you are not under the law, but under grace."*[136] This teaching was scandalous to many Jews because it seemingly undermined the centrality of the Law given to them by God and by which they received their national identity and character. But the world in which the early Christians lived was a different world from that in which the law of Moses was given. Christ had come, they now lived in a newly experienced reality of God's forgiveness, and what had been basic and foundational now needed to be built upon in a new way. Paul would go on to say that this new reality in no way eliminated the need for or the validity of the law of Moses, but that it now had a different role and relationship to God's people. Now, he said, *"the whole law is summed up in a single commandment, 'You shall love your neighbor as yourself.'"*[137]

Many aspects of the law, like the superstructure that supported the Apollo spacecraft on the launch pad, needed to fall away and internal guidance needed to become primary. Among those things that needed to fall away were rites involving animal sacrifice, strict dietary restrictions, and circumcision as the necessary sign of God's special favor. However, just as there was the hard reality of physical laws to which the Apollo needed to remain oriented while still in the earth's atmosphere, the people of God needed to remain oriented to the hard reality of what was right and wrong according to the character of God, particularly as it was revealed in and through Jesus of Nazareth. And now, interiorly, they were promised that God's Spirit would be there and would lead them as the law had led their ancestors.

---

[136] Romans 6:14.
[137] Galatians 5:14.

Just as the Apollo, as it left the earth's atmosphere, needed to transition from a world governed by the laws of aeronautics to one governed by the laws of astronautics, God's people needed to be guided by God's character, not just God's laws, as they moved from an ethnocentric world where God's grace was made known most significantly in the experience of the people of Israel to an omnicentric, post-conventional one in which God's grace, through the good news of the Gospel, was to be experienced by those *"from every nation, tribe, people and language."*[138]

Why all this history? The experience of the people of Israel is the context for what is of the greatest significance to Christians. But the question is no longer one of simply knowing the moral law of God and how it was meant to be applied to the people of Israel, but something much broader. The world we live in today is vastly different from the world of the ancient Israelites. They obviously had no inkling of modern life as it has been shaped by so many intervening realities. These include advances in science and the social sciences, modern medicine, modern warfare, global economies, nuclear power and weaponry, space exploration, advanced understanding of physics, chemistry, biology, genetics, mathematics, linguistics, etc. Thousands of years of history with all the intervening trials, errors and events have brought us to the far different world of today. Is it even possible to have an ethic that is able to connect the ancient past with today? Christian virtue ethics provide an important answer to this. character-based, virtue ethics provide both a link to the distant past and an ethic that can face the enormous challenges of modern life.

One of the most respected voices of virtue ethics in recent years has been a Scottish moral philosopher who converted to Catholicism named Alasdair MacIntyre. He focused keenly on one central virtue upon which any ability to link the past, the present and the future depends. If there is a moral law based on the character of God, that applies in all places and at all times, one virtue in particular is needed if we are to know how to apply that law. MacIntyre puts it this way, *"knowing how to apply the law is itself possible only for someone who possesses the virtue of justice."*[139]

---

138 Revelation 7:9.
139 MacIntyre, Alasdair. *Whose Justice? Which Rationality?* University of Notre Dame Press, Notre Dame, Indiana, 1988, p. ix.

Part II: Virtue and Vice

"There is one vice of which no man in the world is free; which everyone in the world loathes when he sees it in someone else ... There is no fault that makes a man more unpopular, and no fault which we are more unconscious of in ourselves. And the more we have it ourselves, the more we dislike it in others ... The vice I am talking of is Pride or Self-Conceit: and the virtue opposite to it, in Christian morals, is called Humility."[140]

C.S. Lewis

---

[140]Lewis, C.S. *Mere Christianity.* pp. 108,109.

Chapter 6

Whose Virtue?

"But as for me and my household, we will serve the Lord."
Joshua 24:15

Perhaps not surprisingly, given my military background, one of the most formative books I've read is one entitled *War, Morality and the Military Profession*. It is a compilation of significant essays, edited by Malham Wakin, on the many topics related to justice in war. It acknowledges the reality of conflict as a part of human life and is concerned with the management of violence in ways that do not undercut the greater concern for justice even in instances when violence is necessary for the protection of the innocent.

Colonel Wakin (later promoted to General) was the head of the Philosophy Department at the Air Force Academy when my father was the Director of Athletics there and I was in Junior High and High School. I mentioned that my mother was a devout Catholic; my father was a less devout Presbyterian. When they married, my father, in deference to their desire to be married in the Catholic church, had to promise to raise my sisters and me in the Catholic Church. I was baptized in the Catholic church and, though my father did not go to Mass with us each Sunday, he made sure we did. From time to time, while I was in Junior High and High School, Col. Wakin taught our religious education classes at the Catholic chapel for permanently assigned staff and families. He was a thorough-going virtue ethicist and he exemplified the reality that virtue ethics must be taught, learned and practiced. He made a life of teaching virtue not only to the cadets at the Air Force Academy but to the children of those who were in his community of faith.

In an essay entitled "Ethics of Leadership" he said *"Loyalty and obedience, integrity and courage, subordination of the self to the good of the military unit and the nation-state - these are among the moral virtues critical to the military function ... "*[141] These are specific virtues necessary for one who

---

[141] Wakin, Malham, Editor. *War, Morality and the Military Profession.* Westview Press, Boulder, Colorado, 1981. p.214.

leads or otherwise serves in the military. They are focused on and applied to military service and illustrate that the question of "Whose Virtue?" can be specific to the military context in the same way that we might speak of medical ethics, business ethics or political ethics in the context of the medical profession, business or politics. But there is a bigger context, the context of virtues essential for meaningful life itself from a Christian perspective that must be addressed before we dive down to specific virtues needed for different professions or walks of life. This bigger context, this greater perspective, this Christian ethic, applies not just to personal life, but to military life, medicine, business and to politics.

Traditional Catholic teaching identifies four "cardinal" virtues: prudence, justice, fortitude and temperance. They are cardinal because all the others can be grouped around them.[142] We'll discuss each of these in the next chapter, but for now will focus on the fact that with respect to ethics, how we understand justice is key. Our understanding of justice depends substantially, if not entirely, on the school of thought that defines it.

Alasdair MacIntyre's book *Whose Justice? Which Rationality?* focuses on three traditions, each of which has a different rationality or logic and consequently a different understanding of justice. He acknowledges that there are more than three main traditions, but focuses on what he terms the Aristotelian tradition, the Augustinian Christian tradition (his own) and the Scottish rational tradition following the philosophy of David Hume.[143] By the time Hume was twenty he had abandoned his Christian roots and come to believe *"that the Morality of every Religion was bad."*[144] These three traditions have had the most impact on western cultures including our American culture.

In broad generalities, these represent the classical tradition, the Christian tradition and the modern western enlightenment liberal tradition. MacIntyre points out that the tradition of Aristotle influenced the Christian tradition which, in turn, influenced the modern liberal tradition even though being largely abandoned by it. These three distinct traditions have different concepts of justice, and one main theme of MacIntyre's book is that one's view of justice is determined by the tradition from which it comes. Evangelicals would claim that their ethic is pure and that it comes

---

[142] *Catechism of the Catholic Church.* p.443.
[143] MacIntyre, *Whose Justice? Which Rationality?* P. 10
[144] Ibid. p.282.

exclusively from the Christian tradition. Not so. American evangelicals are embracing one particular variety of what MacIntyre described as the modern liberal tradition with astonishing naivete and, in the process, damaging the very ethic they claim to embrace.

One of the primary ways that this is happening is by the conflation of Christianity with conservative American politics. This simply means that many evangelicals lump their religious convictions together with their political convictions. Most would argue that their faith is what drives their politics, but that is highly debatable. As alluded to earlier, for many evangelicals, some of their strongest political convictions come not from Christianity but from the Objectivist philosophy of Ayn Rand which is having a surprising, but huge impact on their thinking. It is surprising because the architect of that philosophy was an atheist, a proponent of abortion and near total sexual freedom, ideas that most evangelicals would find highly objectionable. However, evangelicals have selectively embraced key aspects of the ethic of this philosophy without even knowing its origin. In the process, they have literally contaminated their own ethic. Surely this is overstating the issue and crying wolf or saying that the sky is falling, isn't it? No, it is not.

Again, ethics flow out of the overall philosophy or tradition in which they are rooted. The ethic that comes from the philosophy of Ayn Rand is ethical egoism. This ethic is heavily influencing conservative American politics and, by association, it is also significantly influencing American evangelicals today. Much of her philosophy has been adopted by leaders of the Tea Party movement in America and is reflected in both the language and philosophy of the movement.[145] The profound impact she has had was detailed in the 2009 book *Goddess of the Market: Ayn Rand and the American Right*.[146]

In an April 2016 interview with USA Today's Kirsten Powers, a thoughtful Christian and former Fox News analyst, "[Donald] Trump described himself as an Ayn Rand fan. He said of her novel *The Fountainhead*: "*It relates to business (and) beauty (and) life and inner emotions. That book relates to ... everything.*" He identified with Howard Roark, the novel's idealistic central

[145] Gibson, Megan. "The Tea Party and Ayn Rand's Atlas Shrugged." *The Guardian,* 22 April 2011.
[146] www.theguardian.com/commentisfree/cifamerica/2011/apr/22/tea-party-movement-republicans. Accessed 19 March 2019.

figure, an architect, who designs skyscrapers and rages against the establishment.[147] As earlier indicated, Donald Trump's *The Art of the Deal* is a virtual textbook for personal ethical egoism and illustrates how deep this influence goes.

Mike Pompeo, formerly Director of the Central Intelligence Agency and currently the US Secretary of State for President Trump, has often said that Rand's works inspired him. "*One of the very first serious books I read when I was growing up was 'Atlas Shrugged,' and it really had an impact on me,*" the [then] Kansas congressman told Human Events in 2011."[148] Mick Mulvaney, currently serving as President Trump's Chief of Staff, formerly Director of the Office of Management and Budget and Acting Director of the Consumer Financial Protection Bureau, has read Rand's novels six or eight times each.[149] Former Secretary of State, Rex Tillerson, former CEO of Exxon Mobil, described *Atlas Shrugged* as his favorite book.[150] In a 2009 video explaining that he was not, in fact, named after Ayn Rand, Kentucky Senator and two time Republican presidential candidate, Rand Paul describes himself as a "big fan of Ayn Rand" who "cut my teeth" on her books in high school, and who "*read a lot of the different free market Austrian economists who were sort-of fellow travelers with Ayn Rand.*"[151]

Though Paul Ryan, the former Speaker of the US House of Representatives, now has distanced himself from the overall philosophy of Ayn Rand, he has not distanced himself from major aspects of her ethic. Several years ago he told The Weekly Standard "*I give out Atlas Shrugged as Christmas Presents and I make all my interns read it.*"[152] Paul Ryan is not alone. In *Goddess of the Market: Ayn Rand and the American Right,*

[147]Powers, Kirsten. "Donald Trump's 'kinder, gentler' version." *USA Today*, 11 April 2016. www.usatoday.com/story/opinion/2016/04/11/donald-trump-interview-elections-2016-ayn-rand-vp-pick-politics-column/82899566/. Accessed 10 March 2019.

[148] Hohmann, James. "The Daily 202: Ayn Rand-acolyte Donald Trump stacks his cabinet with fellow objectivists." Washington Post, December 13, 2016. www.washingtonpost.com/news/powerpost/paloma/daily-202/2016/12/13/daily-202-ayn-rand-acolyte-donald-trump-stacks-his-cabinet-with-fellow-objectivists/584f5cdfe9b69b36fcfeaf3b/. Accessed 19 March 2019.

[149] Seabrook, Andrea. "On Capitol Hill, Ayn Rand's 'Atlas' Can't Be Shrugged Off." *NPR*, 20 November 2011. www.npr.org/2011/11/14/142245517/on-capitol-hill-rands-atlas-cant-be-shrugged-off. Accessed 19 March 2019.

[150] Filkins, Dexter. "Rex Tillerson at the Breaking Point." *The New Yorker*, 16 October 2017. www.newyorker.com/magazine/2017/10/16/rex-tillerson-at-the-breaking-point. Accessed 19 March 2019.

[151] Paul, Rand. "Rand Paul on Ayn Rand and his Name." *YouTube*, May 2009. www.youtube.com/watch?v=oD-R_OeP6tU. Accessed 19 March 2019.

[152]Mangu-Ward, Katherine. "Young, Wonky and Proud of It," *The Weekly Standard,* 17 March 2003.

Jennifer Burns noted that today's conservative thought leaders have found that they *"can use the parts of Rand they want to use and not engage the rest."*[153]

Why is it important to know that the ethics of Ayn Rand have had such an impact on the thinking of the President, the current and former Secretaries of State, one of whom is the former Director of the Central Intelligence Agency, the former Speaker of the House, the current White House Chief of Staff and former Director of the Office of Management of the Budget and Consumer Protection Agency, many other influential political leaders and the thinking that has driven the Tea Party? The question is especially relevant here because, like the impact of second-hand smoke, the second-hand impact on evangelicals has been enormous.

First, the point should be made that it is possible to differentiate an ethic from the philosophy that gave it birth, but it is not possible to eliminate the DNA of that philosophy from the ethic. A good example of this is the well written *Confessions of a Secular Jesus Follower: Finding Answers in Jesus for Those Who Don't Believe.* This was written by award winning USA Today columnist, Tom Krattenmaker who shows how the Sermon on the Mount can be a powerful ethical guide for non-religious people. He separates the ethic of Jesus from the overall Christian tradition and philosophy, but he can't do away with its DNA. It is pointedly obvious where it came from. Similarly, American evangelicals have taken major aspects of Ayn Rand's ethic without buying the philosophy as a whole, but what they have taken is full of her DNA.

In the same way that Paul Ryan now describes the overall philosophy of Objectivism as incompatible with his Catholic faith, it is unlikely that Donald Trump, Mike Pompeo, Mick Mulvaney or Rand Paul would embrace all the tenets of Objectivism, especially not its atheism. However, they do embrace the central and most potent elements of the ethic of Objectivism and that raises credible concerns that cannot be ignored. Without going into overwhelming detail, it is necessary to understand a little bit about this philosophy in order to understand how toxic it is to historic Christian ethics.

---

153 Gibson, Meghan. "The Tea Party and Ayn Rand's Atlas Shrugged." The Guardian. 22 April 2011. www.theguardian.com/commentisfree/cifamerica/2011/apr/22/tea-party-movement-republicans. Accessed 19 March 2019.

Objectivism

"Objectivism advocates reason as man's sole means of knowledge, and therefore, for the reasons I have already given, it is atheist."
Leonard Peikoff

Dr. Leonard Peikoff, about whom Ayn Rand said, *"Until or unless I write a comprehensive treatise on my philosophy, Dr. Peikoff's course is the only authorized presentation of the entire theoretical structure of Objectivism - that is, the only one that I know of my own knowledge to be fully accurate."*[154] Ayn Rand left her estate to Peikov who wrote *Objectivism: The Philosophy of Ayn Rand* which is Volume VI in the Ayn Rand Library. In that he said, *"Like all religions, Christianity is incompatible ultimately with every virtue."*[155] Virtue, according to this philosophy, is oriented neither towards God nor other humans, but it is oriented toward "reality."[156] By this philosophy, the proper object of love is neither God nor other people, it is love for what is real and "real" is defined as a reality excluding any presence of or moral requirements of God.

In Lecture 2 of his series "The Philosophy of Objectivism," Peikoff said:

> *"Objectivism advocates reason as man's sole means of knowledge, and therefore, for the reasons I have already given, it is atheist. It denies any supernatural dimension presented as a contradiction of nature, of existence. This applies not only to God, but also to every variant of the supernatural ever advocated or to be advocated. In other words, we accept reality, and that's all."*

As discussed earlier, Christianity values reason very highly, but also says that a reality that excludes God is not reality at all. Compare Peikoff's assertion with the admonition from the Old Testament book of Proverbs, dear to Christians as well as Jews, that says *"The fear of the Lord is the beginning of knowledge, fools despise wisdom and instruction."* [157] My point here is not so much to argue against Objectivism or its ethic but to make it as clear as possible that it is a focused denial of Christianity and Christian

---

[154] Peikoff, *Objectivism: The Philosophy of Ayn Rand.* Cover.
[155] Ibid., p. 290.
[156] Ibid., p. 251.
[157] Proverbs 1:7.

ethics. Additionally, one cannot take the ethic of one philosophy and inject it into another without changing the philosophy into which it is injected.

At what point does something cease to be what it was originally? For example, at what point does a car cease to be a car? One can permanently take the roof off of a car and it can still be a car. One can permanently take off the hood from the front of a car, the backseat, the sound system or the gas cap and it can still be a car. But one can't permanently take the motor out of a car and it still be a car, because that which is essential to its purpose can't be taken from it without it ceasing to be what it was made to be.

If the central problem of humanity is a moral problem, as evangelicals believe it is, how can a Christian ethic be replaced or modified in its central aspects by an ethic that denies it? Looking at it differently, how can the ethic of Christians be placed on a foundation other than its historic foundation, on God's character and commands, without Christianity itself being compromised? If Christ is the motor, then the character of Christ, inseparable from Christ, cannot be taken out of Christianity and it continue to be what it is. When the motor is taken permanently out of a car it becomes a static display, a relic of a car. When the motor is taken out of Christianity the same thing happens.

The very foundation of the philosophy of Objectivism is not just a challenge to but is a direct and intentional repudiation of what Jesus said was the foundation of Christian ethics and the foundation for all virtue. Again, *"The first and greatest commandment,"* Jesus said is *"Love the Lord your God with all your heart and with all your soul and with all your mind and … Love your neighbor as yourself. All the Law and Prophets hang on these two commandments."*[158] Love of God and love of neighbor together are the foundation of Christian life and ethics. Peikoff specifically contrasts the teaching of Ayn Rand's philosophy with that of Jesus and declares Jesus' teaching deficient.

Objectivist ethical egoism dismisses Christian ethics as not only deficient, but unjust.[159] Trump, with a Presbyterian background of sorts, Pompeo, an

---

[158] Matthew 22:37-40.
[159] Peikoff, *Objectivism: The Philosophy of Ayn Rand.* pp. 288-290.

evangelical, Rand Paul, a Presbyterian and Paul Ryan and Mick Mulvaney, both Catholics, would disavow the atheism that Ayn Rand held to so tenaciously, but do embrace key Objectivist values that are the foundation of Objectivist ethical egoism. The ethics of Christianity and the ethics of Objectivism are two different ethics. The two different ethics belong to two different faiths.

In 1964 Ayn Rand wrote *The Virtue of Selfishness*. It became one of her best selling works of nonfiction and by 2014 well over a million copies had been sold. Selfishness, or the pursuit of self-interest, is married with rationality in her philosophy. As Peikoff points out, "*In Ayn Rand's philosophy, virtue consists of allegiance to existence ... In 'Atlas Shrugged,' Ayn Rand defines six major derivatives of the virtue of rationality ... The six derivative virtues are independence, integrity, honesty, justice, productiveness, and pride.*"[160] This may sound high-minded and plausible to some, but it is necessary to understand what is meant by these words in the vocabulary of Objectivism.

For example, "*Justice is the virtue of judging men's character and conduct objectively and of acting accordingly, granting to each man that which he deserves.*"[161] Doesn't sound too bad on the surface, but there is more. "*The Objectivist position is the opposite of the injunction 'Judge not that ye be not judged* [from the Sermon on the Mount].' *Our policy, in Ayn Rand's words is: 'Judge, and be prepared to judge.'*"[162] Peikoff goes further,

> "*Like all religions, Christianity is incompatible ultimately with every virtue ... If men are to have any chance for a future, it is this aspect of Christian ethics above all others - this demand, at once brazen and mawkish, for unearned love, unearned approval, unearned forgiveness - that the West must reject, in favor of a solemn commitment to its moral antithesis: the trader principle.*"[163]

The Trader Principle is defined this way: "*The trader principle states that, if a man seeks something from another, he must gain title to it, i.e., come to*

[160] Ibid, p.251.
[161] Ibid., p.276.
[162] Peikoff, *Objectivism: The Philosophy of Ayn Rand.* p.278.
[163] Ibid., p. 290.

deserve it by offering the appropriate payment."[164] This seems reasonable on the surface, but there is more. Objectivism teaches that *"If justice is the policy of identifying a man's desserts [what a person deserves] and acting accordingly, mercy is the policy of identifying them, then not acting accordingly ... Mercy substitutes for justice a dose of the undeserved and does so in the name of pity."*[165] Objectivism mistakenly sees mercy, Christian or otherwise, as being based on a pathetic pity that defies justice. Contrast this with Jesus' teaching calling us to *"Be merciful, just as your Father is merciful."*[166] Being merciful for a Christian is based not on pity at all, but on God's having been merciful to us. For Objectivism, justice is based on the trader principle. You get what you earn, period. For Christians it is based on the justness of God which becomes the mandate for our being just. Though the word is the same, it is hard to overstate the difference between these two understandings of what justice is and on what it is based.

To the extent that evangelicals have bought into the definitions and foundations of Objectivism they have decisively moved away from historic Christian ethics. By continuing to self-identify as Christians who are witnesses of the Gospel, those who publicly or privately embrace Objectivist ethics are doing tremendous damage to Christian ethics and historic Christianity. It is one thing to say that Jesus' teaching is hard to understand or difficult to put into practice. It is an entirely different thing to say that it is incompatible with every virtue. If love of God and love of neighbor is the North Star of Christian ethics, rational self-interest is the guidestar of Objectivism. The followers of each are following two different stars. These are two different faiths.

Retributive and Distributive Justice

"Do not be deceived. God cannot be mocked. A man reaps what he sows."
Galatians 6:7

Any comprehensive study of justice must address two particularly important aspects: retributive justice and distributive justice. Both of these aspects receive considerable attention in both testaments of the Bible. Retributive

---

[164] Ibid., p. 286.
[165] Ibid., p. 289.
[166] Luke 6:36.

justice is justice based on what we deserve. This is understood both positively and negatively. For example, Jesus taught *"The worker deserves his wages."*[167] Paul, quoting both Jesus and Moses, made exactly the same point connecting consistent New Testament and Old Testament teaching about our receiving positively what we deserve.[168] Concerning the negative aspect of retributive justice, Paul also wrote,*"Do not be deceived. God cannot be mocked. A man reaps what he sows."*[169] The principle is stated bluntly in the Old Testament: *"An eye for an eye, a tooth for a tooth."*[170] But retributive justice is only part of the overall biblical treatment of the subject of justice, and the Bible does not end with an eye for an eye, rather it moves far beyond it as the Sermon on the Mount makes clear.

Earlier it was noted that there was and is much more to the concept of the Sabbath than merely keeping one day a week holy. The Old Testament concept of the Sabbath went far beyond the weekly observance we usually associate with it. One year in seven, a sabbatical year, the people of Israel were to let their fields rest. That is, they were not to plant them, but to let them replenish. Anything that grew on the land during that year was to be not only for themselves, but for their servants, hired workers and the non-Israelite aliens who lived in their communities.[171] Additionally, with regard to their own countrymen, God commanded that *"At the end of every seven years you must cancel debts."*[172] In summing up the requirements for what had to be done every seven years, God said *"Therefore I command you to be open-handed toward your brothers and toward the poor and needy in your land."*[173]

After seven cycles of seven years, after the 49th year, in the fiftieth year they were to observe a sabbath of sabbatical years known as the Year of Jubilee during which there was a massive rebalancing of inequities that had accumulated over those years. It was an agricultural economy and land was the primary means of production. To have to sell your land was to sell the one thing most necessary for your family's livelihood and well being.

---

[167] Luke, 10:7; 1 Timothy 5:18.
[168] Deuteronomy 25:4; 1 Timothy 5:18.
[169] Galatians 6:7.
[170] Exodus 21:24.
[171] Leviticus 25:1-7.
[172] Deuteronomy 15:1.
[173] Deuteronomy 15:11.

Leviticus 25, the Old Testament chapter which succinctly summarizes the content and reasons for this aspect of the Sabbath, assumes that the reason one would sell his land would be major misfortune resulting in poverty because there was no other rational or plausible explanation. In the Year of Jubilee, land that had been sold was returned to its original owners. If not, poverty would become permanent and God's justice made specific provisions to guard against that.

How could God require new owners to return land they may well have been able to acquire, not just because of their neighbor's misfortune, but due to their own industry and productivity? The Scripture makes it simple for God's people: *"because the land is mine* [God's] *and you reside in my land as foreigners and strangers."*[174] Psalm 24 makes clear that this is not just the land of Israel, but all land and lands: *"The earth is the Lord's and everything in it."* In the New Testament, James says it this way, *"What do you have that God hasn't given to you? And if everything you have is from God, why boast as though it were not a gift?"*[175] Paul, encouraging Christians in what we now know as Greece to contribute to the needs of the Christians in Jerusalem, says it this way:

> *"For you know the generous act of our Lord Jesus Christ, that though he was rich, yet for your sakes he became poor, so that by his poverty you might become rich ... the gift is acceptable according to what one has—not according to what one does not have. I do not mean that there should be relief for others and pressure on you, but it is a question of a fair balance between your present abundance and their need, so that their abundance may be for your need, in order that there may be a fair balance. As it is written,'The one who had much did not have too much, and the one who had little did not have too little.'"*[176]

"In order that there may be a fair balance." This is what is meant by distributive justice. The biblical mandate for a fair balance between the poverty of some and the abundance of others is prominent in both testaments of the Bible. Certainly it is a call to generosity, but not

---

[174] Leviticus 25:23.
[175] 1 Corinthians 4:7.
[176] 2 Corinthians 8:9,12-15.

generosity for generosity's sake or for the sake of the kind of pity that Objectivism sees as so pathetic in Christianity. Rather, it is based on what God in Christ has done for us and it is central to the biblical idea of justice. Some believe that this primarily refers to Christians sharing with other Christians. We will explore this further in a later chapter and will find that to be an argument founded on very shaky ground.

Does any of this mean that the Bible does not honor the principle of personal possession of private property? Of course not, the commandment against stealing in the Ten Commandments assumes it. What it does mean is that my right to private property is not absolute; rather, it is bounded by an even greater divine concern for justness in society. My "private property" is meant to serve God's greater concern for justice for all and not just personal well being or the well being of one family or nation over all others. The apostle James was scathing in his denunciation of those who, while neglecting the poor, *"hoarded wealth in the last days"* and *"have lived on earth in luxury and self-indulgence."*[177]

Does any of this mean that the Bible does not recognize an appropriate self-interest or self-love? Not at all; rather, it too is assumed in the Great Commandment that says not just to love your neighbor, but to love your neighbor *as yourself.* Self-love, self-interest is taken for granted in the Scriptures, but is never elevated in such a way that it becomes an end in itself. The way we love ourselves is simply the model for how we are to love others. It was never intended to stop at self-love or self-interest.

The just cited indictment by James is the same as Jesus' indictment of those of his contemporaries who were among the most religious of their day, but whose lack of love for their neighbors was evident in their neglect of the poor. *"Woe to you Pharisees, because you give God a tenth of your mint, rue and all other kinds of garden herbs, but you neglect justice and the love of God."*[178] The clear context of the teaching of both Jesus and James was neglect of the poor. Both retributive justice and distributive justice are powerfully important from a biblical perspective.

---

[177] James 5:4,5.
[178] Luke 11:42.

For Objectivism, justice consists in retributive justice. Period. You get what you earn, what you deserve. It is not that Objectivism has nothing to say about this aspect of justice that is insightful or useful. It's problem is not mainly in what it includes, but in what it excludes. What it excludes is central to Christian ethics and central to Christianity.

In the *Fountainhead*, Ayn Rand describes the fundamental judgment that Objectivist philosophy makes. It divides the world into two camps, the creators and the parasites, or in the words most frequently used by those like many in the Tea Party who embrace her thoughts today, the makers and the takers.

> *"Nothing is given to man on earth. Everything he needs has to be produced. And here man faces his basic alternative: he can survive in only one of two ways - by the independent work of his own mind or as a parasite fed by the minds of others. The creator originates. The parasite borrows. The creator faces nature alone. The parasite faces nature through an intermediary.*

> *The creator's concern is the conquest of nature. The parasite's concern is the conquest of men. The creator lives for his work. He needs no other men. His primary goal is within himself. The parasite lives second-hand. He needs others. Others become his prime motive.*

> *The basic need of the creator is independence. The reasoning mind ... demands total independence in function and in motive. To a creator, all relations with men are secondary."*

> *The basic need of the second-hander is to secure his ties with men in order to be fed. He places relations first."* [179]

This judgment is a judgment regarding one's fundamental being. It makes a judgment and applies a label that tells one everything he or she needs to know about another. As Peikoff says *"the refusal to judge, like any other kind of agnosticism, is itself the taking of a stand. In this case a profoundly immoral stand."* [180] In the Sermon on the Mount, Jesus says *"Do not judge, or you too will be judged. For in the same way you judge others, you will*

---

[179] Peikoff, *Objectivism: The Philosophy of Ayn Rand*, pp. 251, 252.
[180] Ibid., p. 277.

be judged, and with the measure you use, it will be measured to you."[181] Paul said the same thing, *"You, therefore, have no excuse, you who pass judgment on someone else, for at whatever point you judge another, you are condemning yourself, because you who pass judgment do the same things."* According to Objectivism this teaching of Jesus and Paul is not only in error, it is immoral.[182]

The point of both Jesus and Paul is to specifically command that we not do what Objectivism and the American conservative political perspective that embraces its tenets do as a foundational part of their shared ethical philosophy. More than that, both Jesus and Paul see those who do this as accountable to God for engaging in a fundamental injustice. The New Testament divides humanity between those who have experienced God's mercy and those who are yet to experience God's mercy. As Paul put it, *"God ... wants all people to be saved and to come to a knowledge of the truth."*[183] Objectivism divides the world into those who, according to its precepts, know the "truth" and those who are hopelessly out of touch with the so-called truth of Objectivism: the dividing of humanity into the creators and the parasites, the makers and the takers, the winners and the losers. It is a direct repudiation of Christianity and the ethics of Christianity. Large parts of its ethic are being widely embraced by American evangelicals.

---

[181] Matthew 7:1,2.
[182] Romans 2:1.
[183] 1 Timothy 2:4.

Chapter 7

The Golden Mean

'It is in the nature of moral qualities that they are destroyed by deficiency and excess.'[184]
Aristotle

This observation of Aristotle's is powerfully insightful. Jesus, without using the same words, taught the same thing. The earlier example about picking grain on the Sabbath illustrates this. Jesus took the Law of Moses, including the Law of the Sabbath, very seriously. In the Sermon on the Mount he said, *"Do not think that I have come to abolish the Law or the Prophets; I have not come to abolish them but to fulfill them."*[185] Jesus was determined to fulfill the Law, that is, to fill it to its fullest meaning and expression. He was also determined to show that what the Pharisees were doing was opposed to that. There was a right attitude and a wrong attitude towards the Law. The selective, excessive, nitpicking way of the Pharisees was as wrong, on one end of the scale, as it would have been, on the other end of the scale, if the Law were disregarded or abolished. If there is no Law of God there can be no obedience to it. Jesus opposed either extreme. If obedience to God's moral law is the virtue, deficient or no obedience on one hand and excessive or selective obedience on the other each are vices.

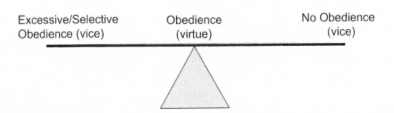

Excessive/Selective Obedience (vice) — Obedience (virtue) — No Obedience (vice)

This idea of balance or proportion when discussing virtue is critical not only when discussing individual virtues, but also when looking at what weight is given to what virtues in any given philosophy. There are many virtues that

---

[184] Aristotle. *The Nicomachean Ethics.* p.34.
[185] Matthew 5:17.

are commended in the Scriptures. The Book of Proverbs contains scores of them. How we group them and what priority we give them are vitally important. The key Christian virtues are grouped under love and, more specifically, love of God and love of neighbor as the inseparable and over-arching Christian virtues. We noted earlier that Paul, calling Christians to that which is the core of their identity, wrote *"Therefore, as God's chosen people, holy and dearly loved, clothe yourselves with compassion, kindness, humility, gentleness and patience ... And over all these virtues put on love, which binds them all together in perfect unity."*[186] The notion that we can leave these behind or that different rules apply when we move into the realms of politics, military service or business has no basis in Scripture.

The North Star

"This is what the Lord says, he who appoints the sun to shine by day, who decrees the moon and stars to shine by night ... "
Jeremiah 31:35

The North Star is the brightest star in its constellation. If "love God and love your neighbor" is the North Star, think of compassion, kindness, humility, gentleness and patience as other stars in the same constellation. When we seek practical guidance for how to love, these virtues that are constellated with the North Star provide just that. For Christians, any ethic that does not recognize the primacy of this constellation of virtues under love misses the mark. While Christianity constellates its virtues around love of God and neighbor, Objectivism constellates its virtues around self-interest and a rationality that does not include any divine mandate. With alarming regularity American evangelicalism is constelling its public values around these same two objectivist "virtues" and others that are shaped by them.

The virtue of "productiveness," which is highly valued in objectivism, can certainly be supported by the biblical record, as in Proverbs 31 where a virtuous woman is described like this: *"She sets about her work vigorously; her arms are strong for her tasks. She sees that her trading is profitable, and her lamp does not go out at night."*[187] This describes an admirable virtue, but not if it isn't constellated as a lesser light with those even

---

[186] Colossians 3:12,14.
[187] Proverbs 31: 17,18.

weightier virtues constituting love. Specifically, apart from the virtues of compassion, kindness, humility, gentleness and patience, its value is diminished substantially and possibly extinguished altogether. When read in context, these verses locate productiveness with an even greater obligation from the same passage to *"Speak up for those who cannot speak for themselves, for the rights of all who are destitute. Speak up and judge fairly, defend the rights of the poor and the needy."*[188] The point is a simple one. All virtues are not equal and, for Christian ethics, the primacy of love cannot be replaced by any other virtue. Any virtue that lacks an accompanying love lacks the one thing that defines that virtue as Christian or not.

As noted earlier and as listed in the Catholic Catechism, the four cardinal human moral virtues of prudence, justice, fortitude and temperance assume the primacy of love and the necessity of our participation in developing these virtues in our own lives. The catechism puts it this way, *"The moral virtues are acquired by human effort. They are the fruit and seed of morally good acts; they dispose all the powers of the human being for communion with divine love."*[189] Starting with prudence, the Catechism defines the virtues: *"Prudence is the virtue that disposes practical reason to discern our true good in every circumstance and to choose the right means of achieving it."*[190] Prudence, as a Christian virtue, is doing the right thing the right way at the right time for the right reason. Along with temperance it weighs the consequences, but does not give consequences more weight than the means to attaining them.

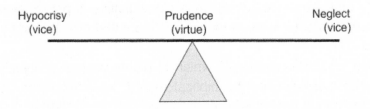

| Hypocrisy (vice) | Prudence (virtue) | Neglect (vice) |

[188] Proverbs 31:8,9.
[189] Catechism of the Catholic Church, Section 1804, p. 443.
[190] Ibid, Section 1806, p. 444.

"Justice is the moral virtue that consists in the constant and firm will to give their due to God and neighbor. Justice toward God is called the 'virtue of religion.' Justice toward men disposes one to respect the rights of each and to establish in human relationships the harmony that promotes equity with regards to persons and to the common good."[191] Justice towards God is summarized in the first four of the Ten Commandments, justice towards mankind is summarized in the last six of the Ten Commandments. Justice, like fortitude, demands consistency. It demands a principle or set of principles by which we know what is right and wrong and it demands the consistent application of those principles.

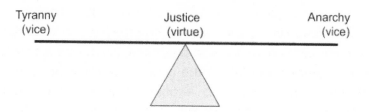

Tyranny	Justice	Anarchy
(vice)	(virtue)	(vice)

Another way to depict this:

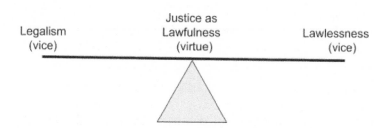

	Justice as	
Legalism	Lawfulness	Lawlessness
(vice)	(virtue)	(vice)

"Fortitude is the moral virtue that ensures firmness in difficulties and constancy in the pursuit of the good."[192] As touched upon above, consistency is a thread that necessarily runs through other virtues, but it is highlighted here. A virtue which is applied selectively or is practiced inconsistently carries the burden of proof that it is a virtue at all. If one is not consistent in the application of moral principles, even in trying circumstances, then regardless of how lofty those principles may be, one lacks the virtue of fortitude. On the other hand, if one is incapable of

---

[191] Ibid. Section 1807, p. 444.
[192] Ibid., Section 1808, p. 444.

necessary change, one also lacks fortitude because there is "too much" of the quality that makes fortitude a virtue.

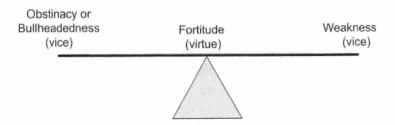

Obstinacy or Bullheadedness (vice)   Fortitude (virtue)   Weakness (vice)

"Temperance is the moral virtue that moderates the attraction of pleasures and provides balance in the use of created goods."[193] Balance is the essence of temperance. Along with prudence, it involves a careful weighing of the consequences and taking the course that maximizes the good and minimizes the evil according to a principle that actually identifies and distinguishes between good and evil. It too requires doing the right thing the right way and for the right reason.

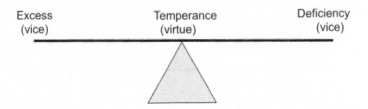

Excess (vice)   Temperance (virtue)   Deficiency (vice)

In light of our earlier discussion of absolutism and the fact that it claims adherence to absolutes but does so inconsistently and excessively, it is as much a vice as is a relativism which recognizes no universal moral principles. We can picture their relationship this way:

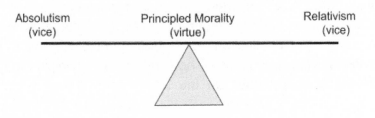

Absolutism (vice)   Principled Morality (virtue)   Relativism (vice)

---

[193] Ibid., Section 1809, p. 445.

Corrie ten Boom's life provides a great picture of what all these mean. She used her practical reason to see that the right thing to do involved saying what was needed to protect the Jewish families and resistance workers she and her family were helping. This was the "true good" spoken of in the catechism, even if it involved saying some things that were untrue. She did the right thing, at the right time, for the right reason. This is prudence. She was clear that all of this was her duty, both to God and to her neighbors. This is justice. She kept at it before she was arrested, while she was in a concentration camp and after her release. This is fortitude. She and her family had a comfortable home and all they needed to live. She appreciated this and at the same time shared what she had with others. She was not attached either to her comfortable home nor to the things she and her family had. This is temperance. None of this happened by accident. It was the fruit of her upbringing. It was taught, learned and practiced.

Here is another picture of this using Ken Wilber's paradigm. In this case, think of this from a Christian perspective. Start with the lower left quadrant.

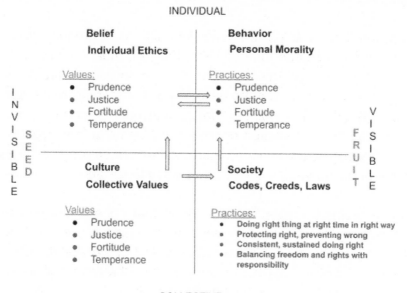

When you see "culture" in the lower left quadrant you don't need to think of a national or ethnic culture though it works at that level too. Think of any group; a family, church, corporation or any other group and its culture. Each group has an innate set of values, those things most important to it. For a Christian community, think of it as ideally having the cardinal moral values of prudence, justice, fortitude and temperance. This is the lower left quadrant.

Those primarily responsible for cultivating these values are also responsible for passing them on and the actual teaching of the values ideally becomes evident in the actual customs or regular practices of the group. This is the lower right quadrant.

These values also need to be learned and adopted by the individual who is a member of the group. The ethic of the group thus becomes the ethic of the individual. This is the upper left quadrant.

When thinking in terms of seed and fruit, the values are the seed. The individual members learn these and, having learned and embraced them, they begin to put them into practice. The fruit of this ethic is that which works out in the life and behavior or morals of the individual. This is the upper right quadrant.

The group, through its actual teaching, its customs, its regular practices, reinforces those values and the behaviors they are meant to produce. The fruit of this behavior contains seeds. As the individual practices the behavior that is consistent with the ethic, his or her morality reinforces and strengthens the ethic. The point is that all four quadrants are necessary. Though this has been presented positively, the same is true negatively. If the values, the seeds, are unsound then the fruit will be too. To the extent that any one of the quadrants is neglected, the fruit will show it.

There is a movement among the quadrants that doesn't just occur, it is actually necessary. In Christian language, though God is Creator, God has made humanity co-creators. We participate in this process and, apart from our involvement, it simply does not come to be. Character and its virtues don't exist by themselves, they must be taught, learned and practiced.

This movement creates a social reality through necessity. This then has a life of its own, a reality that now has a powerful ability to influence and change those who have been involved in its creation. We noted earlier that Peter Berger spoke of this overall process as having the three movements of externalization, objectivation and internalization. Think of the beginnings of our government. It was created in the crucible of conflict, and ideally it was to be characterized by values summed up by Abraham Lincoln years later that called for it to be *"of the people, by the people and for the people."*[194] This is externalization. With this came the necessity not only for a structure, outlined in our Constitution, but for concrete things like taxation in order that we might have roads, hospitals, schools, a military that provides for the security of the people and much more.

The actual formation of a government capable of these things is human objectivation. The government then acts back upon us as a social reality that has an existence that seems as real as the God-created reality of the rocks and dirt. This is particularly experienced when we run afoul of it. Anyone who has been arrested or undergone an audit by the IRS is vividly aware of how real this socially constructed reality is. Government's ability to influence us is the result of successful internalization by which we acknowledge its legitimacy and power, even when we don't like it.

---

[194] These words are from the Gettysburg Address, but most would agree that they reflect the values of the Founders. The words were first penned by John Wycliffe in the prologue to his translation of the Bible in 1384.

Chapter 8

Tension: Virtue, Responsibility and Rights

"The rights of natural life are, in the midst of the fallen world, the reflected splendour of the glory of God's creation ... The duties, on the other hand, derive from the rights themselves ... They are implicit in the rights." [195]
Dietrich Bonhoeffer

Years ago, and for several years, I flew a medical helicopter out of St. Mary's Hospital in Grand Junction, Colorado. One night we responded to an auto accident in the mountains near the town of Aspen. Shortly after landing, we realized that the driver of the car had broken his femur, the major bone in his thigh. His muscles were contracting in spasms and his thigh was bent into a shallow "v" shape. We were able to extract the driver from the car and while the flight nurse and I held the man's waist and chest, the paramedics who had been the first responders, pulled his lower leg. You can imagine the pain and I can still hear his screams, but if we had not applied that tension to straighten the leg it is very likely he would have died. The extreme tension at that moment gave way to the steady tension of the traction devices to which he was attached for a much longer period of time. Both the extreme initial tension and the long term steady tension were needed for his healing.

Still, most of us don't like tension. It begs for resolution. In a talk I heard given by Andy Stanley, pastor of a megachurch near Atlanta, he pointed out the necessity to distinguish between those tensions which need to be resolved and those which need to be managed. The fact is that there are tensions which we cannot live without and these need to be managed, not resolved. There are necessary physical tensions and there are necessary spiritual tensions. Apart from some reference to physical tensions we have no metaphor for understanding spiritual ones. The tensions between virtue and vice as well as those between rights and responsibilities are spiritual ones.

---

[195] Bonhoeffer, *Ethics*, p. 150.

It is impossible to seriously address ethics as a whole and virtue in particular without addressing rights and responsibility. Though our responsibilities or duties may flow out of our rights, our responsibilities also help us define our rights. Some key questions about our responsibilities need to be asked and answered before delving into our rights. At the very least we need to answer "responsible to whom, responsible for what?" Christians would say that we are responsible both to God and to our neighbors and, specifically, that we are responsible to God for our treatment of our neighbors, whoever they may be.

Many who don't buy into Christian theism would still say that we are responsible to and for our neighbors; however, as we have seen, many today, including an increasing number of Christians, see that responsibility as clearly secondary to our responsibility to ourselves. This in itself is a significant ethical issue. Our responsibility "to whom" and "for what" are parts of the same larger question and we need some sort of framework if we are going to answer coherently. Other frameworks have been proposed, but as our topic is evangelical ethics as a subset of Christian ethics, the writing of Dietrich Bonhoeffer is a reasonable place to start. Whether one embraces his thinking or not, Bonhoeffer's insights clearly distill and reflect centuries of Christian thinking.

He spoke of four particular mandates as having been given by God and in relation to which all humans are responsible. A mandate is an order or commission to do something. These are not necessarily the only divine mandates, but in Bonhoeffer's thought they supersede all others. Regarding these four, citing substantive Scriptural proof, he wrote "*It is God's will that there shall be labor, marriage, government and church.*"[196] The order is important. He believed each to be specifically instituted by God, each with its own requirements and each with its own role in human life. If these mandates were described using more general terms applicable to all of humanity, they could be described as work, family, society and religion.

Bonhoeffer, though, took the Genesis creation account and the mandates we find there, first for Adam and Eve to work and care for the garden and

---

[196]Ibid., p. 204.

then for their union in all its aspects, as the foundation for the mandates of labor and marriage. Whether one takes those accounts literally or figuratively, the message is the same. A few brief and preliminary samples will set the stage for what follows. He wrote:

"The divine mandate of government presupposes the divine mandates of labor and marriage ... Government cannot itself produce life or values. It is not creative. It preserves what has been created, maintaining it in the order which is assigned to it through the task that is imposed by God."[197]

Of the church he wrote,

"The mandate of the Church impinges on all these mandates, for now it is the Christian who is at once laborer, partner in marriage, and subject of a government. No division into separate spheres or spaces is permissible here ... The first three mandates are not designed to divide man up, to tear him asunder; they are concerned with the whole man before God ... reality, therefore, in all its multiplicity is ultimately one." [198]

This is a key aspect of Bonhoeffer's thinking. Though it is possible to distinguish between the mandates we must never divide them. Together they constitute reality and there is only one ultimate reality. Though it is possible to distinguish between Christians and those who are not, together they are one indivisible humanity that has its oneness in Christ whether individuals are aware of that oneness or not. It is possible to use words like "separate" when talking about the distinctions among the mandates or among nations or people, but it is ultimately impossible to divide them.

As each mandate has a divine origin, each can be distinguished from the others while, at the same time, being related to the others as parts of a greater whole. As mentioned earlier, Arthur Koestler coined the term "holon" (from the Greek "holos" meaning whole) by which he understood anything that exists to be simultaneously a whole in itself and part of a greater whole.[199] Think of the car we discussed earlier. It has numerous

---

[197] Ibid., p. 207.
[198] Ibid., p. 208.

whole entities like a whole motor, whole tires, transmission and steering mechanism. They rest upon or are attached to a whole chassis and must function together as a greater whole that we call a car.

Similarly, the mandates rest upon or are attached to God's overall purpose for the world and its people. Each mandate is separate and whole, but each is simultaneously a part of the greater whole which is God's overall purpose. If they don't work together, they don't work. This applies to the church as much as it does to any of the other mandates. Each mandate has equal right to speak to overlapping issues yet they are subject to the other mandates in those areas that are unique and essential to the very existence and function of that particular mandate.

Though God-ordained, at the same time, these mandates are institutions that require the activity and participation of people. They do not come into being nor do they continue to exist without human involvement. With regard to labor, Bonhoeffer wrote: *"The labor which is instituted in Paradise [Adam and Eve's mandate to 'work and take care of' the Garden of Eden] is a participation by man in the action of creation. By its means there is created a world of things and value ..."*[200] Along with the mandate of labor, it is also true that government, marriage and the church obviously require human participation and none can exist apart from it.

Government, understood in the broadest way as any institution whereby a society regulates itself, is what Peter Berger described as an anthropological necessity. Different cultures do this differently, but all cultures do it in some way. Government is not a necessary evil; rather, as a divine mandate, it is simply necessary. Whether government is freely chosen or forced upon a people by a tyrant, it must be "accepted" even when that acceptance is nothing more than grudging toleration. Whatever else it may be, though God-ordained, government cannot exist apart from those who govern and those who are governed and, as history testifies, it can be changed by those who are governed.

Christians in general share the belief with Bonhoeffer that government is ordained by God. This is rooted in the fact that Jesus assumed its validity,

---

[199] Koestler, Arthur. *The Ghost in the Machine*. Penguin Group, London, reprint edition 1990.
[200] Bonhoeffer. *Ethics*. p.206.

even that of a pagan government, when he taught that we are to *"render to Caesar the things that are Caesar's and to God the things that are God's."*[201] Because Jesus acknowledged both the reality and legitimacy of government and our responsibility towards it, Christians are called to recognize its importance. In America this is true of government at all levels including local, state and federal.

From Bonhoeffer's perspective, the mandates apply even when people are unaware of the mandates or their requirements. They apply to Christians and non-Christians alike. It is highly interesting to note that the mandate of the church existed and applied long before there was a Christian church. Though "church" has a distinctly Christian connotation, this mandate can include being part of a faith community that is not specifically Christian. The mandate of the church was first recognized in the specific context of the creation accounts in God's presence with and care for Adam and Eve, and later for the people of Israel in their relationship with God long before Christ was born. That said, those outside the church, whether aware or not, are being called to God's grace through the church and that is a distinctive calling of the Christian church today. Bonhoeffer clearly believed that God's grace found its fulfillment in Christ and that the call to the world was one to enter into an already existing oneness with God and each other that is already there in Christ. Those within the church are called to live in the light of God's grace in Christ and to proclaim that grace to all.

Bonhoeffer was clear that none of the mandates is subordinate to the others. The mandate of government is not subordinate to that of the church. Nor is marriage, nor is labor. Each has its unique role in God's purposes for humankind. Each is created by God through the agency of the very ones affected by them. Though they have many overlapping interests, they are distinctly and individually legitimate and they are equal in importance. The church may do government, marriage or labor in a certain way, but each of these is for the whole of mankind and has a unique mandate or assignment over which the church has no authority except within its sphere of direct influence.

---

[201] Matthew 22:21 English Standard Version.

For example, every culture has some way of effecting the mandate of marriage. Each has a way of ordering the relationships necessary for bringing children into the world, ensuring their growth and development and, with that, the continuance and longevity of the community. When any culture does this it is in some sense fulfilling the marriage mandate whether doing so in a way Christians would agree with or think is right or not. Each has a way of governing itself, each has a way of ordering the labor of its community and in so doing fulfills in part the mandates of government and labor.

In biblical history we see this in a comprehensive way in the giving of the Law on Mt. Sinai through Moses. The people of Israel quickly embraced this law as a covenant with God. God commanded them to obey him and promised to provide for them if they obeyed, promised to hold them accountable when they didn't and ultimately to redeem them. They willingly embraced this covenant. The centrality of the Law to this agreed upon relationship is underscored by the fact that the two tablets of stone on which were written the Ten Commandments were sometimes referred to simply as "the covenant."[202] In addition to the creation accounts, the Commandments also addressed each of the four mandates.

The first few commandments detail responsibility toward God. That is, God's people are to have no other gods than God and are to worship no idols, refrain from taking God's name in vain and keep the Sabbath holy. These apply particularly to the mandate of the church. The first part of the commandment regarding the Sabbath is *six days shalt thou labor and do all thy work.*" It is a day of rest in a week involving productive work. The full meaning of the Sabbath Day is realized only in relation to the responsibility for labor.

The commandment to *"Honor your father and mother"* and the commandment against adultery both pertain to the mandate of marriage. The commandments not to kill, steal, or lie have to do with maintaining harmony in society and pertain to the institution of government as much as they do to individual behavior. The commandment not to covet is the one, more so than all the rest, that has to do with cultivating virtue, individually

---

[202] 2 Chronicles 6:11.

and collectively, by requiring the controlling of our desires. We have roles and responsibilities with regard to each of the mandates alluded to in the Ten Commandments and virtue is defined not just by abstract terms, but in relation to those roles and responsibilities.

Many of our individual roles in life are defined in relation to our responsibilities with regard to these mandates. For the role of the Christian church in this, C.S. Lewis put this beautifully:

> "People say, 'The Church ought to give us a lead.' That is true if they mean it in the right way, but false if they mean it in the wrong way. By the Church they ought to mean the whole body of practising Christians. And when they say that the Church should give us a lead, they ought to mean that some Christians - those who happen to have the right talents - should be economists and statesmen ... and that their whole efforts in politics and economics should be directed to putting 'Do as you would be done by' into action ... The application of Christian principles, say, to trade unionism or education, must come from Christian trade unionists and Christian schoolmasters: just as Christian literature comes from Christian novelists and dramatists - not from the bench of bishops getting together and trying to write plays and novels in their spare time."[203]

In this light, Dr. C. Everett Koop was a renowned pediatric surgeon who collaborated with Dr. Francis Schaeffer to write the book *Whatever Happened to the Human Race?* Schaeffer was a well known Christian philosopher and theologian. The collaboration between Schaeffer and Koop had a profound impact on conservative Christians in America from the 1970's forward, me included. Koop wrote about our Christian responsibilities when it comes to abortion, infanticide and end of life issues including euthanasia in his own book, *The Right to Live, the Right to Die.*

In addition to being a surgeon, Koop was a committed Christian and an elder in his theologically conservative Presbyterian church. During the Reagan administration he was appointed Surgeon General of the United States. During his tenure, the AIDS epidemic was reaching crisis

---

[203] Lewis, *Mere Christianity*, p.80.

proportions. He called for the use of condoms and sex education in our schools as part of a strategy to stop the epidemic.

Many conservative Christians strongly criticized Koop for endorsing policies that they believed to be contrary to Christian principles. By advocating the use of condoms, in their estimation, he was promoting the kind of sexual immorality that they believed responsible for the AIDS crisis. Koop, on the other hand, believed that as Surgeon General his responsibility was to all American citizens, including those most impacted by the AIDS epidemic.

Bonhoeffer would have been sympathetic to Koop's position because he believed both government and church to be God-ordained institutions with different responsibilities and different virtues related to those responsibilities. As a medical professional, knowledgeable in epidemiology, Koop knew that to combat an epidemic the use of every means available to reduce the transmission of the disease was necessary. In spite of the strong criticism, and though he might have done otherwise in his role as a church elder, he knew that his governmental responsibility required him to do what he knew to be needed to stop the epidemic.

For most of us the necessity and reality of the government is something we simply take for granted even if grudgingly. We believe that it has the responsibility to protect, but also the power to enforce. The coercive power of government rests in its ability to compel us to comply with the laws of the society it governs. This power has a bright side and a dark side. American evangelicals are committed to the ideals of law and order. Whether it involves issues as contentious as immigration or taxes, or as readily accepted as the "rules of the road" on our highways, or grudging acceptance of security inspections at airports, we know that there is great importance and value in having a society guarded by law and order.

The bright side of this is security and all the good things it brings. The dark side of this emerges when unjust laws are enacted, when otherwise just laws are enforced unjustly and when unjust wars are undertaken. Violations of basic human rights and decency reflected in unjust laws and unjust enforcement of existing laws during the struggle for civil rights in the 1960's were a prime example. The harsh coercive "reality" of the government was acutely experienced by those who had water cannons and dogs turned on them when they were protesting peacefully. The treatment of these protesters was obviously an abuse of the responsibility of government. Sadly this abuse was largely ignored or, worse, the protesters were actively opposed by significant numbers of evangelicals.

The right to vote is at the heart of the mandate of government in a constitutional democracy such as ours. The right to vote guarantees at least a minimal participation in government. To deny this small individual voice in the government to which one is subject is to gut the liberty which our nation's founding documents describe as an "unalienable" human right. Regardless of one's view of current voting rights debates, it is impossible to deny that there has been much abuse of these rights in our nation's history. There is certainly a legitimate need to provide mechanisms that ensure an orderly and fair process by which elections are conducted and voters are reasonably vetted. Since 1993, the National Voter Registration Act (NVRA) has required each State to maintain an accurate and current voter registration list using a process that is uniform, nondiscriminatory and in compliance with the federal Voting Rights Act of 1965.[204] Discrimination based on race or religion is specifically prohibited.

Recent apparent attempts to suppress voting rights remind us that the hard fought battles over civil rights are not merely a thing of the past. However, the larger point is that we, Christians especially, are responsible both to government and for just participation in our governance. Evangelical support has been critical in those states where conservative efforts have been primarily concerned with maintaining the status quo or ensuring that redistricting is carried out in order to enhance control over voting outcomes that often exclude racial minorities who in many cases are at the bottom of the economic spectrum.

A case in point is my home city of Chattanooga, Tennessee. It is the largest city in the 3rd congressional district which is one of nine in the state. The city's population is 35 percent African American in a state that is 17 percent African American overall. The district boundaries are shaped somewhat like an hourglass and stretch from Georgia on the south to Kentucky on the

---

[204]New Mexico Secretary of State. "2018 NM Voter Confirmation Process Fact Sheet and FAQs." www.sos.state.nm.us/Voter_Information/2018-nm-voter-address-confirmation-process-fact-sheet-and-faqs.aspx. Accessed 19 March 2019.

north and are drawn such that the overall percentage of African Americans is 10 percent. One of the largest African American communities in the state is in a district where their voices, to the extent that they have unique concerns, are virtually guaranteed never to be heard. Sadly, this reflects the norm in much of the so-called Bible belt.

The escalated separation of children from their parents in the current immigration context at the Mexican border, a separation that goes to the heart of the marriage mandate, is an example of government overriding one of the basic divine mandates. Secure borders and just immigration laws are undoubtedly warranted and necessary, but for the majority of evangelicals supporting administration policies that actually strike at the heart of a divine mandate is inexcusable. This is particularly the case if we give the biblical narrative its due. God consistently told the people of Israel to welcome the alien and stranger because they, under God's sovereign hand, had been aliens and strangers.[205] When Herod sought to kill the Messiah, Joseph, Mary and Jesus were forced into exile in Egypt where they were immigrant refugees. For evangelicals to ignore the implications of this is beyond baffling. There have been a few peeps from evangelical leaders, but now that this has reached government induced crisis proportions, the current administration and its policies are being as strongly supported as ever by President Trump's evangelical base.

A right is that to which we are entitled. Rights and responsibility are necessarily related. In Bonhoeffer's thought, rights precede responsibility. Both rights and responsibility usually grow with maturity. In that sense they are progressive. That for which we have a genuine responsibility is something to which we have a right and the gravity of the responsibility is directly proportional to the weight of the right. At the very least it is our responsibility to respect the rights of those whose rights are every bit as weighty as our own.

For this discussion, chief among these rights will be those enumerated in the Declaration of Independence: *"We hold these truths to be self-evident, that all men are created equal, that they are endowed by their Creator with certain unalienable rights, that among these are life, liberty and the pursuit*

---

[205] See Deuteronomy 10:19 and Leviticus 19:34 for starters, then the birth narrative of Christ in the Gospel of Luke among literally scores of biblical references.

of happiness." In all that follows and without trying to justify it further, I am going to assume that it is true that these rights actually are ordained by God and that they are unalienable. Though this can be debated, for most evangelicals in America this is indisputable conceptually, but not practically as we shall see.

Entitlement has a negative connotation in much of our public discussion today, so it is necessary to clarify this. Constitutional rights, legal rights, and human rights, can be distinguished. Unlike "entitlements" created constitutionally or legally and therefore through an act of government, like the right to bear arms, an unalienable right is an innate entitlement from which we can never be separated. It is built into our humanity. It is something that is owed to us by others and something that we owe to others.These rights are ours purely on the basis of our having been given them by our Creator. These entitlements are established by God, not by government, and apply to all people regardless of race, religion or nationality. They are foundational human rights.

That said, none of these is absolute. Whatever else it may be, anything for which there is an exception or exceptions, is not an absolute. This is simply true by definition. My rights, even the weightiest of them, are bounded by the rights of others. In many states in the US, if I unlawfully take the life of another, the state may take my life in return. If some number of deaths of innocent individuals improperly convicted takes place, it is seen by many, including many evangelicals, to be a generally unintended consequence thus not sufficient ground to eliminate capital punishment. If innocent life is lost in the course of a just war for the protection of the innocent larger populace, this is seen to be justifiable and even necessary in the eyes of most Americans, including evangelicals. In either case, these are exceptions that allow the taking of innocent lives. Whether this is right or not in an ethical sense needs more discussion.

Sometimes, as in the dropping of the atomic bombs on Hiroshima and Nagasaki, the exceptions involve very large numbers of innocent people. This, along with the examples in the previous paragraph, is simply a statement of current and historic fact, not a defense of, nor is it an argument against, the use of nuclear weapons, capital punishment or of just wars. The point here is that the right to life, from these perspectives shared by many if not most evangelicals, is not an absolute one even for the innocent. Both the military and the police are given considerable latitude and protection under law when it comes to the taking of life in the course of their duties. Many Americans, evangelicals included, concur in the granting of this latitude and protection even when innocent lives are taken. We will return to this in more detail in later chapters.

In the context of the four mandates, as a husband and father, I have all the rights and responsibilities of the marriage mandate (family) and fatherhood which it encompasses. Therefore as a father I have the right to what is needed to fulfill those responsibilities. This would include, for instance, the right to instill in my children the values I believe to be most important in life. The same sort of responsibilities and rights accrue to my wife as wife and mother and to parents everywhere. We together have the responsibility to provide for, protect, and prepare our children for responsible life in community, thus we have the right to the means to do all of these things. That same right exists for those who do not share our values, even when we may disagree substantially. That said, neither we nor they have a right to neglect or abuse our children and the government (the legitimate representative of society) has every right to intervene if we do. If parents lack the necessary means to provide for, protect, and prepare their children for meaningful life in society, then government has both the right and responsibility to step in and assist.

Similar comments can be made regarding the other mandates. The mandate of the church (religion), one that is to be freely undertaken, requires the right of freedom to be part of a faith community or not. If there is no freedom to opt out there is no real freedom. In this light, the church has no right and certainly no obligation to impose its religious beliefs or practices on society as a whole, but this in no way prevents those in the church or other faith communities from full and meaningful participation in the life of the nation of which they are citizens.

Our responsibility for productive work includes the right not to be denied employment for unjust reasons and to be justly compensated for our labor. However, labor is not merely that for which one receives compensation. The work that is done in the fulfilling of any and all of the mandates constitutes labor regardless of whether one is paid for it or not. When one is unjustly prevented from the fulfilling of this mandate (the work mandate), then government has a responsibility to address this injustice and the church has the responsibility to speak out against such injustice.

The responsibility to be a meaningful part of the social system in which we live flows from and brings with it the rights necessary for that. For example, in a democracy such as ours, to be excluded from fulfilling my right and responsibility to participate in the government to which we are subject is in itself unjust. Though unalienable rights proceed not from the government, but by endowment from our Creator, the government has the responsibility to protect these rights which allow the fulfillment of our responsibility to fulfill the divine mandates.

Virtue, in these instances, consists in the proper balance between rights and responsibilities. Vice consists in the denial or diminishing of our rights or the rights of others or in the failure to take the responsibilities that come with these rights. This necessity for proper balance is true both for individuals and among the mandates themselves. For example, we are responsible not to encroach upon the rights of others, and the government must not encroach upon the essential rights inherent to the church, family and laborer.

With the mandate of the church comes both the right and responsibility to articulate its religious beliefs, determine its own membership and establish rules and principles of conduct for its members. There are religious virtues that are strictly the province of the church and the government has no voice or place in these. Such virtues and virtuous practices as worship, study of the Scriptures, prayerfulness and fasting for the purpose of drawing near to God are religious virtues, and cannot be mandated or forbidden by government. In addition to adherence to the religious and moral beliefs of the church, other religious virtues involve things like faithful attendance at services, giving to the needs and mission of the church, obedience to the form of government of the church, etc. Virtue here resides with those who embrace the beliefs of the church, attend its gatherings, pray and fast, give to the work of the church and respect the authority of its leaders.

However, the church may not infringe upon the individual rights of its members by compulsion other than the kinds of moral persuasion that are essential to its identity. Similarly, the religious virtues of the church cannot be imposed upon those not within its fold. It's right and ability to discipline its members or otherwise practice its faith is limited by the government's unique right to protect the rights of all its citizens regardless of church membership.

The marriage of Christianity and democracy isn't always an easy one. That's because the marriage between Christianity and any form of government is not an easy one. Though having used concepts that were clearly articulated by Bonhoeffer, much of what I have written betrays a unique personal perspective and a peculiarly American perspective of that marriage. Bonhoeffer's national heritage was very different from ours and was one in which abuses of the power of the church were much more prominent in its history. At the same time, he was living in a period when much of the mainline church, in both its Catholic and Lutheran expressions, was selling its soul to Naziism. The church's failure to maintain its true identity separate from the politics and government of his day was a sad denial of the faith. But long before that, Germany had experienced the other side of the failure to draw a clear line between the church and the state.

Catholic abuses in the centuries leading up to the Reformation were precursors to Germany's unique history of having been delivered from the tyranny of the church not just by Luther and the Reformation, but by civic leaders outside of the church structure. There was clear warrant to believe that the relationship between the church and state was one that could be abused by either party. The church and the state have different roles and different responsibilities. These differences create a tension. The tension between church and state, far from being a bad thing, is actually a good thing in most instances. American Christians would be wise to learn from Germany's experience in both extremes. The church must not sell its soul to the politics of the day, and the government must not co-opt the church in fulfilling its own ends. The conflation of evangelical Christianity with the current politics of the right is dangerously flirting with both.

One of the key responsibilities inherent in the mandate of government is protecting its citizens internally and, if necessary, in time of war. Though this is the unique responsibility of government, it cannot override the mandate of the church as it applies to those who adhere to its role in their lives. With respect to war, the Christian faith has spoken deeply into the issues involved and has done so through the writing and thinking of some of its greatest sons and daughters.

Part III: Sanctity of Life

Recognizing the dangers and disagreement likely to arise when trying to define such a profound term in just a few words, I'm going to try anyway: The phrase "sanctity of life" encompasses the valuing and safeguarding of God's entire creation and that which makes us truly human, made in the image of God, in terms of life itself and the content and quality of that life.

Chapter 9

Just War

"When the king of Israel saw them, he asked Elisha, "Shall I kill them, my father? Shall I kill them?" "Do not kill them," he answered. "Would you kill those you have captured with your own sword or bow? Set food and water before them ..."
2 Kings 6:21,22

Arguably, the largest shift in Christian ethics took place approximately 1500 years ago. The Christian doctrine known as the Just War doctrine provides for Christians the only historically serious theological warrant for the taking of any lives, not only innocent lives, in war or in any other circumstance. That Christians, prior to the 3rd century A.D., were strongly opposed to the taking of any lives, not just demonstrably innocent lives, even in war, is simply a matter of history. Roland Bainton, noted church historian, asserted that, though there were some Christians in the Roman legions, church teaching was pacifist until the time of Constantine.[206] For more than three hundred years from the time of Christ, the church, in its official teaching and practice, was pacifist. That is a span of time greater than the existence of the United States.

Apart from instances like those in the gospels and Acts where John the Baptist, Jesus, Peter, and Paul encountered soldiers, sometimes positively, there is no evidence of there being even one Christian soldier in the Roman Army from NT times until 170 A.D. [207] In the fourth century, in light of the growing numbers of conversions among soldiers, the Canons of Hippolytus (c. 340 AD), a guide for church discipline, allowed service in the military as long as the role of soldiers was one that did not involve killing. The "christianization" of the empire under the Roman Emperor Constantine created a need for further development of Christian thinking about involvement in war.

---

[206] Bainton, Roland. "The Early Church and War." *The Harvard Theological Review, Volume 39, Number 3,* July 1946, p. 189.
[207] Elwell, Walter A., Editor. *Evangelical Dictionary of Theology.* Baker Book House, Grand Rapids, Michigan,1984, p. 1153.

"The Emperor Constantine's official toleration of Christianity (A.D. 312) and deathbed conversion (A.D. 337) foreshadowed a great change in the Christian attitude toward war: 'A Christian empire and a Christian army defending the nucleus of the civilized world against heretics and vandals created an atmosphere more favorable to the conception of a holy war waged by a Chosen People than did a pagan empire persecuting a Christian minority.' In this state of flux, St. Augustine emerged as 'the great coordinator' of Christian doctrine upon peace and war." [208]

The Just War doctrine first articulated by Augustine (354-430 AD) put significant limits not just on what was allowable for Christians in military service, but limits as to what constitutes a just war in the first place.[209] For a Christian, the taking of life in war is justifiable only if the war itself is just. Augustine, borrowing from and developing the thought of Greek philosophers, formulated many of the principles for establishing whether a war was just or not.[210]

Just War doctrine has several key facets that are essential. In short, *"if the war is declared by legitimate authority, is embarked upon for a just cause, is waged with the right intention, and employs just means, then that war may be morally justified."*[211] As this thought developed over the centuries, other refinements were articulated. For a "just cause" to exist, any war undertaken has to be in response to the commission of an actual injustice. Military force may be used only when all peaceful means of resolution have been exhausted. It cannot be for national prestige, territorial expansion, conversion to a particular religion or political philosophy and there must be a reasonable chance for success. Any use of force in war has to be proportional. For example, a country cannot respond to a border infraction with nuclear weapons. Finally, the objective of the war must be to establish a just peace in its aftermath.[212] As other Christian thinkers contributed to this over the years, the fruit of that thought greatly influenced the Geneva Conventions that were adopted in whole or with reservations by 196 nations, including the US, in the aftermath of World War II.[213]

---

[208] Wakin. *War, Morality and the Military Profession,* .pp. 246,247.
[209] Ibid.
[210] Ibid.
[211] Ibid., p. 238.
[212] Thiroux and Krasemann. *Ethics: Theory and Practice,* p. 112.

The impetus behind the first Geneva Convention in 1864 was driven by Henry Dunant. Though a marginal student and not successful in business, Dunant was the founder of the International Committee of the Red Cross and was the winner of the first Nobel Peace Prize. This should be especially meaningful to evangelicals because Dunant was one. He was born into a deeply Christian Swiss family, and few people can argue the significance of his founding work and the resulting Geneva Conventions of 1906, 1929 and 1949. What kind of man was Dunant?

> *"As a young man, Henri Dunant participated in the kind of free-wheeling association that seems to be typical of evangelical religion everywhere. In about 1848, at age 20, he organized a group of like-minded young men known first as the Thursday Meeting, and soon after as the Union of Geneva. Their aim was to be 'more effective in Christian charity,' 'to heat up the lukewarm' believers, and to 'convert those who had not met God.'"* [214]

The Geneva Conventions of 1906, 1929 and 1949 deal primarily with the treatment of people in war and provide for the protection of non-combatants and humane treatment of prisoners, including the outlawing of torture. The Geneva Protocols of 1977 and the Hague Conventions of 1899 and 1907 deal with means of warfare itself and outlaw such things as the use of bio-chemical weapons. The influence of classical Christian Just War doctrine on all of these agreements is very significant and the principles underlying them should be of great importance to all Americans today and especially so for evangelicals.

Though the advent of nuclear weapons and the rise of international terrorism strain the application of just war principles, for Christians they

---

[213] There were four Geneva Conventions between 1864 and 1949. All have been signed and ratified by the US and 195 other nations. In 1977 two protocols (amendments) were added, both of which have been signed by the US, but not ratified. **Protocol I** is a 1977 amendment protocol to the Geneva Conventions relating to the protection of victims of *international conflicts*, where "armed conflicts in which peoples are fighting against colonial domination, alien occupation or racist regimes" are to be considered international conflicts.**Protocol II** is a 1977 amendment protocol to the Geneva Conventions relating to the protection of victims of *non-international* armed conflicts.**Protocol III** (2005) relates to the Adoption of an Additional Distinctive Emblem.

[214]Neff, David. "Compassionate in War, Christian in Vision." *Christianity Today,* 8 August 2008. www.christianitytoday.com/history/2008/august/compassionate-in-war-christian-in-vision.html. Accessed 19 March 2019.

cannot be abandoned. There is a spirit to these principles and, just as our ethics are challenged by new developments on technological and medical frontiers, we have to continue to embrace that spirit and rise to the challenge without abandoning the principles. The key to addressing these new challenges may well be the careful building of international consensus and not just the endeavors of individual countries.

The American military has a proud history and a vital role in defending our nation and the world. When one becomes a member of the US military, Christians included, it is essential that the individual soldier trust and be able to trust that the nation and its military leaders are justified in the military decisions they make. The individual soldier is not privy to all that goes into the decision to employ military force in any particular circumstance and, even in instances where he or she does not understand or agree with the decisions made, lawful orders must be obeyed consistent with the oath one takes at the outset of one's service. At the same time, the soldier is required, morally and by law, not to obey an unlawful order. If it becomes evident that the leadership of the country and its military are failing to abide by just war principles, then Christians have an obligation to confront the injustice or step back from their military service in an honorable way.

It is critical at this point to make a distinction between American interests, American policy, and American military activities and what constitutes justifiable participation by Christians when it involves the taking of innocent lives. American interests and military involvement may overlap with just war principles, but they are not the same thing. Many, if not most, American evangelicals do not make such a distinction. It is reflexive to believe that, if the US military is involved, the question of the morality of a Christian participating is simply assured.

Religious legitimation of the kind discussed earlier is profoundly important in this regard. Peter Berger describes as "marginal" human situations those which most unsettle us. Impending death or the impending putting to death of others often drive us to seek God's blessing. Prayers offered before the execution of a criminal for a capital crime are supposed to comfort the criminal, if that is possible, and to legitimate what is being done by those doing the executing. Prior to the launch of the bombers which dropped the atomic weapons on Nagasaki and Hiroshima, the missions were blessed by a Catholic priest and a Lutheran minister, one of whom later deeply regretted the role he had played in legitimating the missions.

Contrary to conventional opinion, there was substantial opposition by American military leaders in World War II to the use of atomic weapons to end the war. This included six of the seven five star admirals and generals. President Dwight Eisenhower, Allied Supreme Commander during the war, recalled that he had made his opposition known to Secretary of War Henry Stimson before the use of the bombs: *"I told him I was against it on two counts. First, the Japanese were ready to surrender and it wasn't necessary to hit them with that awful thing. Second, I hated to see our country be the first to use such a weapon."* Admiral William Leahy, who was White House Chief of Staff and Chairman of the Joint Chiefs of Staff during World War II, wrote in his 1950 memoirs: *"the use of this barbarous weapon at Hiroshima and Nagasaki was of no material assistance in our war against Japan. The Japanese were already defeated and ready to surrender."* He went on to say, *"in being the first to use it, we had adopted an ethical standard common to the barbarians of the Dark Ages. I was not taught to make war in that fashion, and wars cannot be won by destroying women and children."* Admiral "Bull" Halsey, famed 3rd Fleet Commander in the Pacific, said in 1946, *"the first atomic bomb was an unnecessary experiment."* The Japanese, he noted, *"'had put out a lot of peace feelers through Russia 'long before' the bomb was used."* [215]

The atomic bombs ultimately killed more than 200,000 people. Japan was on the verge of surrendering, Stalin's army was racing towards Japan to retake land lost in a previous conflict and there was strong desire to force the Japanese into unconditional surrender before the Russians arrived. Father George Zabelka, Catholic chaplain for the 509th Composite Group whose planes dropped the bombs, recanted his role in the aftermath of the bombing when the enormity of what they had participated in became obvious.

---

[215] Hohan, Uday and Maley III, Leo. "Hiroshima: Military Voices of Dissent." *Origins: Current Events in Historical Perspective,* Published by the History Departments of Ohio State University and Miami University, 26 July 2001. origins.osu.edu/history-news/hiroshima-military-voices-dissent. Accessed 19 March 2019.

Ironically, the largest concentration of Christians in Japan was in Nagasaki. Their presence was the fruit of the evangelistic work of Francis Xavier who planted a church there in 1549. Being a Christian was a capital crime in Japan from 1600 to 1850. As is often the case in times of persecution, the church not only survived, but thrived. An American bomb nearly wiped out the largest Japanese Christian community in seconds; something the Japanese government had not been able to do in over two and a half centuries.[216]

In dropping these bombs, it is hard to argue that there was no intent to kill the victims. There were few soldiers killed and a massive number of civilians. The mission facing the crews cried out for divine legitimation because, even if some crew-members may have had qualms about what they were doing, there was no doubt about the outcome if they were successful. Without believing that God condoned it, most religiously sensitive Americans could hardly have condoned the carnage that resulted from the dropping of these bombs. Most evangelicals today, particularly those of my vintage, see no discrepancy between what happened in Nagasaki and Hiroshima and their Christian faith because it has been thoroughly religiously legitimated.

In the My Lai massacre during the Vietnam War, a company of American soldiers massacred hundreds of fleeing villagers. Approximately 350-500 villagers, mostly women, children and the elderly were systematically killed by American soldiers. The massacre was stopped only when an American helicopter pilot, Hugh Thompson, landed between the soldiers and a group of the fleeing villagers and threatened to open fire on the American troops if they didn't stop. Only one soldier, Lt. William Calley, was held responsible for his role. Though originally sentenced to life in prison, Calley was released after three and a half years of house arrest. This is largely due to the fact that there was massive public support, including strong evangelical support, for our military whether right or wrong. Perhaps the most visible evangelical supporter of Calley was Jimmy Carter, governor of Georgia at the time, who felt that Calley was being used as a scapegoat though he personally had killed more than twenty of the villagers.[217] Mendel Rivers, a

---

[216] Kohls, Gary G. "Christianity and the Nagasaki Bomb." *Consortium News*, 22 February 2019. consortiumnews.com/2016/08/09/christianity-and-the-nagasaki-bomb/. Accessed 19 March 2019.

respected congressman from South Carolina and then Chairman of the House Armed Services Committee, stated that the only person who should be punished was Hugh Thompson.[218] Despite that perspective shared by many, some years later Thompson received military honors for his role in stopping the massacre.

Our involvement in the Saudi Coalition in Yemen up till now (2019) has produced a similar or greater magnitude of deaths of innocents as did Nagasaki and Hiroshima, minus the atomic weapons. The famine that has ensued will claim many thousands more before it is finished.[219] Shiite Muslims and Sunni Muslims are engaged against each other in a deadly religious war. Our involvement began late in the Obama Administration when the government of Yemen was overthrown by Shiite rebels. Even if justified at first, it has stepped up under the Trump Administration in large part due to substantially increased arms sales to the Sunni majority Saudis. This includes sales of laser guided bombs which were banned for sale to the Saudis by the previous administration.[220] The level of concern for our national security in this age of terrorism is so high that most Americans, including most evangelicals, are more than willing to look the other way and grant significant latitude to those we believe to be protecting our larger national interest.

What are the implications of all this? The requirement that any war participated in by a Christian must be a just war rules out the justification for killing in wartime simply because one is a citizen of a particular nation and that nation is at war. Rather it requires that participation by a Christian in any war undertaken by a particular nation, the US included, must be a just war based on clear and compelling principles and it must employ just means. When America has been at its best, its leaders, while protecting the

---

217 Rothman, Lily. "My Lai Verdict at 45: Read TIME's Original Story on the Case." *Time*, 29 March 2016. time.com/4268062/my-lai-verdict-1971/. Accessed 19 March 2019.

218 Russell, Shahan. "Helicopter Pilot Who Stopped My Lai Massacre Was Called A Traitor In America & Almost Court-Martialed." *War History Online,* 12 November 2015. www.warhistoryonline.com/featured/helicopter-pilot-stopped-my-lai-massacre.html. Accessed 16 March 2019.

219 Karasz, Palko. "85,000 Children in Yemen May Have Died of Starvation." *The New York Times,* 21 November 2018. www.nytimes.com/2018/11/21/world/middleeast/yemen-famine-children.html. Accessed 19 March 2019.

220 Cohen, Zachary. "Trump administration touts 33% increase in foreign arms sales." *CNN,* 10 October 2018. www.cnn.com/2018/10/10/politics/trump-administration-foreign-arms-sales-2018/index.html. Accessed 19 March 2019.

nation, were also protecting the consciences of its soldiers by not committing them to an unjust cause or the use of unjust means of waging war.

Please note that this is not a political point based on contemporary issues. This is a theological point firmly rooted in more than fifteen hundred years of church history. The basis for participation in war for a Christian cannot merely be ethnic or national interest. A war protecting the vital interests or honor of America does not rise to the standard of a just war unless the nation is responding to an actual injustice or an undeniable threat of injustice in a measured, incremental, proportional way and when there is no other alternative solely regarded from the perspective of justice. Most Americans, evangelicals included, have a much lower standard.

Whatever else it may be, an ethic which embraces *"America right or wrong"* is not a Christian ethic. It may be patriotic from the perspective of American nationalism, but a Christian patriot has a higher calling. If one's allegiance *"to the flag of the United States of America and to the republic for which it stands"* is equal to or conflated with one's allegiance to Jesus, it is a departure from a Christianity that allows no allegiance to modify what is required by one's allegiance to Christ.

A Christian in the military cannot delegate his or her conscience to anyone, including the military chain of command. When Hugh Thompson landed his helicopter between the Vietnamese women, children and elderly fleeing American soldiers who were perpetrating the massacre at My Lai, he was demonstrating what this means. This was also true of John McCain when he spoke out strongly against President Trump's call to reinstate and use the kind of torture that McCain had suffered at the hands of his captors during the Vietnam War. McCain's concerns regarding torture, and the President's advocacy of it, were echoed by Gen. James Mattis, who resigned his position as Secretary of Defense with carefully measured words for a Commander in Chief, whose only previous notable relation to the US military was his avoiding service by questionable means when he was a young man.[221]

---

[221] Eder, S. and Philipps, D. "Donald Trump's Draft Deferments: Four for College, One for Bad Feet." *The New York Times,* 1 August 2016. www.nytimes.com/2016/08/02/us/politics/donald-trump-draft-record.html. Accessed 19 March 2019.

This section of the book is focused on the sanctity of life. It is virtually self-evident that the issues surrounding justice in war need to be part of that discussion and it is appropriate that we started there. We will soon focus in on other specific issues that are central to our understanding of the sanctity of life. Before doing that, however, we need to give attention to a few more serious matters of values and perspective that play a strongly influential role in shaping our thinking and understanding our responsibilities.

Chapter 10

Making America Great Again

"Do not say, 'Why were the former days better than these?'
For it is not from wisdom that you ask this."
Ecclesiastes 7:10

"Make America Great Again" was the campaign slogan of now President Donald Trump. It struck a chord with many Americans and particularly so with many evangelicals. The slogan begs the question, though, great again for whom? Great again for some Americans or all Americans? Great again for some people made in God's image or all people made in God's image? Along with the majority of voters in the 2016 presidential election, many minority Americans, including African Americans, Latino Americans, Muslim Americans, Asian Americans and recent immigrants from parts of the world that do not have a European heritage reacted much differently to the election from those who supported the new President.

As a campaign against the political status quo, President Trump's campaign was remarkably and, for many, surprisingly effective. Trump supporters had mounting concerns and fears regarding terrorism, illegal immigration and stagnant wages. Though particularly important to Trump supporters, these were and are concerns shared at some level by almost all Americans. These fears were coupled, however, with substantial reaction to "political correctness" and with discomfort regarding social changes related to the assertion of rights of women and minorities, including increasing acceptance and normalization of those with a host of related sexual identity issues.

There is something else behind the strong evangelical support for this administration, and this has to do with something much more fundamental identified decades ago by Francis Schaeffer. In the book *How Should We Then Live?* he noted that the controlling values for Americans in general and most American Christians were what he called "personal peace" and "affluence." On the surface these seem like reasonable values to hold. It is a fact that these values have a very strong affinity with the American

Dream; however, they have much less of one with historic Christianity. Because many American Christians conflate the American Dream with the Gospel, Schaeffer's words have fallen largely on deaf ears.

"With such values, will men stand for their liberties? Will they not give up their liberties step by step, inch by inch as long as their own personal peace and prosperity is sustained and not challenged, and as long as the goods are delivered? The lifestyles of the young and the old generations are different. There are tensions between long hair and short, drugs and non-drugs, whatever are the outward distinctions of the moment. But they support each other sociologically, for both embrace the values of personal peace and affluence. Much of the church is no help here either, because for so long a large section of the church has only been teaching a relativistic humanism using religious terminology.

I believe the majority of the silent majority, young and old will sustain the loss of liberties without raising their voices as long as their own lifestyles are not threatened. And since personal peace and affluence are so often the only values that count with the majority, politicians know that to be elected they must promise these things. Politics has largely become not a matter of ideals—increasingly men and women are not stirred by the values of liberty and truth—but of supplying a constituency with a frosting of personal peace and affluence. They know that voices will not be raised as long as people have these things, or at least an illusion of them." [222]

The first step in this is allowing the liberties of others to be infringed. Usually this occurs because those whose liberties are infringed are on the margins of society and are seen to be a threat to the stability of society. It is fascinating that at the present moment there is suddenly a huge concern with how to respond to opioid addiction and its ravaging effect on many communities. There is loud and growing support for medical treatment of this rather than criminal prosecution. The opioid problem is a huge problem in largely white communities similar in its devastating effects to the earlier and ongoing crack cocaine problem in largely black communities. Law

---

[222] Schaeffer, Francis. *How Should We Then Live?*, 2005, Crossway Books, 1300 Crescent Street, Wheaton, Illinois, p. 227.

enforcement met the crisis in black communities with criminalization and, due to mandatory sentencing laws, the incarceration of significant numbers of black offenders. African Americans and whites use drugs at similar rates, but the imprisonment rate of African Americans for drug charges is almost six times that of whites.[223]

Now that it is a growing problem in mostly white communities, those voices that called for non-criminalization of nonviolent drug offences are finally being heard, or are they? Former Attorney General Jeff Sessions doubled down on mandatory sentencing and time will tell if that policy continues to prevail and is applied to white offenders with anywhere near the ferocious application of it to blacks. Recent efforts by evangelical leaders to implement criminal justice reform across party lines are welcome indeed, but they need to go far enough to redress the disproportionate past impact on African Americans, prevent that from happening in the future, and somehow address the disproportionate killings of African American men by police. The latter has been largely ignored by evangelicals.

Other People's Sins

"When the Pharisees saw this, they asked his disciples, "Why does your teacher eat with tax collectors and sinners?"
Matthew 9:11

When I first became involved in a serious study of the Bible during my military flight training, one of the things I reacted against from my Catholic upbringing was the Catholic distinction between mortal and venial sins. Mortal sins were the really big ones and venial sins were those that didn't matter so much. Mortal sins were the kind one could go to hell for while venial sins were not. My thinking on this was challenged at the very outset. Confronted with the idea of an infinitely holy God who could tolerate no moral imperfection, it seemed clear that all sin, no matter how venial, was offensive to God and demanded full accountability. As a young evangelical, I believed that all evangelicals felt the same way. Not so as it turns out.

Because, according to evangelical orthodoxy, all ultimate accountability for my sins was borne by Christ on the cross, temporal accountability for my

---

[223] NAACP. "Criminal Justice Fact Sheet." www.naacp.org/criminal-justice-fact-sheet/. Accessed 19 March 2019.

sins lost much of its sting. Surely God didn't like it when I sinned, but it made little difference in eternity where my acceptance was assured and my salvation not in doubt. This assurance of salvation was vigorously reinforced by the memorization of verses that conveyed this truth. But as time went on I realized that for evangelicals there are mortal sins and venial sins too. For the born again Christian all personal sin is venial. As it turns out, the sins that are mortal are other people's sins. People other than those who are born again with full assurance of their salvation, that is.

Also, though it is at odds with centuries old Christian teaching originating with Jesus, who welcomed prostitutes ahead of the religious zealots of his day, and including such respected works as Dante's "Inferno" (c. 1300 AD), for evangelicals the "hot" sins (read sexual) are the really bad ones and the "cold" sins like pride, greed and envy, not as bad. This is an exact reversal of the understanding of generations of thoughtful Christians in the past. In *Mere Christianity,* CS Lewis put it like this:

> *"Finally, though I have had to speak at some length about sex, I want to make it as clear as I possibly can that the centre of Christian morality is not here. If anyone thinks that Christians regard unchastity as the supreme vice, he is quite wrong. The sins of the flesh are bad, but they are the least bad of all sins. All the worst pleasures are purely spiritual: the pleasure of putting other people in the wrong, of bossing and patronising and spoiling sport, and back-biting; the pleasures of power and hatred. For there are two things inside me, competing with the human self I must try to become. They are the Animal Self, and the Diabolical Self. The Diabolical Self is the worse of the two. That is why a cold, self-righteous prig, who goes regularly to church may be far nearer to hell than a prostitute. But, of course, it is better to be neither."* [224]

For evangelical America, sin is thoroughly sexualized. As discussed previously and to be discussed in more detail later, two major moral issues for American evangelicals are abortion and LGBTQ[225] sexual issues led historically by homosexuality. A major part of the evangelical opposition to abortion is that a usual cause of unwanted pregnancies is regarded as

---

[224] Lewis, *Mere Christianity,* p.95.
[225] LGBTQ: Lesbian, Gay, Bi-Sexual, Transgender, Queer.

sexual sin, specifically fornication understood as sexual intercourse outside of a monogamous heterosexual marriage.

Increasing American openness to religious beliefs at odds with historic Christianity, including not only those who hold what have been described as "New Age" beliefs, but also liberal Christians who allow more latitude in sexual matters, has led many evangelicals to believe that America is in danger of being judged by God for tolerance of abortion and homosexuality, though Jesus had nothing to say about either.

The following are extreme examples, but they do illustrate the point. When I was first writing this, Hurricanes Harvey and Irma had left coastal states Texas, Louisiana, Alabama, Florida, Georgia and South Carolina reeling from the historic damage wrought by these major storms. Newsweek magazine reported:

> "LGBTQ Americans have caused the country billions of dollars in structural damage, killed dozens of people, and displaced thousands more from their homes, according to the evangelical figures who believe gay people caused Hurricane Harvey.
>
> Despite overwhelming evidence that adverse weather and climate change had a hand to play in the storm that has devastated parts of Texas, numerous voices emerged that suggested the biblical proportions of the flood were, well, literally biblical.
>
> Among those crying "science be damned" and waving their pitchforks in the general direction of the LGBT community over the past week were minister Kevin Swanson, who believes the Bible preaches death to gays, and the similarly delightful radio host Rick Wiles, who thinks Ebola would be a handy way to wipe out the LGBT community.
>
> Swanson said on his show: 'Jesus sends the message home, unless Americans repent, unless Houston repents, unless New Orleans repents, they will all likewise perish.'" [226]

---

[226] Sinclair, Harriet. "Did Gay Sex Cause Hurricane Harvey or Was it Climate Change? Some On the Right Blame LGBT Americans (No Seriously). *Newsweek*, 3 September 2017. www.newsweek.com/gay-americans-are-blame-hurricane-harvey-apparently-659059. Accessed 19 March 2019.

These guys are the lunatic fringe, but Ann Coulter, conservative commentator and conservative Presbyterian, whose writing and speaking has energized many evangelicals most supportive of a conservative agenda, wrote this on Twitter: "*I don't believe Hurricane Harvey is God's punishment for Houston electing a lesbian mayor. But that is more credible than 'climate change.'*"[227] Just a playful remark from someone who specializes in controversy? Those familiar with her writing and speaking know better. On a truth scale, this elevates the credibility of those claiming God sent a hurricane in judgment of homosexuality above that of those seriously concerned about what is being done to the environment. It elevates seriously antagonizing rhetoric over serious justifiable concern.

Compare this with Pat Robertson's remarks as reported by NPR in the aftermath of the Haiti earthquake in 2010 that took more than one hundred thousand lives:

> "*The scientific experts will tell you that Tuesday's magnitude 7.0 earthquake in Haiti was caused by tectonic forces along a seismic fault line that runs through the island of Hispaniola which Haiti shares with the Dominican Republic.*
>
> *But Pat Robertson, the Christian televangelist, has a different explanation guaranteed to scandalize untold numbers. On the "700 Club" he said Haitians made a pact with the devil to be freed from their French colonizers in the 18th Century.*
>
> *So, as far as Robertson is concerned, the fault is not in the ground; it's in the Haitians.*" [228]

This was widely reported and not only by NPR. Are we to believe that God punished the Haitians, including tens of thousands of Haitian evangelicals, for a pact supposedly made with the devil more than two hundred years ago? If that is truly so then perhaps God is judging America for our toleration of abortion and homosexuality; but if we are looking for moral

---

[227] Ibid.

[228] James, Frank. "Pat Robertson Blames Haitian Devil Pact for Earthquake." *NPR,* 13 January 2010. www.npr.org/sections/thetwo-way/2010/01/pat_robertson_blames_haitian_d.html. Accessed 19 March 2019.

causes for which America should be judged, are there other more striking possible causes?

Our tragic national history involving Native Americans and African Americans dates back fewer years than when some superstitious Haitian allegedly made a pact with the devil. Hundreds of thousands died in Vietnam and Iraq and are dying in Yemen, including huge numbers of unborn and children, because of conflicts in which our participation was initiated for reasons even recent history has shown were unwarranted. Even if we end our involvement in Yemen, as signs are showing we might, what about the tens of thousands of already dead Yemeni non-combatants including children, born and unborn, and the victims of the famine which our cooperation has unleashed?

Many evangelicals would resist being put in the same category with any of the extreme examples of evangelical intolerance noted above. At the same time, though, many more genteel evangelicals do feel that God may well be judging or will be judging America because of our toleration of abortion and homosexuality. This despite these other major injustices with which evangelicals have had few or no apparent moral problems. These constitute far greater reason for God's judgment, but not to those who are *"straining gnats while swallowing camels"* as Jesus quaintly put it.[229] Should we just drop this line of thinking altogether? It really is time to lay this nonsense aside.

Top Down Morality

"Then they hurled insults at him and said, 'You are this fellow's disciple! We are disciples of Moses! We know that God spoke to Moses, but as for this fellow, we don't even know where he comes from.'"
John 9:28,29

One of my most valuable spiritual disciplines has been regularly reading the Bible cover to cover on an annual basis according to a daily schedule. I've now done this well over thirty times and still do it while varying the translation from year to year. In doing this over the years, one thing has become increasingly clear. In the unfolding history of Israel's emergence and growth as a nation, the biblical acceptance of what is now obsolete like

---

[229] Matthew 23:24.

the kind of total war waged by Joshua, slavery, restrictive dietary laws, harshly punitive social and religious prohibitions, and polygamy, to name a few, show that God's revelation can and does progress as humanity develops.

This does not mean that God progresses and develops, it means that humans do. As a professional pilot, I was highly dependent upon radio communications. Two way communication was essential to working with Air Traffic Control in crowded airspace, communicating with the tankers that refueled our long range rescue helicopters in the Air Force, or relaying the condition and needs of patients to physicians who, in turn, communicated instructions to the nurses and paramedics aboard emergency medical helicopters. Radio systems require both transmitters and receivers. Modern systems use digital components, older systems used analog components. Digital two-way radio provides better quality communication over greater distances by resisting interference from other signals. A modern digital receiver can receive analog transmissions, but an analog radio cannot receive digital transmissions. The older systems simply lack the capacities of modern ones, resulting in a level of communication that differs substantially from the kind of communication we experience today. God's revelation is similar to this kind of two-way communication. It too involves a transmitter and a receiver.

This could be pushed too far, but by this analogy, Moses was an early generation receiver, Jesus was not. The Scripture is getting at this when it says *"For the law was given through Moses, grace and truth came through Jesus Christ."*[230] Certain things can only be "seen" and heard at certain levels of development, but not at others. What Jesus heard and taught could not have been heard and taught by Moses. This had nothing to do with Moses' intelligence or his commitment to doing what he thought was right. It had to do primarily with his "altitude," the stage of human development, and the altitude of those around him. What Moses heard and taught the Israelites was preparation for, but differed from, what Jesus brought, not just to Israel or to the church, but to all of humanity.

---

[230] John 1:17.

Moses was a man who lived in and influenced an infant culture that was moving from the pre-conventional to the conventional level of human moral development. Especially in the early stages, conventional, ethnocentric humanity can, and often does, kill those who are perceived to be non-compliant with their rules and their interests and therefore are perceived as a threat to their way of life. Jesus, however, is the essence of post-conventional, omnicentric humanity. God's love and favor is no longer the province of an ethnic chosen people, but those *"from every nation, tribe, people and language."* [231] The Transmitter didn't change. The receiver(s) did.

This explains the necessity to tread carefully when we are prone to pronounce this or that as an absolute. What the Bible says that God ordered and condoned, as well as much that God forbade in Israel's history, is not applicable today and is recognized not to be applicable by thoughtful Christians of all stripes. On the other hand, the unfolding biblical account is critical for establishing a trajectory. Over time and history, principles emerge that are crucial to any mature understanding of ethics.

A graphic example of this is the scripturally condoned killing of a woman believed to have committed adultery because of her husband's jealousy as described in Numbers 5:11-31. His jealousy, apart from any other proof, was warrant enough for her to undergo a trial by ordeal whereby she would drink a bitter concoction. If it caused her to miscarry or made her abdomen swell she was presumed guilty and could be stoned to death, which was the penalty for adultery. She had to be proven innocent by passing the trial by ordeal.

The need given for this is *"since there is no witness against her and she has not been caught in the act."*[232] There is no presumption of innocence here. It acknowledges that there is a possibility that she may be innocent, but the burden of proof rests with her body's ability to withstand the drinking of the noxious concoction and the humiliating ordeal through which she alone must go. It goes on to say:

---

[231] Revelation 7:9.
[232] Numbers 5:13.

"This, then, is the law of jealousy when a woman goes astray and makes herself impure while married to her husband, or when feelings of jealousy come over a man because he suspects his wife. The priest is to have her stand before the Lord and is to apply this entire law to her. The husband will be innocent of any wrongdoing, but the woman will bear the consequences of her sin."[233]

In the recent difficult Supreme Court confirmation of Judge Brett Kavanaugh, he was accused by Dr. Christine Blasey-Ford of sexual assault when they were teenagers. The alleged assault was much more than a "boys will be boys" attempt at sex with a girl and would have been serious grounds for not confirming him, particularly if he lied about it. Much was made of the fact that Judge Kavanaugh was being presumed guilty by many. The same could be said of Dr. Ford. By many, including the President of the US, she was loudly proclaimed to be guilty of perpetrating a hoax.[234] Because she could not prove the alleged sexual assault by Kavanaugh, she was presumed guilty of making false charges.

The trial by ordeal for these two was having to drink the bitter concoction of highly partisan rhetoric accusing each of evil motives and evil conduct. This shows that it was not entirely unreasonable for the OT people of Israel, an infant culture and society seeking justice as best they could, to seek some sort of solution for the resolution of the unresolvable. However, it is important to see that the Old Testament solution was a trial by ordeal stacked heavily against the woman. The earlier discussed case of Jesus intervening when a woman was caught in adultery and was on the verge of being put to death by stoning is similar. The fact that Dr. Ford's testimony would ultimately make no difference is also similar. This is life in a top down world.

Women in America today, even with a balancing of the scales brought about by the "Me Too" movement, still suffer the most when a grave sexual injustice has been done that cannot be proven in a court of law. The presumption of innocence is an incredibly valuable part of our legal and

---

[233] Numbers 5:30-31.
[234] Jackson, David. "Donald Trump calls assault allegations against Kavanaugh a 'hoax.'" *USA Today*, 8 October 2018. www.usatoday.com/story/news/politics/2018/10/08/donald-trump-calls-assault-allegations-against-brett-kavanaugh-hoax/1564801002/. Accessed 19 March 2019.

judicial heritage, but Dr. Ford had little to gain and much to lose in bringing forth her accusation. Judge Kavanaugh has a lifetime appointment that is virtually unassailable. By the very nature of what took place all those years ago, we will never know what actually happened. Given the incredible importance of our Supreme Court and its Justices, were we to presume, for a moment, her innocence of the charge of lying, it was incredibly brave of her to come forward knowing what was likely to follow. In the aftermath of his confirmation, numerous allegations of judicial misconduct against Kavanaugh were received by the Supreme Court and referred to a lower Appeals Court panel of judges. The lower court judges confirmed that the allegations were serious, but couldn't be pursued because his intervening confirmation to the Supreme Court made him immune to the charges.[235]

Predictably, evangelical leaders like Robertson, Franklin Graham and Jerry Falwell Jr. strongly supported Judge Kavanaugh even though they know no more than you or me. As much or even more telling, in a Marist poll, 48 percent of white evangelicals polled said they still supported Kavanaugh's confirmation even if he was guilty of the allegations.[236] Evangelical women who have been sexually violated know what this means and how much this kind of reaction hurts in and of itself. They are not a small number, yet they generally have a small audience in church communities which, by and large, feel that the women involved shouldn't have gotten themselves in those situations in the first place, or shouldn't say anything unless they can prove it in a court of law. Some prominent evangelical women leaders, like Beth Moore, have spoken out bravely, and their efforts including the #ChurchToo and #SilenceIsNotSpiritual efforts are badly needed exceptions to the rule.

What the "Me Too" movement has done is show that we can't presume that a woman is simply lying or trying to destroy a man's life when she claims that she has been wronged. Do some women lie? Yes, as do many men, but the fact that a woman can't prove it in court no longer warrants her keeping her mouth shut simply for that reason. This may be uncomfortable,

[235] Mauro, Tony. "Judicial Ethics Panel Dismisses Brett Kavanaugh Misconduct Complaints," The National Law Journal, 18 December 2018. www.law.com/nationallawjournal/2018/12/18/judicial-ethics-panel-dismisses-brett-kavanaugh-misconduct-complaints/. Accessed 19 March 2019.
[236] Burton, Tara Isabella. "Poll: 48% of white evangelicals would support Brett Kavanaugh even if the allegations against him were true." Vox, 27 September 2018. www.vox.com/policy-and-politics/2018/9/27/17910016/brett-kavanaugh-christine-blasey-ford-white-evangelicals-poll-support. Accessed 19 March 2019.

it is certainly messy, but it is illustrative of Martin Luther King's observation that *"the arc of the moral universe is long, but it bends toward justice."* This is true even when something demanding justice can't be proved in court.

At first, reading passages like the one describing the jealousy test led me to sense that something was happening here that I didn't yet understand. Years later I would hear a lecture by Richard Rohr that would answer a question that had bothered me for decades. He made the observation that many in America read the Bible from the top down while the Gospels and the rest of the NT were written from the bottom up. They were written by people who were poor. The Savior they proclaimed was poor. With the exception of the Apostle Paul, they were denied citizenship by the Roman Empire that controlled their lives. They were denied legitimacy by the religious leaders of the Jewish people. They were at the bottom and wrote what they did from the perspective of those on the bottom. A light went on for me.

My father's family received a large land grant in southwestern Virginia from the British Earl of Dunmore in the mid 1700's. Back Creek was the family estate near a little town called Dublin. Though lost to our family during the Great Depression, it still stands, a proud and stately main house with a large stone barn and other buildings including a long log building that was our family's slave quarters. For any who have read *Pilgrim at Tinker Creek,* this is the same part of the country and it is beautiful.

For years I had been bothered by the fact that a conservative, evangelical theology that had been influential in my father's Southern Presbyterian heritage had strongly defended slavery from a biblical perspective. This is a classic case of reading bottom up texts from a top down perspective. When the apostle Peter wrote, *"Slaves obey your masters,"*[237] Christian contemporaries of my ancestors read this as a defense of slavery. When Christian slaves read this, it was a survival instruction for a life that they could endure only if they acquiesced to a social structure that had placed them at the bottom and could punish them severely if they resisted it. Peter urged them to rest in the fact that their suffering was a reflection of the suffering which Christ had experienced. Both their suffering and Christ's

---

[237] 1 Peter 2:18.

were unjust. By this comparison, as Christ's position was morally superior to those who caused his suffering, their position was morally superior to those who caused their suffering. In any case, their masters certainly held no superiority, moral or otherwise, even when those on the top might never see it. Paul's teaching was similar.

Paul's brief New Testament letter to a Christian slave owner named Philemon had to do with Philemon's runaway slave named Onesimus. At the time the letter was written, Onesimus, whose name meant "Useful," had apparently fled his master for refuge with Paul and was helping with his ministry. Paul did not assume that Philemon would necessarily see that Onesimus was his equal as a brother in Christ, but he pressed him strongly. We don't know the conclusion to the story of Philemon and Onesimus, but Paul sent Onesimus back to Philemon praying that Philemon would see the truth and Onesimus would flourish.[238]

Were there good Christian masters? Probably so, but in the day when Paul wrote this, any master could severely beat his slave with impunity. For slaves who were Christians, wise pastors like Peter and Paul advised them to do that which was most likely to enable them to flourish and grow in their faith, often in unchangeable circumstances where the master was not a Christian or, like Philemon, hadn't fully grasped the implications of the Gospel. "*Slaves obey your masters*" was practical advice, not a biblical endorsement of slavery. Those on the top read this one way, those on the bottom read it differently.

As I have read through the Bible again and again, God's concern and special affection for the poor as a major theme has become increasingly clear. In the Gospel of Luke, apart from a conversation with his parents and the account of his private temptation following a forty day fast, the first publicly spoken words of Jesus were a quote from the prophet Isaiah: "*The Spirit of the Lord is on me, because he has anointed me to proclaim good news to the poor.*"[239] When Jesus announced, "*Blessed are you poor, for yours is the Kingdom of God*" in the opening words of the Sermon on the Plain,[240] it inescapably established that God's calling for the church cannot

---

[238] Epistle to Philemon, New Testament.
[239] Luke 4:18, Isaiah 61:1.
[240] Luke 6:17-49.

be realized apart from a central concern, not just for spiritual poverty which is universal, but for those in physical poverty. If we cannot read the Scripture through the eyes of those on the bottom then it is fair to question whether we are viewing it through the eyes of Christ. Looking at things through the eyes of the poor changes things dramatically.

Chapter 11

Poverty Matters

"Overcoming poverty is not a gesture of charity. It is an act of justice."[241]
Nelson Mandela

There are two instances in the teaching of Jesus where he pictures someone actually in hell or literally going to hell. One is in the Gospel of Luke 16:19-31 where Jesus tells a story that involves a rich man and a poor man named Lazarus. Here is the story:

"There was a rich man who was dressed in purple and fine linen and lived in luxury every day. At his gate was laid a beggar named Lazarus, covered with sores and longing to eat what fell from the rich man's table. Even the dogs came and licked his sores.

"The time came when the beggar died and the angels carried him to Abraham's side. The rich man also died and was buried. In Hades, where he was in torment, he looked up and saw Abraham far away, with Lazarus by his side. So he called to him, 'Father Abraham, have pity on me and send Lazarus to dip the tip of his finger in water and cool my tongue, because I am in agony in this fire.'

"But Abraham replied, 'Son, remember that in your lifetime you received your good things, while Lazarus received bad things, but now he is comforted here and you are in agony. And besides all this, between us and you a great chasm has been set in place, so that those who want to go from here to you cannot, nor can anyone cross over from there to us.'

"He answered, 'Then I beg you, father, send Lazarus to my family, for I have five brothers. Let him warn them, so that they will not also come to this place of torment.'

"Abraham replied, 'They have Moses and the Prophets; let them listen to them.'

---

[241] Mandela, Nelson. *"Address by Nelson Mandela for the "Make Poverty History" Campaign, London - United Kingdom."* 3 February 2005, www.mandela.gov.za/mandela_speeches/2005/050203_poverty.htm. Accessed 8 March 2019.

"'No, father Abraham,' he said, 'but if someone from the dead goes to them, they will repent.'

"He said to him, 'If they do not listen to Moses and the Prophets, they will not be convinced even if someone rises from the dead.'"

This story is a fascinating one if just from the standpoint that it is the only story in the Bible that actually pictures an identifiable person in hell. In the end, though, the story isn't about who is going to heaven and who is going to hell. Why he is there is far more important for us than that he is there. A few things to note here:

The rich man believed he was one of God's people. He immediately recognizes Abraham, the patriarch of God's people who is in heaven, and addresses him as "father." He believed in the Bible. He is obviously familiar with "Moses and the Prophets" though, like many today, he wrongly doubts that Scripture is clear in warning against that for which he has been held accountable. He believed that if someone rose from the dead it would really make a difference. He wants Abraham to send Lazarus from beyond the grave to his brothers so they might repent of their indifference to the poverty of those like Lazarus. Abraham's chilling reply: "*If they do not listen to Moses and the Prophets, they will not be convinced even if someone rises from the dead.*" Not even Jesus? It's a serious question.

Lazarus is in great need. He suffers from disease, disability and hunger. Both he and the rich man are not just single characters in this story, but are apt representatives of the "haves" and the "have-nots." Though Lazarus is laid at his gate, the rich man pays no attention to him until he himself is in torment and thinks that Lazarus may be of some use to him in relieving his pain and being a messenger to his brothers. The gap between the rich man and Lazarus, a gap of indifference and superiority, is one that the rich man cultivated before either of them died and it persisted into life after death.

The rich man is a pathetic man, but not an unbeliever. Then why is he in hell? It is not because he is rich. There are two rich men in this story. Abraham was rich too. As one member of his household testified: "*The Lord has blessed my master abundantly, and he has become wealthy. He has given him sheep and cattle, silver and gold, male and female servants, and camels and donkeys.*"[242] As Martin Luther King Jr. pointed out, the rich man is in hell, not because he is rich, but because Lazarus was invisible to him. This is a terrible story and one that is powerfully relevant today. Though there are occasional encouraging signs, the world's poor are still largely invisible to many Americans including many evangelicals. The "personal peace" and "affluence" that Francis Schaeffer described as our culturally controlling values breed the same kind of indifference and superiority that plagued the rich man in the story.

World poverty statistics are gathered in arrears and much of the data after 2015 is based on projections rather than actual figures. Measurements based on dollars of income are often tied to the economic reality of an American at that income level in dollars. For example, unless a dependent of another, a single man or woman in the US living on $10 a day is most likely sleeping in a car or a shelter. If farmers in Kenya live at the same level as Americans with an income of $10 per day, they are considered for research purposes to have a $10 daily income regardless of whether the local economy is a barter economy or uses another currency.

According to the World Bank, 10 percent of the world's population now lives on less than $2 a day.[243] This, along with other considerations such as access to basic sanitation, clean drinking water and similar considerations establishes the line below which people are deemed to be living in extreme poverty. According to a Pew Research report analysing 2015 income data from around the world, 70 percent lived on less than $10 per day and 84 percent of the world's population lived on less than $20 per day placing them below the US poverty level.[244]

Though major strides have been taken in the fight against extreme poverty since 1990, the rate of improvement is decreasing. Due to the fact that economic gains are disproportionately aggregated at the top, the gap between those at the top and those on the bottom widens rather than declines even when the poor experience incremental increases. Despite

---

[242] Genesis 24:35.

[243] World Bank. "Poverty and Equity Data Portal." povertydata.worldbank.org/poverty/home/. Accessed 19 March 2019.

[244]Boland, Barbara. "84% of world lives at or below U.S. poverty line." *Pew,* 9 July 2015, www.washingtonexaminer.com/pew-84-of-world-population-lives-at-or-below-us-poverty-line. Accessed 19 March 2019.

advances, the vast majority of the world's population lives below the poverty level.

It is symptomatic of how deeply seated our indifference is that these facts barely startle most of us. A profoundly impoverished world is obvious to anyone with eyes to see, but invisible for practical purposes in the same way that Lazarus was. Our collective national response, strongly bolstered by evangelical ownership of our current policies, despite inevitable denials that we own them, is to reduce humanitarian aid or tie it to provable benefit to American interests, tighten our borders and increase and protect what we've got.

For many evangelicals a sufficient response is to evangelize. This misses the point that a very large number of these "statistics" are already Christians, as were many we served in Congo, so we can't plead that if they would just give their lives to Jesus things would be different. We also can't just say that it is somebody else's problem.

The other scriptural account is found in Matthew 25. It is a picture of the last judgment. Again, it is important because here and in the earlier passage are the two instances where Jesus places an identifiable person in hell or an identifiable group being banished to hell. Here is an excerpt:

> "When the Son of Man comes in his glory, and all the angels with him, he will sit on his glorious throne. All the nations will be gathered before him, and he will separate the people one from another as a shepherd separates the sheep from the goats. He will put the sheep on his right and the goats on his left.
>
> Then the King will say to those on his right, 'Come, you who are blessed by my Father; take your inheritance, the kingdom prepared for you since the creation of the world. For I was hungry and you gave me something to eat, I was thirsty and you gave me something to drink, I was a stranger and you invited me in, I needed clothes and you clothed me, I was sick and you looked after me, I was in prison and you came to visit me.'
>
> Then the righteous will answer him, 'Lord, when did we see you hungry and feed you, or thirsty and give you something to drink?

When did we see you a stranger and invite you in, or needing clothes and clothe you? When did we see you sick or in prison and go to visit you?' The King will reply, 'Truly I tell you, whatever you did for one of the least of these brothers and sisters of mine, you did for me.'

Then he will say to those on his left, 'Depart from me, you who are cursed, into the eternal fire prepared for the devil and his angels. For I was hungry and you gave me nothing to eat, I was thirsty and you gave me nothing to drink, I was a stranger and you did not invite me in, I needed clothes and you did not clothe me, I was sick and in prison and you did not look after me.'

They also will answer, 'Lord, when did we see you hungry or thirsty or a stranger or needing clothes or sick or in prison, and did not help you?' He will reply, 'Truly I tell you, whatever you did not do for one of the least of these, you did not do for me.' Then they will go away to eternal punishment, but the righteous to eternal life." [245]

The sheep and the goats are not separated by race or nationality or religion. Both the sheep and the goats call God "Lord" yet they are separated solely based on their response to the physical needs of the poor. There are wonderful Christian people and others who are deeply concerned for the poor and who give of their time, labor and money in very sacrificial ways. But the average evangelical, who to his or her credit, gives twice as much as other Americans to charity, still gives less than 3 percent of his income to the church and charity combined. This is less than the 3.3 percent churchgoers gave during the Great Depression. [246] The almost total separation of faith and works by evangelicals makes the idea of the kind of "sheep and goats" judgment almost unintelligible for those evangelicals who feel little personal responsibility for the poverty of the poor and little sustained inclination to help them.

Both stories above are ones from the life and teaching of Jesus. One from the present is needed too, but first a bit of context: As the American

---

[245] Matthew 25:31-46.

[246] N/P Source. "The Ultimate List of Charitable Giving Statistics for 2018." nonprofitssource.com/online-giving-statistics/. Accessed 19 March 2019. Giving to churches is considered giving to charity in these statistics.

economy has continued to prosper over the past several years, the rate of homelessness began to creep up in 2017 and 2018 after declining nearly 10 percent between 2008 and 2016.[247] According to the US Census Bureau, "*On a single night in 2017, 553,742 people were experiencing homelessness in the United States. For every 10,000 people in the country, 17 were experiencing homelessness. Approximately two-thirds (65%) were staying in emergency shelters or transitional housing programs, and about one-third (35%) were in unsheltered locations. Homelessness increased for the first time in seven years.*"[248] Though there had been notable decreases between 2007 and 2016, the number of homeless veterans and chronically homeless people increased by 2 percent and 12 percent respectively.[249]

A significant part of this increase in homelessness is due to rising rents as well as reduced government assistance. Our current administration has recommended major budget cuts to the agencies responsible for addressing homelessness. This has most impacted those who were living right at the margin and it is a sad reminder that the financial benefit of our prospering economy is not experienced by those on the bottom. It's also a reminder that this is a stubborn problem. If more traditional ways of dealing with it aren't producing what we need, perhaps a fresh approach is in order.

My daughter is the director of the Interfaith Works homeless shelter in Olympia, Washington. In 2007, she overdosed on heroin. It scared me more than anything I have experienced in my life, including Vietnam and Congo. My wife and I checked her into a psychiatric medical hospital where she remained for weeks until admitted to a rehab facility for a 28 day program. Following rehab, a friend in Olympia opened her home and committed to help her put things back together. She began working as a caregiver at a home for mentally and physically disabled adults and also immersed herself in an outreach program to the homeless in Olympia called the Emma Goldman Youth and Homeless Outreach Program (EGYHOP). She eventually entered the Master of Social Work program at the University of Washington, Tacoma.[250] Her Master's thesis was a

---

[247] Thrush, Glenn. "Homelessness Rises Slightly Despite Strong Economy, Federal Report Finds." *The New York Times*, 17 December 2018. Accessed 9 March 2019.
[248] The US Department of Housing and Urban Development. "The 2017 Annual Homeless Assessment Report (AHAR) to Congress." December 2017.
[249] Ibid.
[250] This is told with her full approval. She tells her own story in a TEDx talk:

detailed plan for a "low barrier" homeless shelter in Olympia. Upon graduation, with the help of friends who shared her deep concerns, the groundwork was laid for a shelter based on two overriding principles: Harm Reduction and Housing First. Both of these principles were foreign to me. I was used to thinking of outreach to the poor as a mission of mercy, a charitable undertaking. She insisted that it wasn't an issue of charity, but of justice.

A charity perspective makes an unconscious, but very real, vertical distinction between the helpers and those who are being helped. It's us and them. Both Harm Reduction and Housing First start from the premise that if we respect those who are in need and view them not as people who need to be fixed, but just as people, profound change is possible. Like the rest of us, the homeless have real potential that can be realized if the things that are harming them the most are remedied, whether self-induced problems or larger societal ones. If they have stable housing first, their ability to deal with all the other issues in their lives increases measurably.

After dinner while on a memorable trip to Olympia to see her, my daughter said, "*Dad, I want you to come with me.*" We started walking the streets of downtown Olympia and turned down an alley. There was a barrel with a blazing fire around which were huddled a group of people moving into and out of the firelight. My strong inclination was to turn and get out of there as quickly as possible. She grabbed my arm and took me right to the group. As we got close to the barrel, several of the people who were crowded around the fire recognized her and one said, "*Hey girl!*" She said, "*Hey guys, I want you to meet my Dad.*" By this time she had been doing sock and needle exchange in this community of people for a couple of years and she knew them and they knew and trusted her. For those horrified that anyone would think that needle exchange is a good idea, please stay with this story.

There are two noteworthy aspects to this seemingly counter-intuitive outreach. Unless and until something changes in their lives, drug users are going to use. For those using drugs, needle exchange is often the very first step in taking responsibility for their own health. Clean needles measurably reduce the threat of harm from serious diseases like hepatitis and HIV. Strains of hepatitis are highly contagious among people experiencing homelessness, but they are also a threat of harm to the community as a whole. The exchange of needles protects the users, but also keeps dirty needles off the street. Needless to say, these needles are a threat to others. The potential harm to both users and the public is reduced. A meaningful first step has been taken, but it is only the first step.

The level of stress experienced by the homeless, the majority of whom experience high levels of mental illness, is enormous. For those who don't know where they are going to sleep next, have little or no material or internal resources, no place to keep their meager belongings and regularly face the real dangers that come with living on the street, the level of stress is intense. The energy expended just staying alive is often overwhelming. Assistance programs with daunting administrative requirements are almost impossible to navigate by street people. The least helpful thing is telling them to get a job. Worse is thinking *"if they just cleaned up their act or at least got out of our backyard, we wouldn't have to worry about them."* On the other hand, for people who have regular, adequate housing and skillful help in addressing the root causes of the medical and mental stresses in their lives, the rate and pace of healing is remarkable.

Also remarkable is one particular church. First Christian Church of Olympia, whose pastor and congregation were fully behind it, provided the needed space for the shelter on their campus in the middle of the downtown area. Strenuous efforts by numerous groups had been aimed at keeping the facility as far from there as possible, but the church was not deterred. The forty-two bed shelter is now in its fourth year of full occupancy. There is not a requirement for sobriety for those who agree not to "use" while in the shelter. There is no limit on the number of nights that one can spend there. "Guests" with partners (often their only meaningful connection in life) or with dogs (often the only form of security for those who live in almost total insecurity) are allowed to stay … with their partners and their dogs or other animals. There are separate areas for men, women and couples. The focus is not on cleaning up their bad behaviors, but on meeting their immediate needs and getting them into permanent housing. It has been powerfully effective. When their needs are met, their behaviors change. That said, this is not Shangri La. Shelter staff are trained to administer Narcan (a drug overdose antidote) and to use non-violent conflict resolution when it is needed; however, peace within the shelter is guarded as much by the guests who regard it as home as it is by the staff. Seemingly against all odds, it is a peaceful place.

After much initial resistance, there has been a slow changing of heart in the city due in part to a welcome reduction in homeless-related crime in the city-center. This change is also partly due to the opening of a day shelter and a Community Care Center that the shelter opened in partnership with the largest hospital in the city. Many of the guests are now in permanent homes and the initially reluctant city government is now partnering with the state, the county and the shelter to build a multi-million dollar facility to provide overnight shelter, on-site connection with assistance agencies, medical and mental health services, and long term housing in a multi-story complex near downtown. This is being done in partnership with a developer who is experienced in dealing with housing needs and issues facing the homeless.

A further noteworthy piece in the change of attitude resulted from the editor of the local paper taking an after-dark walk with my daughter to the same part of town to which she took me. When he actually met people who had been on the streets for years in the town that is both his and theirs, his outlook began to change and the editorial stance of the paper did too. When our concern is primarily about the people to whom rules apply rather than just the rules themselves, major change can happen. For those familiar with the Gospel accounts, this is strongly reminiscent of Christ's identification with those on the margins of society, living among them and meeting them where they were.

Most churches have or support ministries that reach out to the poor in their communities and this is surely evidence of the grace of God at work. It is important to point out, though, that the complex problems surrounding poverty, including the needs of the homeless poor, cannot be adequately addressed by the church alone. It is necessary to partner with other people of good will and all levels of government if we are to see real progress. It is also necessary to be realistic about the actual level of impact the church really has on the addressing of these needs.

The vast majority of what is given to the church goes for the operating expenses of the church. That is, it goes to property, utilities, equipment, supplies and staff. I know this to be true. As the Executive Pastor of a large, generous evangelical church and the Chief Operating Officer of Food for the Hungry, it was a required part of my job to research and understand giving and spending patterns in churches. Do the churches serve their communities? Of course they do, but it is necessary that we not overestimate or overstate how much is being directed towards meeting the needs of those who are actually on the bottom. Sadly, it isn't that much.

We give an enormous amount through our taxes, don't we? Whatever one believes about the level or effectiveness of tax supported social assistance programs (see the detailed discussion in Appendix 5), the trajectory supported by evangelicals as an identifiable block is neither to increase or sustain these programs at current levels, but to roll them back. Many believe the false assertion that the poor pay little or nothing in the way of taxes. Even a cursory glance at taxation reveals that it is impossible to avoid gas taxes and other federal and state taxes on commodities, sales taxes, property taxes and most payroll taxes. These impact the poor disproportionately and account for the fact that those making less than $20,000 annually pay approximately 17 percent of their income in local, state and federal taxes that are virtually unavoidable, whether one is here legally or not.[251] This amounts to more than $80 billion annually.

Much of our tax money goes for foreign aid doesn't it? According to a Kaiser Foundation poll, on average those Americans polled believed that 26 percent of our national budget goes for foreign aid.[252] Not even close. According to the nonpartisan Congressional Research Council (CRS), foreign aid, including military foreign aid, accounted for 1.2 percent of the 2016 US federal budget. Of that, more than half went to military and political aid. Less than one percent of our federal budget went for humanitarian foreign aid. In fact, long term economic development and shorter term humanitarian aid accounted for just over half a percent of the

[251]Klein, Ezra. "The one tax graph you really need to know." *The Washington Post,* 19 September 2012. www.washingtonpost.com/news/wonk/wp/2012/09/19/heres-why-the-47-percent-argument-is-an-abuse-of-tax-data/?noredirect=on&utm_term=.f1eab88fc480. Accessed 15 March 2019. See Appendix 5.
[252] Rutsch, Poncie. "Guess How Much of Uncle Sam's Money Goes For Foreign Aid? Guess Again." *NPR, Stories of Life In a Changing World,* 10 February 2015. www.npr.org/sections/goatsandsoda/2015/02/10/383875581/guess-how-much-of-uncle-sams-money-goes-to-foreign-aid-guess-again. Accessed 20 March 2019.

$4.15 trillion budget in 2017. This included US contributions to the United Nations. [253] With one of our largest federal budgets ever, that amount has been reduced for 2019. President Trump has repeatedly called for substantial cuts to our foreign aid and that it be directed only towards those who respect the US and are our "friends."[254] The world is facing an incredible, unprecedented, refugee crisis and worldwide deaths due to malnutrition resulting from famine and war are at an alarming level. The US is actively reducing our contribution to facing these crises and is doing so with our blessing. Since taxes apply to us all, when all is said and done, the average evangelical gives a little more towards the mitigation of poverty than does the average American who is not an evangelical.

Why should this matter for evangelicals? We should first ask *"Does our response to the poor matter to Jesus?"* If the answer to that is yes then we have answered the first question. If Jesus meant what he said in the story of Lazarus and the story of the sheep and the goats it is hard to conclude anything except that it matters a lot. Whatever final judgment involves, according to the teaching of Jesus, it has both an individual and collective aspect to it and it includes those who call God "Lord" and it will be largely concerned with their response to poverty in all its manifestations, not just spiritual poverty.

If we claim to have been chiefly concerned with the spiritual needs of others and our faith has not also led us to the determined meeting of their physical needs, our faith will not have led us where Jesus would have us go. When we look back at who we have become personally and collectively, the one measure that will mean most is how we responded to those in need. This is not my opinion. This is clearly stated again and again in the Scriptures that we evangelicals insist are the Word of God and our guide in life.

As mentioned before, the passages about Lazarus and the rich man and the sheep and the goats, are not chiefly about who is going to heaven and who is going to hell. They are about what constitutes worthwhile living by

[253] McBride, James. "How Does the US Spend Its Foreign Aid." Council on Foreign Relations backgrounder, updated 1 October 2018. www.cfr.org/backgrounder/how-does-us-spend-its-foreign-aid. Accessed 20 March 2019.
[254] Ibid.

people of lasting substance and what does not. They are about whether "*God so loved the world that He sent His only Son*" means anything for the world we live in or primarily for the world to come. Jesus plainly said the world we live in matters … a lot. His message to us all? Trust me, live as I call you to live and leave the future to me.

Chapter 12

"Thou Shalt Not Kill"
Exodus 20:13 KJV

In the early 1980's, as mentioned earlier, I was a pilot flying the emergency medevac helicopter out of St. Mary's Hospital in Grand Junction, Colorado. This was before GPS and the flying was both exhilarating and extremely challenging. We routinely flew patients from the scenes of accidents or from small rural hospitals or clinics unable to adequately cope with a life-threatening illness, injury or other medical condition. We regularly flew hundreds of miles through rugged, mountainous terrain, often to Denver or Salt Lake City with few navigation aids and usually without radar assistance from Air Traffic Control.

One night I flew to the town of Rifle, Colorado where a pregnant woman at 26 weeks gestation was in extreme medical distress. The neonatal team carried their equipment into the local hospital and, after stabilizing the mother and assisting with the birth, made the decision to transport the baby to the Neonatal Intensive Care Unit at St. Mary's. The whole process had taken several hours and by the time we took off to return to St. Mary's the weather had deteriorated badly. Given the life threatening circumstances, a ground ambulance ride was too long and out of the question. I had to follow the interstate highway at low altitude to stay below the icing conditions in the thick clouds above and had to follow a police car with flashing lights to mark the way for the first part of the journey through heavy sleet. We made our approach into St. Mary's over a newly opened abortion clinic advertising abortions through the second trimester. You can read the scathing, pro-life, anti-abortion letter I wrote to the editor of the local newspaper in Appendix 3. Sadly, despite enormous efforts on the part of many professionals, the baby died as they often did at that age at that time.

Fast forward to 2005. On loan from a large evangelical church in Denver where I had been pastoring for years, I was serving as Country Director for Food for the Hungry in the Democratic Republic of Congo. At this point there had been ten years of uninterrupted war in eastern Congo, millions of deaths far surpassing the number of deaths in neighboring Rwanda during the genocide and, as has been widely reported, sexual violence at a level that has never before been seen.

Eastern Congo, where our work was focused, has been called the worst place on earth to be a woman. At that time it was estimated that half of all females over the age of eleven had been sexually assaulted often in the most brutal ways imaginable. It was then estimated that there were more than forty thousand women and girls who needed fistula surgery to repair their torn vaginal walls from almost unimaginable sexual violence, and raped young girls having babies when their bodies were sufficiently developed to conceive, but not sufficiently developed to give birth without major damage to themselves.

The women who had been assaulted and their thousands and thousands of babies were absolutely shunned in communities that had been torn apart and were too primitive to cope psychologically or any other way with the weaponization of sexual violence and its destructive impact on their lives. In areas that were already on the brink of starvation, the violated women, many of whom smelled continually of urine and feces due to the damage to their bodies, and their children, were at the absolute bottom of the food chain. Permanent stunting of the children was common. This means that they would never grow to normal proportions, many were profoundly affected mentally and prone to illness with immune systems that would never develop adequately. I was stunned to realize that a weighty shift was taking place in my thinking. Fair warning, much of what follows is extremely blunt and some will find it offensive.

Given the circumstances I witnessed with my own eyes, were my daughter one of those women or girls, I would do everything in my power to find a way for her to have a safe abortion if she wanted it. Things are little better in Congo today than they were then. The same is true of similar countries in similar circumstances. No one is ever going to adequately care for these women and children, including an evangelical America more concerned with maintaining the current American policy that ensures that the likes of them never cross our borders from their "shithole" countries, as our president describes them, while we are busy making America great again. Unfair? Too harsh? Maybe not.

Nothing that follows should be taken to imply that there are not legitimate issues that need to be discussed and decided among people of good will. For better or for worse, Christians are in the center of the conversation regarding abortion and will continue to be. Regardless of the rhetoric from the "other" side, Christians are admonished to *"Let your conversation be always full of grace."*[255] If ever there was an issue that required the intentional, repeated application of this admonition, it is this one. For those who have made the hard decision to forego an abortion or are the children of women who did, they deserve our unqualified appreciation. Allowing someone else to make a different decision, in no way detracts from that experience of courage and grace because it is a choice and an outcome that easily stands on its own merits. However, if we never recognize any validity to the experience of those who took a different course, there will never be a conversation. For years there have been only monologues on both sides of the issues. If ever there is going to be a serious "conversation" about this, it requires a larger context.

In 1979, Francis Schaeffer and C. Everett Koop published *Whatever Happened to the Human Race?* They awakened evangelicals to the issue of abortion as never before. Though the book also dealt with euthanasia and end of life issues, most evangelicals had given at least some thought to those particular issues and many already had strong convictions regarding them. For many the phrase *"Sanctity of Life"* entered their vocabulary for the first time. Because the first association of many, if not most, evangelicals with the idea of the sanctity of life was specifically in its application to abortion, many did not and do not realize that the phrase has far broader application.

Long before American evangelicals were introduced to this idea, Catholic theologians had been thinking, writing and applying a growing body of insights regarding the sanctity of life. One Catholic writer, Eileen Egan, gathered these teachings through the analogy of a *"seamless garment."* The men who nailed Jesus to the cross divided his clothes among themselves. The last of these garments was the seamless tunic Jesus wore. It didn't make sense to divide it among themselves because it would

---

[255] Colossians 4:6.

be worthless if they did, so they drew lots for the whole garment. The analogy of the seamless garment speaks to the impossibility of separating any life issue from all the others. By this thinking, the sanctity of life applies across the broad spectrum of issues that includes war, militarism, poverty, refugees, social justice, capital punishment, contraception, healthcare, genetics and beginning and end of life issues. It has also been described as a "consistent life ethic," an ethic expounded by Cardinal Joseph Bernardin and many other Catholic and sympathetic writers and theologians.

Schaeffer and Koop made a hard division between the sanctity of life and the quality of life. The unintended consequence of this was to allow their evangelical readers to continue to separate issues that can be distinguished from one another, but cannot be separated. Many issues surrounding life and death are as important to an understanding of the sanctity of life as are the signature issues of abortion and euthanasia. A truly "consistent life ethic" gives appropriate weight to them all, but many American evangelicals would take strong exception to a number of the positions advocated by the chief architects and expounders of a consistent life ethic. Large among these issues with which many or most evangelicals would disagree are those concerning capital punishment, gun control, the unjust distribution of wealth, and the criticism of the use of American military power in ways not consistent with Just War ethics. That said, evangelicals would be in strong agreement regarding abortion.

There are many, many women, evangelical and otherwise, including members of my own family, who could never contemplate having an abortion under any circumstances. Some women who have had abortions have lived to regret it and believe that other women should know what they have experienced before making a decision they too might live to regret. Their convictions are powerful and they have been instrumental in shaping the consciences of many others. Many are Christian women whose character, compassion, intelligence and learning are of the highest caliber. When I recall the strong exemplars of Christian character who have most impacted my life, several are among these women I have just described. Hurting or discouraging those who have impacted my life so positively is the last thing I would ever want to do ... but there is a conversation that must be had.

While in the final stages of flight training, my earlier mentioned friends and I were in a thriving Christian fellowship of young adults. We were mostly novice Christians and many were reading the Bible for the first time. In one study we focused on verses quoting Jesus like this one: "*Whatever you ask in my name, I will do it, that the Father may be glorified in the Son; if you ask anything in my name, I will do it.*"[256] After the study a young woman approached two of us and asked if the verse was really true. Sensing that she was going to ask something that tested that, my friend and I, one of the guys who had walked out of the porno flick with me, looked at each other nervously because this was going to be an obvious stretch to our faith. Without knowing what she was going to say, we simply told her that it was true. She then said that she was pregnant, but felt she was in no way prepared to be a mother. At her request we prayed and simply asked God to take care of her. She called us the next day and told us that she had miscarried that morning. We knew deep in our hearts that the timing was not coincidental.

This is a story that I have rarely shared, because when I did share it with a strongly pro-life friend it was highly disconcerting to her. When this happened it was long before I had read Schaeffer and Koop. It was also before Roe vs. Wade, and I doubt that I had given five minutes of thought to abortion in my whole life. The idea of God terminating a pregnancy in response to a prayer was not something I had ever given any thought to ever. Because we didn't have any idea that we should feel otherwise, our collective response was not that this was somehow sad or incongruous; rather, it was unmitigated joy that God had heard our prayer and had acted powerfully in response to it.

As I have reflected upon this, it underscores for me that God is concerned about the whole of our lives, and is not stuck on a concept of the sanctity of life that elevates unborn life in an absolute way that subordinates other significant life concerns equally included among God's concerns for us. I believe that God was concerned about this young woman's life and heard her prayer. We didn't mourn then and I have never felt that we should have felt anything but the joy that we did. Not many years later, I would adopt a

---

[256] John 14;13,14 RSV which is the version which I had memorized and probably used in that study.

strong ideological position that didn't have a space for this story, so it went onto the back shelf until another time and another place.

Just as abnormal psychology gives us critical insights into normal psychology, extreme human situations give us insight into human situations that are less extreme. Though deeply committed to the truthfulness of God's commandment, "*You shall not murder,*" Dietrich Bonhoeffer came to the conclusion that the decidedly unlawful killing of Hitler, without judicial process, was warranted because he presided over a regime that was antithetical to everything true to the meaning and purpose of life. In the same way, it is incumbent upon Christians today to understand that some circumstances that occur in life are antithetical to any reasonable understanding of what human life is meant to be.

The idea that tens of thousands of raped women and girls in Congo with offspring destined for stunting, being shunned by their communities and consigned to starvation and disease, should be given no option to ease this burden of misery, purely on ideological grounds, is also antithetical to the meaning and purpose of life. The same can be said of thousands of women who, because of the Zika virus, have faced giving birth to children who lack any capacity for normal human life and whose profound need for unceasing care will guarantee that these women and families will never climb out of a grinding poverty.

Though they are genetically identical, the Bible regularly distinguishes between a tree and its fruit. We make a distinction between a chicken and the egg from which it comes. Using an example outside the realm of biology, the point of this book thus far has been to separate one kind of ethic (an undamaged one) from another (a damaged one). Though both are part of the overall classification we call "ethics" they are, in fact, different. One is not the other. A developing chicken, in the egg from which it comes, is genetically identical to a fully developed one, but there is a difference. The fact that a developing child is genetically human is simply a matter of fact, but that does not end the discussion. One can insist upon calling a fertilized human egg at the moment of conception a "baby," and one can insist that anyone who uses terms like "conceptus" or "fetus" or "zygote" or "embryo" is simply trying to deceive and divert attention from what is really happening, but this fails to do justice to a serious conversation that must be undertaken by people of good will trying to deal with a complex issue.

The crux of the argument revolves around the question *"what is being aborted?"* Evangelicals typically assert that there is only one possible perspective and that is the genetic one. What is being aborted from the moment of conception on is a baby ... end of discussion. As we shall see, that is hardly the end of the discussion and, if it is the only possible perspective, it actually opens a whole arena of very problematic ethical and theological issues for evangelicals. Others argue that there is a valid developmental perspective and, when viewed from that vantage point, as many other important aspects of human life regularly are, one comes to a different conclusion. As already noted, rights and responsibilities increase as humans develop biologically, intellectually and morally. As the current detention and family separation policy at the Mexican border clearly shows, this also applies to serious issues like protection under the law. This protection is strong for those resisting "invasion" by "caravans" of aliens, but almost non-existent for many fully developed human beings seeking a new life.

As discussed in detail below, abortion per se is never addressed either in the Old or New Testaments of the Bible. This may make little difference for Christians who dogmatically place abortion in a category all by itself; however, the extreme situations noted above, and ones like them, underscore the importance for Christians to identify a principle which forbids abortion. Some will say that this is simple. Murder is wrong and abortion is murder.

Murder is wrong, but the assertion that abortion is murder is an assertion that is, at best, difficult to prove by biblical standards as we shall see. By virtue of the fact that the Bible does not address it specifically, if it is truly wrong at all times and in all circumstances, it must belong to a class of forbidden actions of which it is an example. If abortion is universally wrong then it requires a universal principle which makes it so. Apart from such a principle, it is a selectively applied ideology that militates against the provision of safe abortion as an option for women heavily impacted by poverty among other things. That is the case for 75 percent of women in the US who choose not to proceed with their pregnancies. This too is discussed below in more detail.

What can and should non-evangelical Americans expect of evangelicals? As a minimum they should expect consistency from us in the application of our Christian beliefs. If we fail to see the connection between abortion and other life issues, many outside of evangelicalism do not. If we are challenged for that, it is not being treated badly for our faith in Christ; rather, it is being held accountable for what in some instances amounts to grave inconsistency. An ethic that is not consistently applied is a deficient ethic and it certainly isn't a Christian ethic.

The Eyes of the Beholder

"I see people; they look like trees walking around."
Mark 8:24

Is it valid for Christians to look at the abortion issue through the lens of poverty? Is there ground between the two examples I described above that calls for us to look again into a very difficult and disconcerting issue? Before we can answer that question, it is necessary to ask again some very basic questions like *"how do we know that abortion is wrong?"* Because it is taken for granted among evangelicals that it is wrong, the question itself evokes suspicion of the asker, but we are going to ask it anyway.

Here is the answer given by one prominent evangelical, R.C Sproul:

> *"Abortion is a monstrous evil, and if I know anything about the character of God, I am totally convinced that this is an outrage to him. From the beginning to the end of sacred Scripture, there is a premium on the sanctity of human life. Anytime we see human life cheapened—as it clearly is in the wanton destruction of unborn children— then those who have an appreciation for the value and the dignity of human life need to stand up and protest as loudly as they possibly can."* [257]

---

[257] Sproul, R.C. "Abortion is a Monstrous Evil." Facebook, 16 March 2017. www.facebook.com/notes/ending-abortion/abortion-is-a-monstrous-evil-rc-sproul/432700430396010/. Accessed 20 March 2019.

First, it is necessary to point out again that the Bible does not address abortion directly. We will discuss Psalm 139 and similar passages dealing with God's involvement in notable pregnancies, but the Scripture passage most closely associated with a biblical prohibition of abortion is Exodus 21:22-25 quoted below from the Revised Standard Version.[258] This passage refers to a miscarriage or premature birth resulting from a fight between two men in which the pregnant wife of one of the men is incidentally injured. Because there is punishment involved in the resolution of this incident involving a pregnant woman, it is seen to have possible application to the abortion issue.

> *"When men strive together, and hurt a woman with child, so that there is a miscarriage, and yet no harm follows, the one who hurt her shall be fined, according as the woman's husband shall lay upon him; and he shall pay as the judges determine. If any harm follows, then you shall give life for life, eye for eye, tooth for tooth, hand for hand, foot for foot, burn for burn, wound for wound, stripe for stripe."*

It isn't just a fight between two men which would call for a fair adjudication of fault if adjudicated at all. The presence of a pregnant wife and the fact of her *"miscarriage"* (RSV) or *"premature birth"* (NIV and NASB) that apparently gives her husband the presumption of lesser culpability and entitlement to compensation.

As rendered in the NIV and the NASB, the text simply states that the baby is premature and not whether it is dead or alive. Those who use this text in addressing the abortion issue understand that the offender will pay a fine if the baby is born live and only the mother is hurt and *"an eye for an eye"* if the baby dies. The NASB notes a variant reading of *"untimely birth"* instead of premature birth and the King James Version says *"her fruit depart from her."* Neither of these specify whether it is a live birth or not.

In the passage it is unclear whether it is further injury to the woman or to the premature baby (if alive) that calls for the penalty of an *"eye for an eye, tooth for a tooth."* The Revised Standard Version of the Bible, quoted above

---

[258] The abbreviation for Revised Standard Version is RSV. The abbreviation for New International Version is NIV. The abbreviation for New American Standard Bible is NASB.

and translated long before the current acrimonious debates about abortion, indicates that it is further injury to the woman that is punishable; that is, injury beyond the miscarriage. That further injury to the woman might be the cause for the penalty cannot be ruled out in any of the other versions.

Suffice it to say that it is one brief passage that is debatable by scholars of good will. It does not address abortion directly, and the immediate context of the verses mentioned hardly supports the idea of a universal sanctity of life. The verses immediately preceding it excuse a master from punishment if he strikes a male or female slave and the slave survives for a day or two after the beating. The King James Version puts it quaintly: *"And if a man smite his servant, or his maid, with a rod, and he die under his hand; he shall be surely punished. Notwithstanding, if he continue a day or two, he shall not be punished: for he is his money."*[259]

The lack of direct scriptural prohibition of abortion is not because abortion was unknown in biblical times or places. Abortion was widely known and practiced in the ancient world.[260] It is often thought to be modern and scientific when, in fact, it is as old as recorded history. There is actually quite a large amount of documentation of this that is easily accessible.[261] The Ebers Papyrus from Egypt (1550 BCE) describes inducing an abortion by means of a plant fiber tampon and is thought to be drawn from even more ancient documents dating back to the third millennium before Christ.[262] The papyrus itself dates to the time that the people of Israel were in Egypt prior to the Exodus. Four hundred years before the New Testament was written, Hippocrates, from whom we get the Hippocratic Oath which calls for physicians not to induce abortions, nevertheless advised a prostitute how to induce miscarriage through a curious regimen of strenuous physical activity. He elsewhere described instruments to dilate the cervix and curette the uterus.[263]

---

[259] Exodus 21:20,21.
[260] British Broadcasting Corporation. "Historical attitudes to abortion." BBC Ethics Guide, 2014. www.bbc.co.uk/ethics/abortion/legal/history_1.shtml#findoutmore. Accessed 20 March 2019.
[261] ProCon.org. "Footnotes and Sources." Updated 9 November 2018. abortion.procon.org/view.resource.php?resourceID=003721. Accessed 20 March 2019.
[262] Head, Tom. "The Ancient History of Abortion and When it Began." ThoughtCo, Updated 5 July 2018. www.thoughtco.com/when-did-abortion-begin-721090. Accessed 20 March 2019.
[263] Lefkowitz, Mary R. and Fant, Maureen B. "Women's Life in Greece and Rome." Hippocrates. "On the Generating Seed and the Nature of the Child." 4th Cent. B.C. www.stoa.org/diotima/anthology/wlgr/wlgr-medicine341.shtml. Accessed 20 March 2019.

There are passages of Scripture referring to God's calling of Samson, Isaiah, Jeremiah, John the Baptist, and Jesus while in the womb and many passages of Scripture that extol the blessing of pregnancy, children and childbearing, but none that speak directly of abortion. The fact that the Bible does not address abortion directly does not mean that it has nothing relevant to say about it, but for Christians the Bible's silence would require that there be a clear and universal biblical principle by which we know that it is always wrong.

What is that principle? What is the progression of thought that concludes with *"Therefore abortion is a monstrous evil?"* Is it *"Thou shalt not kill"* (KJV) from the Ten Commandments? Most newer translations render the commandment *"You shall not murder."* If this is the principle then the syllogism would go like this: God considers murder a monstrous evil. Abortion is murder. Therefore abortion is a monstrous evil. Though this is perhaps the most likely candidate for a universal biblical principle, the fact that the same books of the Bible which contain the accounts of the giving of the Ten Commandments, Exodus and Deuteronomy, not only condone, but specifically call for the killing of all sorts of innocent people. This includes infants and pregnant women, often killed in brutal ways and under circumstances that we would consider to be murder or genocide today. Yet it never addresses the subject of abortion, much less says that abortion is murder.

If murder is the taking of innocent life, Moses and Joshua and those under their command were certainly the killers of innocent unborn and infants on a huge scale. Read the account of the defeat of kings Sihon and Og and the total destruction of their subjects in Deuteronomy 2 and 3. Are we comfortable saying that Moses and Joshua were mass murderers? Clearly the definition of murder in Exodus and Deuteronomy and any universal definition we use today, even by the most conservative among us, are not the same.

Why is it important that we consider that murder as it was understood then and murder as we understand it today are not identical? Similarly, marriage then was generally polygamous and totally accepted as a moral norm. Marriage today is not. If we insist that murder then and murder now are the same, on that principle, should we not insist that marriage then and marriage now are the same? Did the early Mormons get it right? Most of us would say not. This doesn't necessarily prove anything one way or the other, but it means we must define our terms carefully and we can't end our search for a principle quite yet.

This also begs the question of what Sproul means when he says: *"From the beginning to the end of sacred Scripture, there is a premium on the sanctity of human life."* The sentiment is admirable, but we immediately run into a problem here because there are numerous passages in the Old Testament that clearly state that God either directly killed infants (through His angel) as during the final plague visited upon the Egyptians just prior to the Exodus,[264] or God raised up thus and so for the express purpose of killing the unborn or infants along with others. Sometimes it was the children of the enemies of Israel, sometimes it was the children of the Israelites.

For a further sampling of what the Scripture has to say see Exodus 12:29, Exodus 13:15, Judges 21:1-15, 1 Samuel 15:1-3, 2 Kings 8:7-15, Psalm 137:7-9, Isaiah 13:13-18 and Jeremiah 19:7-9. Read these in context. There must be a lens through which we can view these passages by which we can maintain that, from the beginning to the end, Scripture puts a premium on the sanctity of life as we understand it today, because clearly in the early and middle parts of the OT that is not the case according to the clear and plain sense of often repeated words. This is not an argument against the sanctity of life, but it is an attempt to define what we mean when we talk of the sanctity of life and establish some sort of principle by which we can protect it in a meaningful way.

If the principle is that God forbids the taking of **innocent** human life we are immediately aware that there are clear exceptions from the perspective of most evangelicals when it comes to our national security. Being as generous as possible, the scriptural examples to the contrary cited above would have to fit in the same sort of category. For evangelicals, the sad but presumably necessary killing of innocents for American national security reasons is generally accepted, but there is no more Scriptural warrant for that than there is for any other country's national security interests with the

---

[264] Exodus 12:29.

possible exception, from a debatable theological perspective, of Israel in OT times.

Clearly God's laws allowed the taking of innocent lives in OT times unless we begin to quibble about the definition of "innocent." If the unborn and infant children of Israel's enemies were simply enemies and, by that reckoning, not innocent, then the problem is avoided at least for that time in history. However, that does us no good if we are seeking a universal principle today by which we understand that abortion is wrong for all. In any case, if it is US law or the laws of any other sovereign nation that either allow it or make it wrong then a major corner has been turned in the discussion.

Is the principle then that God forbids the **unlawful** taking of innocent human life? We may be getting closer to the heart of the issue, but we are immediately faced again with deciding whose laws apply, God's or ours. When we talk about our laws do we mean the laws of the US or human laws in general? Most evangelicals would be repelled by the notion that the laws of Nazi Germany or the laws of Imperial Japan in WWII would justify the taking of innocent European or American lives in that conflict, but on what principle do we decide that they would not be justified but we are?

When America dropped atomic bombs on Hiroshima and Nagasaki killing 200,000+ people, including the unborn, infants and the non-combatant elderly, was it morally acceptable? Was it acceptable during saturation bombing runs by scores of cohorts of B-52s in North Vietnam? Everything that breathed was obliterated in swaths two miles wide and four miles long in the wake of each cohort. This killed hundreds of thousands of Vietnamese non-combatant peasants including many unborn, infants and elderly. This in a country that posed no direct threat to America in the way that Germany and Japan did in WWII.

Right now there is a humanitarian crisis of massive proportions in Yemen with tens of thousands dead and millions at risk of starvation because of the tactics of our coalition with Saudi Arabia and our status as "allies." The Saudis are using American equipment and active military support to indiscriminately kill the unborn, infants and other innocents as collateral damage in a regional religious war. Is this acceptable? If it is thought to be necessary for American national security, and the threshold for believing this is a low one, most evangelicals say the answer is yes. Thankfully, our Congress may resolve this, but that doesn't bring back to life those for whose deaths we are responsible.

Is the principle that the **intentional** taking of innocent human life is wrong therefore abortion is wrong? When weapons designed to kill everything they are turned upon were fired into a compound in Yemen where there were innocents, including an eight year old American citizen,[265] as well as enemies, how can one say that there was no intent to kill? There may have been no desire to kill innocents, but that is different from no intent. When the atomic bombs were dropped, it is mere sophistry that says there was no intent to kill innocents both on the part of the decision makers and those who carried out the decision.

The intentional decision to use a weapon of mass destruction or saturation bombing is an intentional decision to destroy without reference to innocence. When, in the wake of cohorts of B-52s, everything that breathed was destroyed, how can we say that there was no intent to kill the innocents who went up in smoke along with everything else? Our collaboration with Saudi Arabia in Yemen is the same. In each instance we may not have wanted to take innocent life, but that is completely different from not intending to take those lives. We evangelicals have a rather large tolerance for the intentional taking of innocent life.

Back to the point, let us start from the premise that what is conceived in a woman's womb is genetically human from the start. Japanese, Vietnamese and Yemeni unborn children are as genetically human as are those in America. The same kind of special lens that must be used to enable us to see that the Scriptures place a premium on the sanctity of life from beginning to end apparently enables some of us to see that it is okay to take innocent life for American national security reasons, even when it is difficult to argue that our security is at risk as in Vietnam and now in Yemen. When trying to determine when an unborn heart begins to beat or when an unborn baby feels pain, why is there so little outcry from evangelicals when hearts that we know to be beating and children whom

---

[265] Rascoe, Ayesha. "Donald Trump authorised air strike that killed eight-year-old American girl 'without sufficient intelligence.'" *Independent,* 2 February 2017.

we know to be experiencing pain are being killed or neglected and allowed to die from human induced famine and with our permission? Something else is going on here.

For many American evangelicals today, the special glasses that allow them to see that Trump is God's man for the times also allow them to see that America is God's special nation, thus our national security interests are presumably special ones in God's sight. If the Scriptures don't teach this, and I would argue that only a tortured reading of the Scriptures does, then we still need to ask the question *"upon what principle do we say that abortion is wrong?"*

Is the principle that because of the gruesome nature of some procedures abortion is evil? When appealing to the gruesome image of what happens during an abortion procedure as proof of its evil nature, one should also consider the gruesome carnage from the bombs dropped in Hiroshima, Nagasaki, North Vietnam and Yemen on the innocents incinerated or ripped to shreds by them. One might also consider the gruesome image of a panicked innocent crowd racing to escape the stream of military grade bullets from a Las Vegas hotel room high above the crowd, or Jewish worshippers huddled in a Pittsburg synagogue while they were gunned down by an anti-Semite, or worshippers in evangelical churches in South Carolina and Texas similarly gunned down. Where is the evangelical voice calling for sane gun laws? The argument that the gruesome nature of some abortion procedures makes it evil is an argument from disgust, but there is a lot of disgust to go around and the moralization of our disgust still requires a principle. If we hold that abortion is universally wrong then we need a universal principle by which we know that to be true.

Is the principle that because God is actively involved in shaping and forming us in our mothers' wombs, as Psalm 139 indicates, that therefore the taking of unborn life is a monstrous evil as Sproul indicates? This still evades the question of how do we justify taking the lives of both the unborn and infants in conflict situations, but it also raises a much thornier question. According to the Mayo Clinic, the estimated rate of miscarriage is 10 to 20 percent in women who know they are pregnant,[266] but as many as half of all

---

[266] Mayo Clinic. "Miscarriage." 20 July 2016. www.mayoclinic.org/diseases-conditions/pregnancy-loss-miscarriage/symptoms-causes/syc-20354298. Accessed 16 March 2019.

fertilized eggs may spontaneously abort, often before a woman realizes she is pregnant.[267] A 2010 Stanford University study, reported in Science Daily, notes that as many as two thirds of all human embryos fail to develop successfully.[268]

Pro-life evangelicals believe that human life begins at conception. I share this belief from a genetic perspective, but the fact that a fertilized embryo is genetically human is self-evident and doesn't even begin to solve the ethical issue. Starting from the premise that human life begins at conception, unless someone or something more powerful than God is involved, to the same extent that God is actively involved in knitting us together in the womb, God either intentionally stops knitting or actively unravels what has already been knitted in an enormous number of human conceptions. We are left in the puzzling situation that what God does directly on a routine basis, we may never do. But we may do directly, even when it involves very large numbers, what God never does as in the case of our perceived national security when hostilities are pursued even when they don't rise to Just War standards.

It is not sufficient to say that this huge number of failed conceptions is simply a result of sin in some general sense as some evangelicals believe or, even less tenable, that somehow this is the work of the devil. It is not possible to have it both ways. Either God is actively involved in the process or God is not. If God is involved then the good work of the transmission of life can be thwarted only if something (sin) or someone (the devil) is stronger than God and able to thwart God's purposes. There is another possibility: God's sovereignty covers both the procreation and miscreation that is simply what happens in the wombs of women in the real world, fallen though it may be.

Because the charge of murder has been so freely used by those opposed to abortion at any time or place or under any circumstances, it has resulted in an inability to hear (or be heard by, sadly) anyone who has more to say on the issue. One relevant argument, though, involves revisiting our

---

[267] March of Dimes. "Miscarriage." Last reviewed November 2017. www.marchofdimes.org/complications/miscarriage.aspx. Accessed 16 March 2019.

[268] Stanford University Medical Center. "Which fertilized eggs will become healthy human fetuses? Researchers predict with 93% accuracy." 4 October 2010. www.sciencedaily.com/releases/2010/10/101003205930.htm. Accessed 20 March 2019.

understanding of what is taking place, particularly with regard to abortion in the early stages of pregnancy which is when the vast majority of both abortions and miscarriages take place. Why is this relevant? It is because humanity is a part of nature not so removed from the rest of creation that we cannot see valid comparisons with other forms of life. As noted earlier, even though they are genetically identical, there is a major difference between a chicken and the egg from which it comes. Similarly, there is an order of magnitude difference between a human embryo and a fully developed human being. This developmental understanding seems much more consistent with what happens in so many human fertilizations that never result in live births totally apart from induced abortions. When sperm and egg unite, no one questions the innocence of that which has been conceived. However, if we insist that from this moment on we can speak only of a baby then the ethical problems for Christians have just begun.

At the risk of being overly repetitive, most evangelicals simply take it for granted that the taking of innocent life for reasons of American national security is acceptable and presents no moral problem at all. Regardless of that conviction, it still could be the case that the taking of innocent life for national security interests is as wrong as doing it in the case of abortion. This is a consistent position, and it resolves the difficulty of coming up with another clear principle, which is proving to be very difficult to do. Here, the same principle that disallows abortion disallows the killing of the innocent by Christians in the military, but most evangelicals would resist this.

There must be some sort of witness of the Spirit by which it can be said "killing of innocents for American national security is okay, but abortion is not because the Spirit convinces us that it is so." With more than two centuries of early Christian history forbidding Christians from taking any life in wartime, not just innocent life, one apparently needs special insight by which a distinction can be seen that no one else can see. For those for whom this special insight is not available, because the Spirit presumably does not bear witness to unbelievers as to believers, it sounds like evangelicals are simply saying, "Taking innocent life in cases involving American national security is sad but necessarily allowable, but taking innocent life by abortion is always wrong … because we say so."

It still leaves the question, if in fact the taking of innocent life for reasons of American national security is acceptable, why could there not be other circumstances that would allow it? This prohibition of abortion is viewed by many, if not most, evangelicals as an absolute. Many are not comfortable even with allowances for rape or incest. Though less dogmatically, many suspect that even in situations where there is a threat to the life of the mother the effort should be made to treat it medically without resorting to abortion. An absolute, by definition, allows no exceptions. Whatever else "*Thou shalt not kill*" is, it is clearly not an absolute either in the Scriptures or in practice by evangelicals in the US today.

We've touched on other instances besides national defense where evangelicals tolerate the loss of innocent life for the sake of what in practice amounts to a higher principle. Uncomfortable as it may be, it is necessary to dig a bit deeper. It may well feel as though we are on a "slippery slope." This may be true, but the slope is at least as much behind us as it is in front of us. Though it usually has a negative connotation, it is the context which determines whether a slippery slope is a good thing or not. For somebody on crutches it's a bad thing. For somebody on skis it's not.

Chapter 13

Slippery Slope

"Put your sword back in its place," Jesus said to him, "for all who draw the sword will die by the sword."
Matthew 26:52

The slippery slope was first encountered long ago when Augustine articulated the Just War doctrine. It was meant to be a Christian doctrine from the start, but it was also a departure from historic Christian practice. Though it justified the taking of human life, including the inadvertent taking of innocent life in wartime, Augustine carefully sought to protect innocent life to the extent possible. But while the taking of human life was substantially restrained by the doctrine he articulated, most importantly, it no longer prohibited it in any sort of absolute way.

What could possibly justify this? Augustine saw that, when confronted with a danger that threatens all that is sacred and good about life in society, as did Bonhoeffer centuries later, the use of force to protect that society and those who comprise it was not only justified, but necessary ... but not without limitations. When C.S. Lewis wrote the powerful piece "Why I Am Not a Pacifist" he was invoking the same thinking. By this reckoning, there is a virtue that lies between two vices. When the injustice of unwarranted mortal danger faces a society, we might diagram it like this:

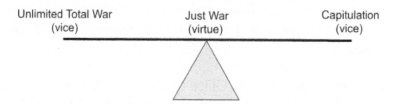

| Unlimited Total War (vice) | Just War (virtue) | Capitulation (vice) |

This kind of thinking should move us in our understanding of how to respond to other issues and not simply to those related to justice in war. In all that follows, two things should be clear. First, balance and compromise are not the same thing. Sometimes compromise is good, but if we compromise between a bad thing and a good thing, that compromise is a bad thing. Second, if we balance a bad thing with another bad thing, that is a bad thing. Two wrongs don't make a right. However, when there is no actual absolute, such as *"Love the Lord your God with all your heart and with all your soul and with all your mind ... Love your neighbor as yourself"*[269] then virtue does not consist in making an absolute out of that which is not. That is absolutism which, in fact, is a vice. Our duty is to find that virtue which comprises the right balance between too much of something that is otherwise good and too little of it. Other circumstances cry out for the kind of balance Augustine, Bonhoeffer and Lewis sought.

Which Innocent Lives Matter?

In the pages that follow we are going to discuss the taking of innocent lives as it relates to gun control, capital punishment, the taking of life by police and preventable deaths due to poverty related issues. All of these are "sanctity of life" issues though, along with the taking of innocent life in war, they are often not recognized as such by evangelicals. Nonetheless, evangelicals play a very large role in how these issues impact the lives of all Americans and many outside of America as well. The final portion of this section will focus on issues for which evangelicals are responsible, positively and negatively, that relate to this broader group of issues.

There are more than eleven thousand gun murders in the US annually. Virtually every other highly developed country in the world has stricter gun laws and far lower murder rates than does the US. According to Pew Research Center data analyzed in 2017 for *Christianity Today* magazine, *"white evangelicals are more likely than members of other faith groups or the average citizen to own a gun; 41 percent do, compared to 30 percent of Americans overall."*[270]

The first chart below, from the UN Office of Drugs and Crime, lists countries in their order of development. It shows only murders using guns. The second chart from the World Health Organization shows total murders, not only murders using guns. As the second chart shows, fewer gun murders in these countries does not mean that they murder people at the same rate as

---

[269] Matthew 22:37-39.
[270] Shellnutt, Kate. *"Packing in the Pews: The Connection Between God and Guns,"* Christianity Today, 8 November 2017. www.christianitytoday.com/news/2017/november/god-gun-control-white-evangelicals-texas-church-shooting.html. Accessed 20 March 2019.

in the US just using other means. The third chart shows the impact of allowing or denying the purchase and possession of assault type weapons.

There are way more gun murders per 100,00 people in the US and way more murders of all kinds per 100,000 people in the US than in other developed countries. There are fewer gun deaths in these countries by a factor of ten and fewer murders in these countries by a factor of five. *US News and World Report* has done a highly informative study on homicide in America. It shows that in the US, despite highly exaggerated claims by Donald Trump to the contrary, the vast majority of homicide victims are killed by people of their own race.[271] Even if we take out all African American murders, which no legitimate study would, and take into account only white American murders, the rate of murders per 100,000 people is about three times as high as any other developed nation.

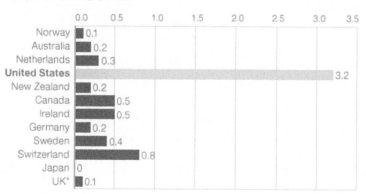

Gun murders in developed countries
Listed in Human Development Index order

Rate per 100,000 of population

Country	Rate
Norway	0.1
Australia	0.2
Netherlands	0.3
United States	3.2
New Zealand	0.2
Canada	0.5
Ireland	0.5
Germany	0.2
Sweden	0.4
Switzerland	0.8
Japan	0
UK*	0.1

*England and Wales only
Source: UNODC. Latest data available for each country (2004-2010)

---

[271]Cella, Matthew and Neuhauser, Alan. "Race and Homicide in America, by the Numbers." *US News & World Report,* 29 November 2016. www.usnews.com/news/articles/2016-09-29/race-and-homicide-in-america-by-the-numbers. Accessed 20 March 2019.

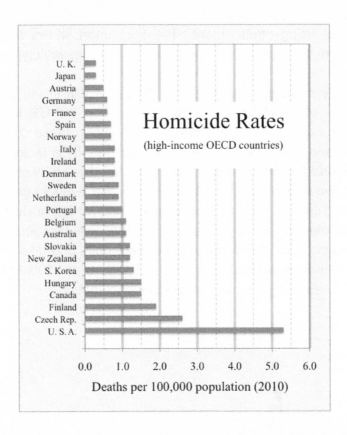

*OECD: Organisation for Economic Cooperation and Development

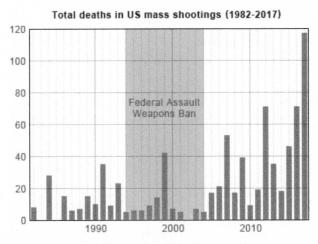

Many American evangelicals are as vigorously supportive of Second Amendment rights as they are opposed to abortion and homosexuality. Here the sanctity of the lives of innocent murder victims, past and future, is

subordinated not just to the right of self defense, but to the right of preparedness for a self defense the occasion for which is statistically negligible. That said, eleven thousand murders annually is a very high number. This is especially so when the number includes atrocities like the school shootings at Columbine, Sandy Hook and Parkland, the concert mass shooting from the MGM Grand Hotel in Las Vegas, the church and synagogue mass murders in Charleston, Sutherland Springs, and Pittsburgh, and other equally tragic occurrences.

None of these were murdered by foreign terrorists. In most mass shootings in the US innocent victims are gunned down by angry white Americans. Clearly mental illness is a factor in some or many of these, but it is also clear that at present there is no effective mechanism available to prevent these weapons from getting into the hands of people who should not have them. Background checks are certainly part of the solution, but in many cases the perpetrators of these violent crimes had passed background checks.

The victims of these shootings and their families are deserving of our utmost sympathy and support, but pretty much everyone is tired of being offered our prayers publicly. In fact, many consider it insulting, and that is our problem, not theirs. The unwavering and absolutely crucial evangelical support of the overall policies of an administration for which easy access to guns is largely non-negotiable gives evangelicals substantial ownership of this regardless of the personal convictions of individual evangelicals. If our concern is for innocent life, we can no more remove gun control from the discussion than we can any other instance whereby we allow or take the lives of innocents.

We tolerate these weapons and the murders committed with them because of a fear driven, highly remote possibility that we will actually need them for our own self defense. Or even more untenable, that we will need them to defend ourselves against our own government. The likelihood of one being murdered with a gun in the United States is less than three in a million. The likelihood of waking up tomorrow to news of a mass murder involving an assault weapon taking place somewhere in the US, often a school or place of worship, is much higher.[272] It is possible to limit the accessibility of these weapons, to institute strong controls, and still provide for an individual's second amendment rights, but we lack both evangelical support and the moral will.

Capital punishment has taken many innocent lives along with the lives of those that many or most would agree were deserving of death for their crimes. The controversial then Republican governor of Illinois declared a moratorium on capital punishment in his state in 1999 when it became clear that the system was totally broken. African Americans were being subjected to disturbing prosecutorial abuses and conviction by all white juries, especially when the victim was white. They were subject to capital punishment at high rates for murders of which many were later shown to be innocent.[273]

About ten years later another Illinois governor, a Democrat, outlawed capital punishment entirely. Today there is strong pressure to restore it there in cases where a law enforcement officer has been killed in the line of duty. Many evangelicals are in favor of capital punishment and many are saddened when it is wrongly applied, but see that as acceptable collateral damage for the perceived deterrent effect and resulting security benefit for all. Again, this is not an argument for or against capital punishment per se, but an example of a willingness to tolerate the deaths of those not deserving it for the sake of a principle that subordinates the innocent individual's right to life to a compelling higher need. This compelling higher "need" is thought to justify the belief that capital punishment is warranted even if there are abuses. There is an actual need for a more just balance.

More recently controversial are the deaths of black males at the hands of law enforcement officers recorded on videos that would result in a level of outrage that would be epic were the officers black and those who were shot white. Convictions of law enforcement officers responsible for these deaths are rare. None of this should be read as an argument against the legitimacy of the Second Amendment, capital punishment or strong law enforcement;

---

[272] This is not to say that more people are murdered with assault weapons than with other weapons; rather, the impact of mass shootings involving assault weapons is disproportionately impactful on our national sense of safety and well-being.

[273] Armstrong, K. and Mills, S. "Part 1: Death Row justice derailed." *Chicago Tribune,* 14 November 1999. www.chicagotribune.com/investigations/ct-xpm-1999-11-14-chi-991114deathillinois1-story.html. Accessed 20 March 2019.

rather it is meant to point out how in these instances the right to life of innocents is subordinated to other concerns deemed to be more compelling. The voices of evangelicals are surprisingly muted in each of these instances, though they cry out for a substantially more just balance.

Perhaps more importantly, poverty and preventable deaths of those living in poverty, is an even larger, more compelling life issue that must be re-addressed in the context of this discussion. The need for humanitarian aid in the world today is as great as it has ever been. The number of refugees fleeing terrible life-threatening situations is perhaps greater than it has ever been before in terms of sheer numbers and the percentages of particular ethnic populations. At just over $30 billion, the United States gives more to foreign humanitarian aid than any country in the world.[274] Though there is a strong move currently underway to reduce that aid, the role America has played needs to be recognized and appreciated. When we look at it from another perspective, though, the picture shifts. When we take the comparative amount of humanitarian aid the US provides as a percentage of national income, America does not even make the top ten of generous nations worldwide. The United Arab Emirates and Turkey, both Muslim majority countries, give higher percentages of national income to humanitarian aid than does the United States.[275]

Let's put the kind of needs we seek to meet by humanitarian aid in very practical terms. According to the United Nations International Children's Emergency Fund (UNICEF), 5.4 million children below the age of five died worldwide in 2017. Nearly a million more who were under the age of fourteen died in the same time frame.[276] This means that more than ten children under five die every minute, plus two more per minute under the age of fourteen, all from largely preventable causes.

With the evangelical focus squarely on abortion, there is little recognition of the necessary connectedness of this with other major life issues. Apart from block support by evangelicals, the sustaining of the current American

---

[274] Myers, Joe. "Foreign aid: These countries are the most generous." *World Economic Forum*, 19 August 2016. www.weforum.org/agenda/2016/08/foreign-aid-these-countries-are-the-most-generous/. Accessed 20 March 2019.

[275] Ibid.

[276] UNICEF. "Child Mortality." March 2018, data.unicef.org/topic/child-survival/under-five-mortality/. Accessed 20 March 2019.

policies and practices that militate against a more broadly understood sanctity of life would be impossible. In addition to lax gun laws and utter disdain for the core issues behind "Black Lives Matter," these include the now senseless support of the Saudis in Yemen, the rollback of spending on behalf of the poor, and the accelerated brutal separation of children from their parents at the border. Along with the assault on vital American institutions and the almost total debasing of political speech in America by the president who is the strong favorite of evangelicals, these constitute an unwelcome part of the "blessing" America is receiving from the hands of conservative Christians.

For a Christian in America, there is never a simply "binary" (either/or) choice when it comes to elections. From the time of Christ, followers of Jesus have believed that we are called first to do the right thing, not the expedient thing, even when the expedient thing "works" or works to our advantage. In the last election, many strong believers wrote in a candidate rather than vote for one of two morally objectionable candidates. Meanwhile, the significant majority of white evangelicals voted for perhaps the most morally objectionable candidate possible by historic Christian standards. He could not have been elected and could not stay in power unless supported by evangelicals. As the strongest voting block in the country today, evangelicals inherit a large portion of the responsibility for what is now unfolding in our midst. Any moral high ground we may have occupied in the past has been abandoned despite attempts to claim otherwise.

About God, war and guns, we need to be clear. It is not God who allows us to kill innocents in the interests of our national security or as a by-product of our personal security fears. It is we ourselves. It is our nation. It is not God or the Scriptures. We can make the valid argument that our government is God-ordained. Though this is true, according to the New Testament, it cannot be unique to a United States which wouldn't even come into existence for more than a millennium and a half after the last writings of the NT. The Apostle Paul was writing to people who were subjects of the pagan Roman empire and subject to the authority of its government when he wrote: *"Let everyone be subject to the governing authorities, for there is no authority except that which God has established. The authorities that exist have been established by God."* [277]

Paul was neither condemning nor was he justifying specific actions of the Roman government which presumably had more to criticize than does our own. He was simply acknowledging its God given authority. At the risk of being overly repetitive, it is solely through the authority of our Constitution and our laws that extreme measures can be taken such as are necessary for our national security, public safety or personal protection. To the extent that these are legitimate functions of government, in the same way that our nation can permit what is needed and desired in such compelling circumstances as these, it can permit it in other compelling circumstances as well.

A strong American military has played an enormously important role in modern world history, and the constitutional right to own a gun can be based on legitimate self defense considerations. Though neither of these is mandated nor specifically allowed by Scripture, we believe them to be consistent with freedoms God allows. Apart from a biblical principle that permits these but prohibits abortion, why should they be treated differently? Abortion laws currently on the books provide for both accountability and limitations while preserving a woman's right to decide such an intensely personal issue. There is legitimate middle ground regarding these vitally important life issues. Are there legitimate evangelical concerns? Yes there are. Is there a needed place for an evangelical voice in these conversations? Yes there is. But if we forfeit the right to be heard by insisting on simplistic absolutist solutions to complex problems, then we need to realize that the fault is ours, not simply that of those around us. When faced with the compelling circumstances which create the tension inherent in each of these issues, we must find a just balance.

Abortion, Adoption, Accountability

What about the compelling circumstance of the relationship between abortion and poverty? As it turns out, there is a very strong relationship and not just of the extreme kind I described in Congo. The two primary sources of research and statistics concerning abortion are the Guttmacher Institute and the US Centers for Disease Control and Protection (CDC).

---

[277] Romans 13:1.

Guttmacher, which does extensive research on reproductive issues, has a very uneasy relationship with Christian pro-life groups which use its research and statistics freely when it serves the pro-life narrative, but are often silent or critical otherwise because of the unambiguous support that the Institute gives to women's reproductive rights.

Though the charge of murder is heard the loudest, evangelicals often see abortion first as a sexual issue for which women must bear primary responsibility, in much the same way as they must bear primary responsibility for sexual encounters of the sort alleged by Dr. Ford regarding Judge Kavanaugh. Why? Because they, in many cases, willingly placed themselves in situations that, in retrospect, they might have, could have or should have avoided.

By this account, the first question for pregnant women considering an abortion, usually unasked but already answered, is *"Why did you have sex when you weren't prepared for the consequences?"* If the first sincere question is *"Why are you contemplating an abortion?"* it reveals something entirely different. Though many will also give answers like *"I'm not ready to have a child"* or *"I'm done having children"* or *"I don't want to be a single mother"* or *"It would interfere with my education or career"* or *"I'm not mature enough to have a child,"* there is one factor that looms over and stands behind almost all of these. According to the Guttmacher research, abortion and poverty are powerfully, closely and increasingly linked, both in the US and in the rest of the world.

Research from the Guttmacher Institute shows that African American and Latino women, as a percentage of the population, are significantly more likely to have an abortion than are white women in the US. Regardless of race, though, approximately half of the women of all races who have abortions are living below the poverty line when they become pregnant. Of the other half who are above the poverty line, half are low income. This means that for 75 percent of American women seeking abortions, whatever other reasons they also may give, their being poor is a powerful factor.[278]

---

[278] Guttmacher Institute. "United States Abortion Demographics." www.guttmacher.org/united-states/abortion/demographics. Accessed 20 March 2019.

According to the most recent statistics, the number of women who self-identify as evangelicals and had abortions was 13 percent (more than 100,000) of all women who had abortions in the US; 24 percent were Catholic and 62 percent self-identified as having religious affiliation. The vast majority of pregnancies resulting in abortion were unplanned, but more than half the women who had abortions were using some form of birth control in the month they conceived, and approximately half were living with their husband or other male partner. 59 percent already had a child or children.Though poor sexual choices, from an evangelical perspective, are part of the picture, the idea that the reason that abortions happen is primarily a matter of irresponsible women making bad sexual choices doesn't nearly convey the reality confronting these women.[279]

Adoption is usually put forward as a legitimate option. Those who have sacrificially opened their homes to adopt children are among the most admirable people in the world, particularly those who are willing to adopt a baby of another race or with challenging physical disabilities. We owe them a debt of gratitude, but this is not anywhere close to a sufficient solution. There were just under 900,000 abortions in the US in 2016 based on state-level statistics, and the numbers have gone down substantially from more than 1.3 million annually in the early and mid-nineties.[280] Compare this with about 135,000 adoptions annually.[281] Black and Hispanic children are somewhat less likely to be adopted than are white children. In addition to adoption as an option, it is true that some infants go into foster care, but the large majority in foster care are older. Approximately 30,000 children under the age of one are in foster care. Still, the overall difference between the number of abortions and the number of adoptions and infant foster care placements is around 650,000. Of these, those for whom poverty is a substantial factor number in excess of 500,000. Adoption is a great solution when it works, but it is not an adequate solution.

Surely, if we evangelicals are going to insist that access to abortions be seriously curtailed or eliminated altogether, we are willing to give increased

[279] Guttmacher Institute. "Induced Abortion in the United States." January 2018. www.guttmacher.org/fact-sheet/induced-abortion-united-states. Accessed 20 March 2019.
[280] Abort73.com. "Facts About Abortion: U.S. Abortion Statistics." abort73.com/abortion_facts/us_abortion_statistics/. Accessed 20 March 2019.
[281] Adoption Network Law Center. "Adoption Statistics." adoptionnetwork.com/adoption-statistics. Accessed 20 March 2019.

special help to the more than 500,000 women seeking abortions for whom poverty is reality, aren't we? Then next year 500,000 more? Many would say *"teach them not to have sex outside of marriage,"* but few would ever even make an attempt to get close enough to these girls and women to have any sort of credible right to teach them anything.

If you are an evangelical, ask yourself a question. If I went to my church and asked the congregation to either give regularly and sacrificially, over and above what they are now giving to the church or Christian causes, in order to help women like this, or to pay more taxes so this help could be given, what would the response be? As a long time pastor of a very giving evangelical church I can tell you. Most would say that this is clearly a sad situation, but few would do any additional practical thing to help because we don't believe we have any personal responsibility for these women. We believe that we have fulfilled our responsibility when we try to keep them from making the choice to have an abortion.

If abortion is a monstrous evil as R.C. Sproul indicated, surely we would be willing to tolerate, for others if not for ourselves, what many evangelicals perceive to be a lesser evil to combat it.[282] This is the dilemma that faced Dr. Koop when, as Surgeon General, he worked to fulfill his responsibility to address the AIDS epidemic and proposed sex education and condoms and was criticized by many evangelicals and Catholics. Promoting sex education in schools and making birth control available either through governmental or non-governmental organizations to reduce the number of abortions has met with exactly the same response from these groups. The fact that this might possibly be construed as encouraging sex outside of marriage makes this a non-starter though this has been a powerful force in reducing the overall number of abortions in the past several years. In Colorado, where we live with family a few months every year, the number of abortions dropped 64 percent in a recent eight year period mostly due to the availability and use of Intrauterine Devices (IUDs) and other contraception methods.[283] Abortions are relatively easily available in

---

[282] The fact that evangelicals might perceive something to be evil that actually may not be evil, which is a distinct possibility, would keep this from being some form of "two wrongs seeking to make a right."
[283] Brown, Jennifer. "IUD program leads to big decline in teen pregnancies, abortions in Colorado," *Denver Post*, 1 December 2017.
www.denverpost.com/2017/11/30/colorado-teen-pregnancy-abortion-rates-drop-free-low-cost-iud/.
Accessed 20 March 2019.

Colorado so this drop is not due to the closing of clinics providing abortions or to restrictive state laws.

Where does this leave us? We are in favor of no abortions, no morning after pill, no public sex education, no availability of birth control through any sort of government funded programs, no increase in ongoing assistance, and almost certainly no personal assistance to women and children once the child is born, no adoptions by same sex couples, even when adoptions come nowhere near the number needed, and no discussion of any real alternatives besides total abstinence.

One common denominator among all of these? For most evangelicals they cost us little or nothing. We can stand against all of these things and never spend an additional penny and never do a single thing except open our mouths and vote. We can do so thinking that we occupy the moral high ground without taking any personal responsibility, because we perceive them to be other people's sins and other people's problems. We loudly proclaim the right to life, but fail to see that the right to life and the right to the means to life are vitally connected. This sounds exactly like those whom Jesus castigated when he said, *"And you experts in the law, woe to you, because you load people down with burdens they can hardly carry, and you yourselves will not lift one finger to help them."*[284] We are demanding only one solution to the problem, one we cannot live up to ourselves, judging from the more than 100,000 evangelical women and girls who have abortions each year.[285] Our "one solution" response is a cheap way to give the illusion that we truly are different from those we believe to be morally deficient. Our response or lack of response to these women and girls would indicate that we are not part of the solution; rather, we are a large part of the problem.

Many evangelicals have strong concerns about accountability. Many buy into the idea that there should be strict work requirements for any sort of public assistance. This is true even if it means that an already financially distressed young woman gives birth to a baby and, after an otherwise reasonable period to adjust, but while the child is still young, must leave her child in order to work. Often this involves working at a job that pays at a

[284] Luke 11:46.
[285] Guttmacher Institute. www.guttmacher.org/united-states/abortion/demographics.

level that she cannot afford child care and may not have enough for food, clothing or adequate housing. The plight of these women evokes little sympathy from those who believe the poor are essentially responsible for their own poverty and are primarily "takers" as opposed to "makers" who earn their keep. If its her own fault, why should we get worked up about it?

Many evangelicals believe that there are millions scamming and abusing the system, and the first step to eliminate this is to cut back on what we spend, or to require that the above mentioned work requirements be imposed for any benefits. Similar to what is being alleged about widespread voter fraud, for which almost no evidence exists, and what is believed by many to be a caravan of the destitute seeking to "invade" America, anecdotal or rare egregious examples are put forward as proof that the problem of scamming is widespread. See Appendix 5. The proposed 2019 US Federal budget will result in large cuts to Medicaid over the next few years. This is one of the primary programs supporting these women. Do you hear loud evangelical opposition to this?

We take for granted that we as a people have the right to seek and provide for our national security. We also take for granted that we as a people have a right to defend ourselves and our loved ones. Because the Scripture, especially the New Testament, does not specifically address either of these with regard to any particular nation or people, we have to infer that these rights are consistent with the freedoms God allows us.

One of the greatest freedoms we Americans have enjoyed historically is freedom of conscience. Our freedom of religion is one element of an even larger freedom of conscience. Most evangelicals believe, for reasons grounded in their faith, that the taking of innocent lives for national security purposes is warranted and acceptable to God. Though not large in number, there are certainly those who would disagree on Christian religious grounds. Though it involves the taking of lives, sometimes innocent ones, would you not resist any attempt to dissuade you from that conviction of conscience? The consciences of most evangelicals would not permit them to have an abortion, but does this warrant denying the same freedom of conscience to those who don't feel the same way? We may and do struggle with how to do that in a way that honors the conscience of both, but by simply working to enshrine in law a "solution" that denies that freedom to many is to impose a religious belief upon those who do not share it.

The lack of a principle that allows the killing of innocents in circumstances involving national security, but forbids abortion, even in light of a compelling developmental understanding of human life that would allow it, means that the prohibition of abortion is an essentially religious dogmatic prohibition. It is thought to be wrong because we say so, and for many Christians that is enough. By what principle do we assert that this is a religious belief we can or should impose upon others?   The 13 percent of evangelical women seeking abortions in the US account for about the same number of abortions as there are adoptions. Perhaps a goal of eliminating, to the extent possible, the perceived need for abortions among evangelicals is a worthy goal for the church. This may be a program for the church, but not for the church to impose.

Rights, Religion and Roe

This brings us to the point where we need to briefly revisit our understanding of rights. As we have seen when it comes to abortion, though not when it comes to our national security, evangelicals generally take the view that there is an absolute universal right to life from conception onward. In every other facet of our national life, rights are progressive in the sense that they are seen as very strong with regard to some, but not so strong with relation to others based on age, citizenship, criminality or other considerations. Take again the rights to life, liberty and the pursuit of happiness. As we have discussed at length, none of these is absolute.

Immigrants who are not yet naturalized or immigrants who are in the US without credentials, do not have the same rights to the liberty and the pursuit of happiness enjoyed by American citizens, even though we say that these rights are *"endowed by their Creator"* and not merely by our Constitution. Additionally, the pursuit of liberty and happiness is appropriately constrained with regard to children who have not reached the age of majority, or those simply constrained by the fact that their rights end where the rights of others begins.

The Roe vs. Wade Supreme Court decision in 1973 provided a framework legalizing abortion that allowed for a progression of rights that shifted as gestational age increased. It focused largely on "viability" defined as the ability of a child to live outside the body of the mother. It provided for a woman to have a largely unlimited right to an abortion in the first three months of her pregnancy. In the second three months of a pregnancy it gave each state a strong right to legislate limitations for the purpose of protecting the mother. The end of the second trimester was the point at which the Court regarded viability to begin. During the last trimester, and after the fetus was considered "viable," state laws were permitted to restrict and prohibit abortion except when an abortion would be necessary to preserve the health of the mother.[286]

Progress in medical technology has resulted in viability at an earlier age, but not much earlier, than when Roe vs. Wade was decided. In 1992 the Court reaffirmed the fundamental right of a pregnant woman to determine whether to bear a child, subject to limitations, but moved from a focus on gestational trimesters. The Court deemed unconstitutional any "undue burden" on women seeking abortions otherwise consistent with Roe vs. Wade, but as the age of viability decreased, it allowed states more latitude in restricting abortions.

Roe has been widely denounced by evangelicals, though the first trimester, when the vast majority of induced abortions take place, is the same gestational period during which God sovereignly receives back into the divine bosom the vast majority of those who are spontaneously aborted for natural causes. Regardless of the circumstances, we can trust that God receives them all. The small numbers of induced abortions during the latter periods largely parallels the small number of unborn whom God takes sovereignly during the second and third trimesters of pregnancy. And the fact remains, unless God is absent from the process, God takes far more unborn lives than does abortion. This is not blasphemy nor is it an indictment of God, but a measurable reality in the world God created and sovereignly sustains.

---

[286] Encyclopedia.com. "Roe vs. Wade." *West's Encyclopedia of American Law*, 2005. www.encyclopedia.com/social-sciences-and-law/law/court-cases/roe-v-wade. Accessed 20 March 2019.

According to the CDC, approximately 91.5 percent of abortions take place in the first thirteen weeks, the first trimester. Approximately 7.2 percent take place between the end of the thirteenth week and the end of the twentieth week, well before the end of the second trimester. After the twentieth week, 1.3 percent of abortions take place.[287] Many of these take place before the end of the second trimester and an extremely small number take place after that. A far greater number of miscarriages occur overall in nature.[288]

The idea that women, many of whom are in abusive relationships, serious emotional instability or are faced with giving birth to a child with serious birth defects … the idea that they don't agonize over a decision to have an abortion anytime, but especially after the 20th week, is just not in touch with their reality. If anyone thinks that there are no deeply committed Christian women who fit into this category they are wrong. One particularly sad case in my experience involved a strongly pro-life family agonizing over but ultimately deciding to have a late term abortion due to profoundly increasing physiological problems with the unborn child and a clear prognosis of death shortly after birth. Similarly, the recent moving story of a strongly Catholic obstetrician, working in Africa and facing a genuine need for a safe abortion well into her second trimester,[289] calls us to look again at this most difficult of issues through the eyes of others whose experience and insight may be far different from ours.

In his 2019 State of the Union address, President Trump said, "*Lawmakers in New York cheered with delight upon the passage of legislation that would allow a baby to be ripped from the mother's womb moments before birth.*" The level of mischaracterization and irresponsibility in this statement is staggering. No one has a third trimester abortion just for the hell of it. This bill had been strongly advocated by a woman named Erika Christensen who, because of the previously existing law in New York had to fly to Colorado for an abortion at 32 weeks gestation. Late in her pregnancy she learned that there were multiple malformations that the

---

[287] Centers for Disease Control and Prevention. "Data&Statistics - Reproductive Health." www.cdc.gov/reproductivehealth/data_stats/index.htm. Accessed 20 March 2019.

[288] One might argue that a significant number of these miscarriages are due to chromosomal problems, but most pro-birth advocates do not recognize fetal defects as a legitimate reason for an abortion so this is a moot point in their opposition to abortion for any reason.

[289] Luckett, Rebecca. "I'm a Catholic Obstetrician who had an abortion.This is not politics or religion. It's life." USA Today, 19 March 2018. www.usatoday.com/story/opinion/2018/03/19/catholic-obstetrician-who-had-abortion-not-politics-religion-its-life-rebecca-luckett-column/416614002/. Accessed 20 March 2019.

doctors said were "incompatible with life" and would result in suffocation during or shortly after birth. She waited to confirm the diagnosis with a sonogram and by the time she got the results she was well past the twenty four week cut-off for an abortion in New York.[290] The New York law referred to by the president and a similar Virginia law provide for late term abortions for reasons of maternal health, non-viability and severe fetal anomaly in circumstances like those experienced by Erika Christensen, the couple described earlier and the Catholic obstetrician. Sadly, the poisonous atmosphere is made even more toxic by many Christians.

Were you in the situation of the family or physician above, would you want your church congregation second guessing your decision? Would you want to have to appear before a judge to approve your decision? Is it not more appropriate that this decision be made by those directly involved? Along with evangelical parents of children with non-conforming sexual identities, evangelical women or parents of women or girls who choose to have an abortion are among the loneliest people in the world. They realize that the ideology of their evangelical circle leaves no room for their actual circumstances which don't fit into a neat ideological package.

The statistics compiled by the Guttmacher Institute and the Centers for Disease Control, are often used by evangelicals when they can be construed to support a narrative that negatively labels those who do abortions and attributes only the worst of motives for their doing it. By this narrative, organizations like Planned Parenthood are akin to the spawn of the devil. They are portrayed as nefarious ghouls, with no regard for the unborn at any stage of pregnancy, as they simply dupe women who don't know any better into having abortions so they can sell body parts. This simply isn't true. Are there bad actors in the mix? There may be, just like there are bad doctors, lawyers, soldiers and pastors. Do others portray evangelicals in opposite but similar untrue ways? They do, but there's a difference. Christians are supposed to follow a higher call. There's room for middle ground here.

---

[290] Belkin, Lisa. 'We are not Monsters': Parents Go Public About Late-Term Abortions." LIFE Parenting, 18 February 2019. www.huffpost.com/entry/we-are-not-monsters-parents-go-public-about-late-term-abortions_l_5c6afe6de4b01cea6b8815ff. Accessed 20 March 2019.

In all that has been said above, I am not advocating for abortion. I am saying that abortion as an issue cannot be separated from the real people and real life circumstances of those who contemplate and perhaps choose it. There are instances, not just limited to rape, incest, health of the mother or poverty, that might be justification for a woman or girl to conclude that it is neither wise nor good for her to see her pregnancy through to term. Whatever justification there might or might not be for that decision, if she does decide to carry to term, she will receive little or no help from her fellow citizens, and that includes evangelicals. Those who have no stake in her decision, one way or the other, have no business making that decision for her, and they have no business placing obstacles in the way.

Chapter 14

Uncomfortable Truths

"'What should we do then?' the crowd asked. John answered,'the man with two tunics should share with him who has none, and the one who has food should do the same.'"
Luke 3:10,11

These words of John the Baptist describe what most of us would consider generosity to a fault. They were not spoken to those who were followers of Jesus. They were spoken to those who were being prepared to be followers of Jesus. Their relative prosperity, and the bar was a low one if having two tunics was the standard, was sufficient to require their generosity. This is a perspective of prosperity and generosity viewed from the bottom. What we would consider generosity to a fault is just the biblical view of generosity.

If not the most prosperous and secure nation in the history of the world, America is certainly among a very small number that could even attempt a rival claim. For those who are the primary beneficiaries of this prosperity, for evangelicals especially, there are a number of biblical truths which are greatly discomforting or fail to be only because we ignore them. Jesus said, *"Truly I tell you, it is difficult for a rich man to enter the kingdom of heaven."* [291] Most of us do not believe that for a minute. But, he was speaking to his followers when he said *"Blessed are you poor for yours is the kingdom of God"* and, in the same breath, *"But woe to you who are rich, for you have already received your comfort."* This didn't come out of nowhere, Jesus first learned this at the feet of his mother. When she learned she was going to give birth to the Messiah, one of the verses she sang was *"He has filled the hungry with good things but has sent the rich away empty."*[292] The point is a simple one: God really cares about how we care about the disparity.

The idea that there are genuine dangers associated with our riches seldom occurs to us. The idea that what little lasting benefit we gain from our riches has already been experienced, except to the extent that those riches are shared in mitigating the needs of those most deeply in need, may sound

---

[291] Matthew 19:23.
[292] Mary's Magnificat, Luke 1:53.

more like a nightmare than a dream, certainly not the American Dream. Incremental increases in the prosperity and security of the most prosperous and secure nation in history have relatively little value in the kingdom of God. The very idea that this could be true seems downright offensive.

History will judge America however it does, and it will judge this generation of Americans however it does. The people of God, totally apart from any final judgment of history or others, will be held accountable by God for their attitude toward and their engagement with and their actual care for the poor. We can argue about how best to do that, but we cannot argue the fact that God requires it of us.

The people of Israel, in the time of Joseph, were refugees and immigrants in Egypt. By the generosity of the Egyptian pharaoh and people, their lives were saved and God's good plans for the world were preserved. Jesus, Mary and Joseph fled to Egypt and were sheltered there as refugees from the wrath of Herod. God's repeated admonitions to the people of Israel to welcome the "alien and stranger" were, as God repeatedly reminded them, because they too had been aliens and strangers. To think this has no implications for us in our attitude toward and treatment of refugees and immigrants defies belief. We can argue about how best to approach immigration and related refugee issues, especially as they apply to the poor, but we cannot argue the fact that God has very high expectations about how we welcome, think of and treat immigrants and refugees. Further, we cannot argue the fact that we are ultimately accountable, not just for our sentiments, but for our actual "doing" in that regard.

We can argue about how best to implement gun control, but we can't dispute the fact that Jesus declined to defend himself and constrained those closest to him to non-violence when they sought to defend him. To think that this has no implications for issues like gun control for Christians is simply not believable. Again, for those who follow Jesus, our support of the use of our military and how we participate or refuse to participate really matters. The Sermon on the Mount calls us to love our enemies. To think this has no implications for Christians regarding our view of the use of military force, especially if the tenets of a Just War are not met, is incomprehensible. Unless, of course, being an American holds equal or greater importance to our being Christian. The two cannot be conflated.

Jesus taught that we can't have two masters. If it is "America first" it can't be "Jesus first." If it is "Jesus first" it can't be "America first."

We can argue about how best to deal with the poor in our own country and abroad, but we can't dispute the fact that God cares mightily about whether we seriously focus on and engage in the mitigation of that poverty or not. The standard God has set, what we might call "generous to a fault," is actually the definition of biblical generosity. Evangelicals, especially those of us who are prosperous, have a difficult time knowing how to apply all of this personally because of the belief that heaven is assured for the believer, regardless of what we do or don't do. This feels uncomfortably different from that. "Poor" is quickly re-interpreted to mean mainly "poor in spirit." It is true that poverty of spirit is universal due to the universality of our sinfulness, but the kind of priority given to poverty of spirit by many evangelicals renders physical poverty less important in such a way that it also renders the clear teaching of Jesus about the priority of the poor in the Kingdom of God not understandable. The primary question raised by many evangelicals is *"How do we get to heaven?"* A more basic question is *"Is there enough substance in our lives even to get to heaven?"*

In the story of the sheep and the goats, Jesus pictured some on the way to heaven and some on the way to hell. In similarly disturbing language, Flannery O'Connor described a vision of those on their way to heaven. Mary Flannery O'Connor was a Catholic writer who was born in Georgia in 1925 and died there thirty-nine years later. She wrote using exaggeration and blunt imagery that many today might find offensive, but not dissimilar to the imagery invoked by Jesus. She wrote a wonderful short story entitled "Revelation" in which she records a vision of sorts experienced by *"Ruby Turpin, a respectable, hardworking, church-going woman"* as she saw herself. The story begins in a doctor's waiting room where Ruby is looking at all the occupants who are ungenerously described through the "top down" lens of her eyes. There is an altercation and a mentally disturbed girl throws a book at her, calls her a "warthog from hell" and tries to choke her. The story ends at the hog pen at Ruby's farm where she is hosing down her hogs and railing at God for the ugly judgment the girl had made. Here is the vision:

"Until the sun slipped finally behind the tree line, Mrs. Turpin remained there [at the hog pen] with her gaze bent to them [the hogs] as if she were absorbing some abysmal life-giving knowledge. At last she lifted her head. There was only a purple streak in the sky, cutting through a field of crimson and leading, like an extension of the highway, into the descending dusk. She raised her hands from the side of the pen in a gesture hieratic and profound. A visionary light settled in her eyes. She saw the streak as a vast swinging bridge extending upward from the earth through a field of living fire. Upon it a vast horde of souls were tumbling toward heaven. There were whole companies of white trash, clean for the first time in their lives, and bands of black n*ggers in white robes, and battalions of freaks and lunatics shouting and clapping and leaping like frogs. And bringing up the end of the procession was a tribe of people whom she recognized at once as those who, like herself and Claud [her husband], had always had a little of everything and the given wit to use it right. She leaned forward to observe them closer. They were marching behind the others with great dignity, accountable as they had always been for good order and common sense and respectable behavior. They, alone were on key. Yet she could see by their shocked and altered faces even their virtues were being burned away. She lowered hands and gripped the rail of the hog pen, her eyes small but fixed unblinkingly on what lay ahead. In a moment the vision faded but she remained where she was." [293]

Four suggestions: First, if you are a Christian and an American, decide whether you are going to be an American Christian or a Christian American. Second, do not simply identify the poor, but learn to identify with the poor (those on the bottom, economically and socially) and learn to see the Scriptures and the world through their eyes. Third, share what you have generously. Fourth, to the best of your ability, do what Jesus calls us to do in the Sermon on the Mount and leave the future to Him. We don't need detailed instructions for any of this. If it is in our hearts to do, we will find a way.

---

[293] O'Connor, Flannery. *"Revelation."* from *Everything That Rises Must Converge."* Farrar, Straus and Giroux, New York, January 1965.

Appendix 1: The Sermon on the Mount

Matthew 5:1-7:29

Now when Jesus saw the crowds, he went up on a mountainside and sat down. His disciples came to him, and he began to teach them.

He said:

"Blessed are the poor in spirit,
*   for theirs is the kingdom of heaven.*
Blessed are those who mourn,
*   for they will be comforted.*
Blessed are the meek,
*   for they will inherit the earth.*
Blessed are those who hunger and thirst for righteousness,
*   for they will be filled.*
Blessed are the merciful,
*   for they will be shown mercy.*
Blessed are the pure in heart,
*   for they will see God.*
Blessed are the peacemakers,
*   for they will be called children of God.*
Blessed are those who are persecuted because of righteousness,
*   for theirs is the kingdom of heaven.*

Blessed are you when people insult you, persecute you and falsely say all kinds of evil against you because of me. Rejoice and be glad, because great is your reward in heaven, for in the same way they persecuted the prophets who were before you.

You are the salt of the earth. But if the salt loses its saltiness, how can it be made salty again? It is no longer good for anything, except to be thrown out and trampled underfoot.

You are the light of the world. A town built on a hill cannot be hidden. Neither do people light a lamp and put it under a bowl. Instead they put it on its stand, and it gives light to everyone in the house. In the same way, let your light shine before others, that they may see your good deeds and glorify your Father in heaven.

Do not think that I have come to abolish the Law or the Prophets; I have not come to abolish them but to fulfill them. For truly I tell you, until heaven and earth disappear, not the smallest letter, not the least stroke of a pen, will by any means disappear from the Law until everything is accomplished. Therefore anyone who sets aside one of the least of these commands and teaches others accordingly will be called least in the kingdom of heaven, but whoever practices and teaches these commands will be called great in the kingdom of heaven. For I tell you that unless your righteousness surpasses that of the Pharisees and the teachers of the law, you will certainly not enter the kingdom of heaven.

You have heard that it was said to the people long ago, 'You shall not murder, and anyone who murders will be subject to judgment.' But I tell you that anyone who is angry with a brother or sister will be subject to judgment. Again, anyone who says to a brother or sister, 'Raca,' is answerable to the court. And anyone who says, 'You fool!' will be in danger of the fire of hell.

Therefore, if you are offering your gift at the altar and there remember that your brother or sister has something against you, leave your gift there in front of the altar. First go and be reconciled to them; then come and offer your gift.

Settle matters quickly with your adversary who is taking you to court. Do it while you are still together on the way, or your adversary may hand you over to the judge, and the judge may hand you over to the officer, and you may be thrown into prison. Truly I tell you, you will not get out until you have paid the last penny.

You have heard that it was said, 'You shall not commit adultery.' But I tell you that anyone who looks at a woman lustfully has already committed adultery with her in his heart. If your right eye causes you to stumble, gouge it out and throw it away. It is better for you to lose one part of your body than for your whole body to be thrown into hell. And if your right hand causes you to stumble, cut it off and throw it away. It is better for you to lose one part of your body than for your whole body to go into hell.

It has been said, 'Anyone who divorces his wife must give her a certificate of divorce.' But I tell you that anyone who divorces his wife, except for sexual immorality, makes her the victim of adultery, and anyone who marries a divorced woman commits adultery.

Again, you have heard that it was said to the people long ago, 'Do not break your oath, but fulfill to the Lord the vows you have made.' But I tell you, do not swear an oath at all: either by heaven, for it is God's throne; or by the earth, for it is his footstool; or by Jerusalem, for it is the city of the

Great King. And do not swear by your head, for you cannot make even one hair white or black. All you need to say is simply 'Yes' or 'No'; anything beyond this comes from the evil one.

You have heard that it was said, 'Eye for eye, and tooth for tooth.' But I tell you, do not resist an evil person. If anyone slaps you on the right cheek, turn to them the other cheek also. And if anyone wants to sue you and take your shirt, hand over your coat as well. If anyone forces you to go one mile, go with them two miles. Give to the one who asks you, and do not turn away from the one who wants to borrow from you.

You have heard that it was said, 'Love your neighbor and hate your enemy.' But I tell you, love your enemies and pray for those who persecute you, that you may be children of your Father in heaven. He causes his sun to rise on the evil and the good, and sends rain on the righteous and the unrighteous. If you love those who love you, what reward will you get? Are not even the tax collectors doing that? And if you greet only your own people, what are you doing more than others? Do not even pagans do that? Be perfect, therefore, as your heavenly Father is perfect.

Be careful not to practice your righteousness in front of others to be seen by them. If you do, you will have no reward from your Father in heaven.

So when you give to the needy, do not announce it with trumpets, as the hypocrites do in the synagogues and on the streets, to be honored by others. Truly I tell you, they have received their reward in full. But when you give to the needy, do not let your left hand know what your right hand is doing, so that your giving may be in secret. Then your Father, who sees what is done in secret, will reward you.

And when you pray, do not be like the hypocrites, for they love to pray standing in the synagogues and on the street corners to be seen by others. Truly I tell you, they have received their reward in full. But when you pray, go into your room, close the door and pray to your Father, who is unseen. Then your Father, who sees what is done in secret, will reward you. And when you pray, do not keep on babbling like pagans, for they think they will be heard because of their many words. Do not be like them, for your Father knows what you need before you ask him.

This, then, is how you should pray:

Our Father in heaven,
 hallowed be your name,
your kingdom come, your will be done,
 on earth as it is in heaven.
 Give us today our daily bread.

And forgive us our debts,
    as we also have forgiven our debtors.
And lead us not into temptation,
    but deliver us from the evil one.

For if you forgive other people when they sin against you, your heavenly Father will also forgive you. But if you do not forgive others their sins, your Father will not forgive your sins.

When you fast, do not look somber as the hypocrites do, for they disfigure their faces to show others they are fasting. Truly I tell you, they have received their reward in full. But when you fast, put oil on your head and wash your face, so that it will not be obvious to others that you are fasting, but only to your Father, who is unseen; and your Father, who sees what is done in secret, will reward you.

Do not store up for yourselves treasures on earth, where moths and vermin destroy, and where thieves break in and steal. But store up for yourselves treasures in heaven, where moths and vermin do not destroy, and where thieves do not break in and steal. For where your treasure is, there your heart will be also.

The eye is the lamp of the body. If your eyes are healthy, your whole body will be full of light. But if your eyes are unhealthy, your whole body will be full of darkness. If then the light within you is darkness, how great is that darkness!

No one can serve two masters. Either you will hate the one and love the other, or you will be devoted to the one and despise the other. You cannot serve both God and money.

Therefore I tell you, do not worry about your life, what you will eat or drink; or about your body, what you will wear. Is not life more than food, and the body more than clothes? Look at the birds of the air; they do not sow or reap or store away in barns, and yet your heavenly Father feeds them. Are you not much more valuable than they? Can any one of you by worrying add a single hour to your life?

And why do you worry about clothes? See how the flowers of the field grow. They do not labor or spin. Yet I tell you that not even Solomon in all his splendor was dressed like one of these. If that is how God clothes the grass of the field, which is here today and tomorrow is thrown into the fire, will he not much more clothe you—you of little faith? So do not worry, saying, 'What shall we eat?' or 'What shall we drink?' or 'What shall we wear?' For the pagans run after all these things, and your heavenly Father knows that you need them. But seek first his kingdom and his righteousness, and all these things will be given to you as well. Therefore do not worry about tomorrow, for tomorrow will worry about itself. Each day has enough trouble of its own.

Do not judge, or you too will be judged. For in the same way you judge others, you will be judged, and with the measure you use, it will be measured to you.

Why do you look at the speck of sawdust in your brother's eye and pay no attention to the plank in your own eye? How can you say to your brother, 'Let me take the speck out of your eye,' when all the time there is a plank in your own eye? You hypocrite, first take the plank out of your own eye, and then you will see clearly to remove the speck from your brother's eye.

Do not give dogs what is sacred; do not throw your pearls to pigs. If you do, they may trample them under their feet, and turn and tear you to pieces.

Ask and it will be given to you; seek and you will find; knock and the door will be opened to you. For everyone who asks receives; the one who seeks finds; and to the one who knocks, the door will be opened.

Which of you, if your son asks for bread, will give him a stone? Or if he asks for a fish, will give him a snake? If you, then, though you are evil, know how to give good gifts to your children, how much more will your Father in heaven give good gifts to those who ask him! So in everything, do to others what you would have them do to you, for this sums up the Law and the Prophets.

Enter through the narrow gate. For wide is the gate and broad is the road that leads to destruction, and many enter through it. But small is the gate and narrow the road that leads to life, and only a few find it.

Watch out for false prophets. They come to you in sheep's clothing, but inwardly they are ferocious wolves. By their fruit you will recognize them. Do people pick grapes from thorn bushes, or figs from thistles? Likewise, every good tree bears good fruit, but a bad tree bears bad fruit. A good tree cannot bear bad fruit, and a bad tree cannot bear good fruit. Every tree that does not bear good fruit is cut down and thrown into the fire. Thus, by their fruit you will recognize them.

Not everyone who says to me, 'Lord, Lord,' will enter the kingdom of heaven, but only the one who does the will of my Father who is in heaven. Many will say to me on that day, 'Lord, Lord, did we not prophesy in your name and in your name drive out demons and in your name perform many miracles?' Then I will tell them plainly, 'I never knew you. Away from me, you evildoers!'

Therefore everyone who hears these words of mine and puts them into practice is like a wise man who built his house on the rock. The rain came down, the streams rose, and the winds blew and beat against that house; yet it did not fall, because it had its foundation on the rock. But everyone who hears these words of mine and does not put them into practice is like a foolish man who built his house on sand. The rain came down, the streams rose, and the winds blew and beat against that house, and it fell with a great crash.

When Jesus had finished saying these things, the crowds were amazed at his teaching, because he taught as one who had authority, and not as their teachers of the law.

Appendix 2: The Sermon on the Plain

Luke 6:17-49

He went down with them and stood on a level place. A large crowd of his disciples was there and a great number of people from all over Judea, from Jerusalem, and from the coastal region around Tyre and Sidon, who had come to hear him and to be healed of their diseases. Those troubled by impure spirits were cured, and the people all tried to touch him, because power was coming from him and healing them all.

Looking at his disciples, he said:

"Blessed are you who are poor,
  for yours is the kingdom of God.
Blessed are you who hunger now,
  for you will be satisfied.
Blessed are you who weep now,
  for you will laugh.
Blessed are you when people hate you,
  when they exclude you and insult you
  and reject your name as evil,
    because of the Son of Man.

"Rejoice in that day and leap for joy, because great is your reward in heaven. For that is how their ancestors treated the prophets.

"But woe to you who are rich,
  for you have already received your comfort.
Woe to you who are well fed now,
  for you will go hungry.
Woe to you who laugh now,
  for you will mourn and weep.
Woe to you when everyone speaks well of you,
  for that is how their ancestors treated the false prophets.

"But to you who are listening I say: Love your enemies, do good to those who hate you, bless those who curse you, pray for those who mistreat you. If someone slaps you on one cheek, turn to them the other also. If someone takes your coat, do not withhold your shirt from them. Give to everyone who asks you, and if anyone takes what belongs to you, do not demand it back. Do to others as you would have them do to you.

"If you love those who love you, what credit is that to you? Even sinners love those who love them. And if you do good to those who are good to you, what credit is that to you? Even sinners do that. And if you lend to those from whom you expect repayment, what credit is that to you? Even sinners lend to sinners, expecting to be repaid in full. But love your enemies, do good to them, and lend to them without expecting to get anything back. Then your reward will be great, and you will be children of the Most High, because he is kind to the ungrateful and wicked. Be merciful, just as your Father is merciful.

"Do not judge, and you will not be judged. Do not condemn, and you will not be condemned. Forgive, and you will be forgiven. Give, and it will be given to you. A good measure, pressed down, shaken together and running over, will be poured into your lap. For with the measure you use, it will be measured to you."

He also told them this parable: "Can the blind lead the blind? Will they not both fall into a pit? The student is not above the teacher, but everyone who is fully trained will be like their teacher.

"Why do you look at the speck of sawdust in your brother's eye and pay no attention to the plank in your own eye? How can you say to your brother, 'Brother, let me take the speck out of your eye,' when you yourself fail to see the plank in your own eye? You hypocrite, first take the plank out of your eye, and then you will see clearly to remove the speck from your brother's eye.

"No good tree bears bad fruit, nor does a bad tree bear good fruit. Each tree is recognized by its own fruit. People do not pick figs from thorn bushes, or grapes from briers. A good man brings good things out of the good stored up in his heart, and an evil man brings evil things out of the evil stored up in his heart. For the mouth speaks what the heart is full of.

"Why do you call me, 'Lord, Lord,' and do not do what I say? As for everyone who comes to me and hears my words and puts them into practice, I will show you what they are like. They are like a man building a house, who dug down deep and laid the foundation on rock. When a flood came, the torrent struck that house but could not shake it, because it was well built. But the one who hears my words and does not put them into practice is like a man who built a house on the ground without a foundation. The moment the torrent struck that house, it collapsed and its destruction was complete."

Appendix 3: Letter to the Editor

The following letter to the editor of "The Daily Sentinel" in Grand Junction, Colorado was published on February 1, 1983 under the byline "Speaking the public mind." My family and I lived in Grand Junction where I was flying the Air Life helicopter out of St. Mary's Hospital. By that time I had been profoundly affected by the writing of Francis Schaeffer, a Christian theologian and philosopher. My thinking has changed since the writing of this letter and I explain that following the text of the letter.

Editor:

I wonder if it has occurred to Jim Fain [Editorial page contributor who had written a then recent pro-choice piece about not legislating morality] that a significant portion of our law has been enacted for the express purpose of legislating morality. Our laws against murder, rape, fraud, robbery and a significant number of other crimes are based on the supposition that those acts are immoral and thus must be prevented.

Jim begged us to "have whatever morals you choose but don't force them on me or anyone else." If we were to grace this emotional and poorly thought through plea with serious consideration we would be forced to conclude that the principle he advocates would leave us with no basis for enacting any criminal legislation (including laws against murder, rape or anything else). Rapists and murderers have chosen their own morals and, according to Jim's simplistic egalitarian principle the rest of us ought to refrain from forcing our morals upon them.

From the beginning of our country's history we have recognized that one person's rights end where another person's rights begin. One of the frightful things about abortion is that up until 1973 conventional morality (as reflected in our laws) recognized that the human fetus is a person and thus was guaranteed rights under our Constitution. It wasn't a law enacted by the men and women we have elected that changed the situation; rather, it was a decision by a small group of judges who are not answerable to us. In other words it makes little difference what we think or what our elected representatives think. The law is whatever the Supreme Court says it is. Does that sound like the tail wagging the dog? It should.

My job brings me in contact with large numbers of premature infants. I have the privilege of flying a medical helicopter and working with outstanding doctors and nurses who are dedicated to the preservation of life no matter how tiny or insignificant. One flight I remember in particular was at night, through the mountains, and in marginal weather in an attempt to save an infant born at 26 weeks gestation.

In essence we risked the lives of three highly trained people and hundreds of thousands of dollars worth of equipment to save a little child who eventually died. Do you know what that makes us? Fools. It makes us fools because babies by the droves are being aborted in just that range. They're being aborted because through ridiculous verbal gymnastics they're referred to as "tissue," or the doctors and women involved justify their actions by pleading ignorance as to whether it is a real human life or not.

In case you are curious, let me assure you that the little baby we went to pick up was indeed a person -- a human person no less! One doesn't need a constitutional lawyer to realize that that baby and the thousands of babies being aborted ought to be protected under the laws of our country.

Maurice L. Martin, Jr.
Grand Junction

What has changed? Though there are aspects of this letter I still believe, there are many aspects with which I no longer agree.

1) During my two years with Food for the Hungry in the Democratic Republic of Congo, I saw the issue from a different perspective for the first time. I saw and worked among real people in Congo whose plight I never could have imagined and saw them not simply through an ideological lens that does not have the capacity to factor in such a desperate plight. See Chapters 12 and 13 for a complete discussion. Then, for the first time, I understood at a deep level that there were actual circumstances I had encountered where safe access to abortion was, in my estimation, not only desirable, but necessary.

2) At the time I wrote the letter, I had assumed that there was an actual and clear biblical absolute prohibiting abortion, but later discovered that it is neither as clear or simple as that. In fact, the Bible doesn't address abortion at all even though there are many instances in the Bible in which the lives of unborn children are intentionally taken with God's knowledge and permission. Previously, I had gone to the Bible with a belief that I wanted to confirm, not simply seeking what the Bible had to say or not say, as explained in detail in the body of this book under the headings "Thou Shalt Not Kill," "The Eyes of the Beholder" and "Slippery Slope."

3) I had no idea how many human embryonic fertilizations do not result in live births due to purely natural circumstances (30-50 percent according to a noteworthy study published through Johns Hopkins University).[294] A later (2010) Stanford University study showed that two thirds of all fertilizations do not develop successfully. The rate of miscarriages for women who know they are pregnant is 10-20 percent and because there are many fertilizations that fail before a woman even knows that she is pregnant, the number is higher and according to the studies cited, much higher.

4) If God is "knitting us together in our mothers' wombs" (Psalm 139) then, for whatever reason, God stops knitting or unravels what has been knit in an enormous number of pregnancies. To the extent that God is positively involved in forming us in the womb, God is also involved in pregnancies that do not develop successfully. We find ourselves in the unusual circumstance of never being able to do directly what God does directly and routinely, yet with respect to personal and national security issues, we can do regularly and directly what God never does. What if the number of failed fertilizations were only 20 percent? That still means that there are more spontaneous abortions than induced abortions. What if the number were only 10 percent? It is still a huge number and does not change the argument.

5) I had not connected abortion with the large number of other sanctity of life issues, including those that deal very seriously with quality of life issues including those related to poverty.

---

[294] Lippincott, Williams, and Wilkins. "The Johns Hopkins Manual of Gynecology and Obstetrics (4 ed.). 2012, pp. 438,439.

6) I began to understand more clearly, and then took seriously, that both humans and human rights are developmental in nature. Even though they are genetically identical, there is a major difference between a chicken and the egg from which it comes. Similarly, there is an order of magnitude difference between a fertilized embryo and a fully developed human being. This understanding is much more consistent with what happens in so many human fertilizations that never result in live births totally apart from induced abortions.

7) Christian opposition to abortion is dogmatic. That is, even though abortion is not dealt with in the Bible and Christians are willing to allow the taking of innocent human life in other circumstances, it is treated as a moral absolute without further proof. This is the purview, that is, it is within the rights of a church to believe this, but it is not mandated by the Scriptures and, in my estimation, ought not to be mandated for others.

It was and is my belief that there is such a thing as a just war and that a nation has the right to undertake it when necessary. In certain circumstances this warrants the death of innocents when it is absolutely unavoidable. It was and is my belief that capital punishment is appropriate in cases where a heinous capital crime has undoubtedly been committed by a convicted perpetrator. A nation has the right to protect its citizenry in this way even though innocent people have been put to death mistakenly in more circumstances than we should tolerate as a people. It was and is my belief that owning and using a firearm for the purpose of protecting my own life or the life of my family should be allowed even if the consequence of that is that innocent lives might be lost at the hands of those who abuse this right. This right, though, is and should be strongly limited. The right of a woman to decide whether to bear a child to term thus, to a large degree, setting the course of her entire remaining life, is certainly of the magnitude of these other rights and as deserving of protection.

It is my belief that all of these circumstances may be limited in ways that provide appropriate protections consistent with developmental stage and the maintaining of the basic right in question. The right of a nation to defend itself and the right of individuals to protect themselves, though important rights, are subject to restrictions. The fact that one or more of these rights might be exercised in ways with which we might not agree does not eliminate the right and does not result in its forfeiture. This includes a woman's right to choose.

Appendix 4: *"You will always have the poor among you ..."*

The following blog which I wrote was posted on the Covenant Theological Seminary website late in 2014:[295]

After many years of ministry experience, I'm convinced this phrase from John 12:8 is the best known reference in the Bible concerning poverty. Christians frequently quote this as proof that poverty will always exist and cannot be overcome. When this is believed to be true, little urgency is felt in dealing with physical poverty. Strong calls to do so are often dismissed as "social gospel" and of secondary importance at best in living out the Gospel.

A friend and fellow pastor often said that a text without a context is a pretext. He is right. In this case, the context of John 12:1-11 and Matthew 25, 26 is critically important for understanding what Jesus meant. The teaching concerning the poor found here is almost always taken out of context and simply does not mean what many Christians take it to mean.

The Story

The story in John 12 is that Mary, sister of Lazarus, took an expensive jar of perfume, anointed Jesus' feet and wiped them with her hair. Judas Iscariot, identified in the same passage as having no concern for the poor, regularly stealing from the common purse and on the verge of betraying Jesus for money, castigated Mary, saying, "Why wasn't this perfume sold and the money given to the poor?" From parallel passages in Matthew and Mark it is evident that Judas' deceitfulness had already influenced his unwitting fellow disciples.

Jesus defended Mary and, in John 12:8, said to Judas, "You will always have the poor among you, but you will not always have me." Jesus' message is powerfully biting: Judas would not always "have" Jesus because Jesus and Judas both knew he was betraying Him. But he would still "have" the poor if he really cared to do anything about their poverty which both Jesus and Judas knew he did not. This "outing" of Judas and

[295]Martin, M. "You Will Always Have the Poor Among You." Covenantseminary.edu. 2014. www.covenantseminary.edu/you-will-always-have-the-poor-among-you-by-marty-martin-of-food-for-the-hungry/. Accessed 20 March 2019.

his stunning lack of genuine concern either for Jesus or for the poor, when taken to teach that physical poverty is an insoluble problem and thus a secondary Kingdom concern, totally misrepresents the point.

Jesus' laser use of sarcasm and the plural "you" in John 12:8 both are important because, to the extent that other disciples buy into Judas' lack of tangible concern for the poor, the powerful irony of Jesus' message is for them too. The point often missed is simple, but profound: relieving the material poverty of the poor is central to the Gospel, not peripheral.

Sheep and Goats

The Kingdom priority of addressing physical poverty is found in the extended teaching of Jesus in continuous, connected narrative starting at Matthew 25: 31 with the "sheep" being separated from the "goats" and culminating in the Matthew 26 rendition of the anointing at Bethany. It provides the immediate larger context for understanding Jesus' response to Judas and the disciples influenced by him. **The unambiguous message: sheep address the physical poverty of the poor, goats do not.** *The point of this teaching is not to identify who is going to heaven and who is going to hell. It is to underscore the profound Kingdom importance of responding together to the poverty of the poor and the tragedy of not so doing. The Gospel everywhere assumes that all alike are spiritually poor, but it reserves and repeats, again and again, a central importance of responding to the material poverty of the poor (Luke 4:18; Luke 6:20; Luke 16:19-31; Galatians 2:10; 1 John 3:16-18; James 2:14-17 for starters).*

Several reasons this should matter to a pastor

- *The greatest resistance among Christians to sustained, strategic response to poverty is theological and is usually based on misreading of Scripture, a reductionist view of the Gospel and a false dichotomy between faith and works.*
- *Looking back over their lives, if the Gospel has not led our people to significantly, tangibly address the material needs of the needy, then it has not accomplished one of its central purposes for their lives.*
- *Many people, Christians included, struggle to find purpose in life. Responsibility and purpose are inextricably tied together. When Cain asked "am I my brother's keeper?" God answered with chilling silence*

241

conveying the loudest possible "yes." When people accept their responsibility, they find their purpose.

- Given our responsibility as pastors to prepare people for eternity, we first need to introduce them to present reality. Twenty percent of the world's people live on less than $1.25 per day; another twenty percent live on less than $2 per day; eighty percent live on less than $10 per day. The gap between the upper twenty and the lower eighty is widening. This is not okay and we are responsible, not for the ultimate solution, but to weigh in for the long haul on the side of the lower eighty. Otherwise, what real meaning does "God so loved the world" have?

A final note: Many feel pangs of shame when exposed to the plight of the poor and the magnitude of world poverty. Pastors profoundly influence how people resolve guilt and shame. Guilt and shame have little or no long term transformational value. In fact they usually paralyze. We must move beyond them to a settled resolve in order to take meaningful steps. When Jesus told the paralytic to take up his mat and go home, the most meaningful and toughest step was the first one.

Appendix 5: Myths Regarding the Poor

The Poor are lazy
The Poor are to blame for their own poverty
The Poor pay no taxes
The Poor are scamming the System

The Poor are lazy: During my two years in DR Congo, I had the privilege of working with some of the most outstanding people I have ever worked with, including those I worked with during my time in the US Air Force. By almost any American standard, these Congolese men and women were poor, but I can attest that they were among the most devoted, hard-working people anywhere. Many were well educated and, had they been born in America, they would have been successful in anything they undertook. Imagine yourself in a place where hard work is not rewarded. In eastern Congo, those farmers who work hard and create a surplus which they can sell if there are markets available (often there are no markets) are often rewarded by having their crops harvested or stolen by regional armies that earn their living at the point of a gun. It isn't laziness that accounts for the poverty in Congo, but what about the US? See the next three sections and decide for yourself.

The Poor are to blame for their own poverty: If you make ten dollars an hour, work forty hours a week and take two weeks unpaid vacation or time off because you are sick, as is the case with most workers at this level who only get paid when they work, your annual salary is $20,000. This describes 35 percent of working Americans. If 17.3 percent of that or more goes to taxes over the course of the year (see below), then you have an after tax income of $15,540 or less which amounts to about $1380 per month for rent, utilities, food, transportation, phone, clothing, medical and dental expenses, etc. If you are supporting yourself this doesn't go very far and leaves no margin for error. If you are supporting a child, certainly the child is not to blame for his or her poverty, but at this level, both parent and child are in poverty. Approximately 21 percent of children in America live below the poverty level. This amounts to 15 million children living in poverty in the US. We feel little personal responsibility for these children and justify our lack of concern for the poor by blaming them for their own poverty when there are mountains of data that paint a very different picture.

The poor don't pay taxes: In 2017, according to figures published annually by the US Government Social Security Administration, as noted above, 35 percent of all American wage earners earned less than $20,000. 41 percent of all wage earners earned less than $25,000. Nearly 50 percent of all wage earners made less than $30,000.[296] Family incomes are higher because a number of these wage earners are spouses or children of wage earners. However, as shown in the chart and table below, the lowest twenty percent of wage earners in the US annually pay an average of 17.3 percent of their income in local, state and federal taxes that are virtually unavoidable.[297] Though those at the bottom may not pay federal income taxes, unless they have employers who do not pay into the system, they cannot avoid federal payroll taxes nor can they avoid federal excise taxes like the $.184 per gallon that everyone pays on each gallon of gasoline. Federal excise taxes are also levied on health related goods and services, as well as on alcohol, tobacco and on your phone (3 percent of your bill). The point? Even if a person doesn't pay federal income taxes, that person still pays significant federal taxes of other kinds and those taxes are virtually unavoidable. The poor pay even more in unavoidable state and local taxes. The notion that the poor (including those who are undocumented) pay no taxes is simply false.

It should be noted that the figures in the graph and table below were all compiled before the tax reform bill passed subsequent to President Trump's election. Due to the fact that the reforms disproportionately favored the very wealthy, the percentages depicted here will not improve (if by improvement one means that those on the lower end of the spectrum will pay less of a percentage of our overall tax bill).

---

[296] U.S. Social Security Administration. "Wage Statistics for 2017." Social Security Online. www.ssa.gov/cgi-bin/netcomp.cgi?year=2017. Accessed 20 March 2019.

[297] Klein, Ezra. "*The one tax graph you really need to know.*" Washington Post, 19 September 2012.

State, local and federal taxes by income Group

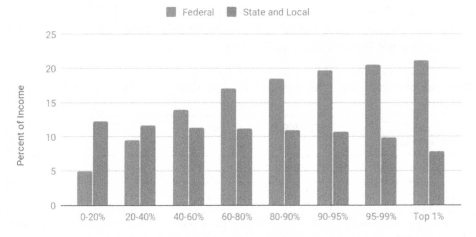

State local and federal taxes by Income Group

Income Percentile	Federal Tax as a Percent of Income	State & Local Tax as a Percent of Income	Total Taxes Paid as a Percent of Income	Total Income per U.S. Gov. Social Security Administration 2017 (approximate)
0 - 20%	5%	12.3%	17.3%	$1 - $10,000
20 - 40%	9.5%	11.7%	21.2%	$10K - $25K
40 - 60%	13.9%	11.3%	25.2%	$25K - $40K
60 - 80%	17.1%	11.2%	28.3%	$40K - $70K
80 - 90%	18.5%	11%	29.5%	$70K - $100K
90 - 95%	19.7%	10.7%	30.4%	$100K - $135K
95 - 99%	20.6%	9.9%	30.5%	$135 K- $300K
Top 1%	21.1%	7.9%	29%	$300K - $50M+

The poor are scamming the system: The biggest social assistance program is Medicaid. 70 percent of Medicaid beneficiaries are children, disabled or elderly. Most of the remaining 30 percent are employed full or part time. Many of the remainder are care providers for the children, disabled or elderly. The stepped up calls for additional work requirements are a solution looking for a problem and are consistent with the narrative that views those on the bottom as takers largely responsible for their own plight. Here are the US Census Bureau statistics:[298]

Category of Participant	Number in 2015	Percent	Cumulative Percent
Child/Youth (under age 19)	30,419,902	45.8	45.8
Ages 65 and Older	7,155,401	10.8	56.6
Disabled (ages 19-64)	8,781,327	13.2	69.8
Institutionalized (ages 19-64)	380,517	0.6	70.4
Recent Mother (ages 19 and older)	1,040,193	1.6	71.9
Working Full Time Year Round* (ages 19-64)	4,678,142	7.0	79.0
Working Part Time or Part Year* (ages 19-64)	3,319,811	5.0	84.0
Other	10,641,447	16.0	100.0
TOTAL Means-Tested Public Health Insurance	**66,416,740**	**100.0**	**100.0**

*Notes: Categories are mutually exclusive. Full-time, year-round work includes those working 35 hours or more per week, 50 or more weeks per year. Part time includes those working at least 10 hours per week, at least 47 weeks per year, excluding full-time, year-round workers.

As noted earlier, a number of the "Other" listed above are primary caregivers for the children, elderly, disabled and institutionalized listed

---

[298] Lee, Amanda and Jarosz, Beth. "Majority of People Covered by Medicaid, and Similar Programs, Are Children, Older Adults or Disabled. *PRB*, 29 June 2017. www.prb.org/majority-of-people-covered-by-medicaid-and-similar-programs/. Accessed 20 March 2019.

above. What about those who are not? As mentioned earlier, my daughter is the director of a homeless shelter. I've had the privilege of working with her as part of an advisory board and can attest what she has said for years. Mental illness is a huge component in the level of homelessness in the US. In the 1980's there was a substantial cut back in federally funded programs and institutions for the mentally ill. The privatization of mental health care made it virtually impossible for the majority of mentally ill persons or their families to afford such care. As a result, many of these people end up on the streets. When they show up in a hospital Emergency Department they are counted among the "Other." Were you to spend a day or night shadowing those who provide shelter for the homeless, though you might be frightened at first, you would soon realize that the people being served are not fearful, but in desperate need of care. Can we find anecdotal evidence of those who are actually scamming the system? Of course we can, but to use that to pardon ourselves for not really tangibly caring for the poor is an evasion.

Following the passage of the American Health Care Act in 2017, the nonpartisan Congressional Budget Office estimates 23 million additional people will lose health insurance by 2026 compared to coverage under the Affordable Care Act and that while insurance premiums would decrease for many of the individual market plans over the same period, the savings would come from a reduction in coverage.[299] Blanket support of the current policies insure that millions fewer Americans will have access to only recently gained health care benefits and virtually all of them are at the bottom of the economic stack. Again, regardless of one's personal convictions, self-identified evangelicals have ownership of this policy as the one most powerful voting block in the US and still strong supporters of current policy.

How might Jesus feel about all of this? Let's end close to where we began, with the Sermon on the Plain.

Looking at his disciples, he said:

---

[299] Levy, Gabrielle. "Congressional Budget Office Releases Trumpcare Score." *US News and World Report.*, 24 May 2017. www.usnews.com/news/politics/articles/2017-05-24/cbo-score-23-million-lose-coverage-under-american-health-care-act-deficit-trimmed-119-billion. Accessed 20 March 2019.

"Blessed are you who are poor,
    for yours is the kingdom of God.
Blessed are you who hunger now,
    for you will be satisfied.
Blessed are you who weep now,
    for you will laugh.
Blessed are you when people hate you,
    when they exclude you and insult you
    and reject your name as evil,
        because of the Son of Man.

"Rejoice in that day and leap for joy, because great is your reward in heaven. For that is how their ancestors treated the prophets.

"But woe to you who are rich,
    for you have already received your comfort.
Woe to you who are well fed now,
    for you will go hungry.
Woe to you who laugh now,
    for you will mourn and weep.
Woe to you when everyone speaks well of you,
    for that is how their ancestors treated the false prophets.

"But to you who are listening I say: Love your enemies, do good to those who hate you, bless those who curse you, pray for those who mistreat you. If someone slaps you on one cheek, turn to them the other also. If someone takes your coat, do not withhold your shirt from them. Give to everyone who asks you, and if anyone takes what belongs to you, do not demand it back. Do to others as you would have them do to you.[300]

---

[300] Luke 6:20-31.

Acknowledgments

My deepest thanks to all the following: my wife, Rosemary, who encouraged me to stay at this and is my best critic and a thoughtful editor; my sister, Joan, who painstakingly edited the entire manuscript and provided many needed insights along the way; to my sons, Lang and John, who together with their wives, Charity and Julia, read and critiqued important parts of the book; to my sister, Michele, who also read and provided wise commentary on much of the key content; to my daughter, Meg, who inspires me daily by her pure love for the homeless poor and her husband, Kevin, without whom she could not keep on; to all the guys in the "reading group" (no one wants to call it a "book club") who have challenged my thinking for years; especially, Joe, Jim, Larry and Mike who read and debated the final draft and, even when they disagreed, were a great support; to Bryan, classmate, fellow helicopter pilot and pastor for his confirmation of details and encouragement; to Niki, Gary, Barby, Bruce and Sally, who also read, discussed and thoughtfully critiqued much of the first part; to those alongside whom I have worked and from whom I have learned so much, both at Cherry Creek Presbyterian, a great and giving church, and at Food for the Hungry ... they have inspired me with their commitment to know and follow the Truth; and, finally, to my ethics students at (then) Mesa College, Colorado, and Cleveland State Community College, Tennessee, who have challenged me to go deeper into the study of ethics. Not all of these good people agree with all in this book, but all have helped me to do the best job I can.